The CALVIN INSTITUTE OF CHRISTIAN WORSHIP LITURGICAL STUDIES Series, edited by John D. Witvliet, is designed to promote reflection on the history, theology, and practice of Christian worship and to stimulate worship renewal in Christian congregations. Contributions include writings by pastoral worship leaders from a wide range of communities and scholars from a wide range of disciplines. The ultimate goal of these contributions is to nurture worship practices that are spiritually vital and theologically rooted.

PUBLISHED

Singing God's Psalms: Metrical Psalms and Reflections for Each Sunday in the Church Year
   Fred R. Anderson

The Pastor as Minor Poet: Texts and Subtexts in the Ministerial Life
   M. Craig Barnes

Arts Ministry: Nurturing the Creative Life of God's People
   Michael J. Bauer

Touching the Altar: The Old Testament and Christian Worship
   Carol M. Bechtel, Editor

Resonant Witness: Conversations between Music and Theology
   Jeremy S. Begbie and Steven R. Guthrie, Editors

God against Religion: Rethinking Christian Theology through Worship
   Matthew Myer Boulton

From Memory to Imagination: Reforming the Church's Music
   C. Randall Bradley

By the Vision of Another World: Worship in American History
   James D. Bratt, Editor

Inclusive yet Discerning: Navigating Worship Artfully
   Frank Burch Brown

What Language Shall I Borrow? The Bible and Christian Worship
   Ronald P. Byars

Visual Arts in the Worshiping Church
   Lisa J. DeBoer

A Primer on Christian Worship: Where We've Been, Where We Are, Where We Can Go
   William A. Dyrness

VISUAL ARTS IN THE WORSHIPING CHURCH

LISA J. DeBoer

WILLIAM B. EERDMANS PUBLISHING COMPANY
GRAND RAPIDS, MICHIGAN

Wm. B. Eerdmans Publishing Co.
2140 Oak Industrial Drive N.E., Grand Rapids, Michigan 49505
www.eerdmans.com

22 21 20 19 18 17 16   1 2 3 4 5 6 7

ISBN 978-0-8028-6951-7

Library of Congress Cataloging-in-Publication Data

Names: DeBoer, Lisa J., author.
Title: Visual arts in the worshiping church / Lisa J. DeBoer.
Description: Grand Rapids : Eerdmans Publishing Co., 2016. | Series: The Calvin Institute of
    Christian Worship liturgical studies series | Includes bibliographical references and index.
Identifiers: LCCN 2016032273 | ISBN 9780802869517 (pbk. : alk. paper)
Subjects: LCSH: Christianity and art. | Worship.
Classification: LCC BR115.A8 D45 2016 | DDC 261.5/7 — dc23
    LC record available at https://lccn.loc.gov/2016032273

CONTENTS

CONTENTS

FOREWORD

Beginning in the 1960s, a stream of books has appeared addressing the topic of the church and the visual arts. Some of these books have presented theological arguments for integrating the visual arts into the life of the church, the basic theological category employed usually being either *creation, incarnation,* or *sacrament.* Others have approached the topic from a philosophical angle, exploring how we in the West have come to think about the arts and how that way of thinking shapes the role we give to the arts in the church. Yet others have approached the topic historically, narrating the diverse ways in which different branches of the church have engaged the visual arts over the centuries.

In *Visual Arts in the Worshipping Church,* Lisa DeBoer takes a distinctly different approach to the topic. Rather than adding one more book to the stream of theological, philosophical, and historical treatises, she looks at how congregations in different ecclesiastical traditions actually engage the arts and explores what this tells us about how they understand the arts and how they understand themselves as church. Though her discussion is deeply informed by Scripture, theology, philosophy, and history, her overall approach is sociological rather than theoretical or historical. She identifies and analyzes the practices of actual congregations and brings to light the ways of thinking that underlie those practices. Along the way she offers evaluative judgments. But her dominant concern is not to tell readers how the church *should* engage the arts but to uncover how actual congregations in different traditions *do in fact* engage the arts and why they engage them as they do. It's a ground-breaking approach, full of fascinating details and perceptive analyses.

Rather than sending surveys to a large number of congregations, Professor DeBoer conducted detailed "field studies "of twenty or so congregations in southwest Michigan that she judged to be representative. She observed their practices, talked to their leaders, and read the documents, if any, that these congregations used to guide them in their practices, her aim being to dig beneath the details to discover general similarities and differences. Her observations confirmed her expectation that the major "fault lines" would run between the thought and practices of Orthodox, Catholic, and Protestant congregations.

It was especially DeBoer's discussion of the role of the visual arts in contemporary Protestant congregations that proved eye-opening for me. Her discussion of the role of the arts in Orthodoxy and Catholicism is rich and deep, thoroughly versed in the relevant literature and grounded in close observation of the thought and practice of actual congregations. One knows in advance, however, that the tradition of icon painting will prove decisive for Orthodox congregations and that declarations emerging from Vatican II will be decisive for Catholic congregations. What comes as a surprise is that, whereas initially it appears that the ways in which Protestant congregations engage the arts are "all over the place," here too there proves to be a pattern: usually it is not a Protestant congregation's self-understanding as church that shapes the way it engages the arts, nor its standing in a certain tradition, but the influence of a few member artists or art instructors who have been inducted into our present-day secular art system and think about the arts as they were taught. Let me quote what DeBoer says in one place:

> Scripture, theology, and confessional identity, while influential, do not ultimately determine how the visual arts are integrated into the life of any given Protestant church. Rather, particular people in a congregation shape what is happening on the ground. Their commitments, in turn, may be couched in whatever scriptural, theological, confessional, or stylistic language is native to a particular congregation, but the starting point is the visionary, whose ideas about art are a product of the varied sectors of our art system. If there is enough resonance between the visionary's ideals and the mission and identity of the church, the program has a chance at embedding itself into the finances and governance of the congregation. If not, not.

Foreword

With respect to the visual arts, art-committed Protestant churches are basically arenas of intense, mostly unexamined cultural exchange. (p. 157)

Of course, it's not just true of Protestant congregations but of Orthodox and Catholic congregations as well that there is "resonance" between how the congregation engages the visual arts and how it understands itself as church. Analyzing how a congregation engages the arts not only opens a window onto what it asks and expects of art but also opens a window onto how it understands itself as church. What is fascinating about DeBoer's use of her field studies is how she not only uses the ways in which these congregations understand themselves as church to illuminate what they ask and expect of art, but also uses the ways in which they engage art to illuminate how they understand themselves as church.

I have no doubt that Professor DeBoer's turn away from abstract theory and general history to the lived thought and practice of actual present-day congregations will shape subsequent discussions of the role of the visual arts in the worshipping church.

Nicholas Wolterstorff

ACKNOWLEDGMENTS

Those who know me know how long this book has been in the making.
After two paradigm shifts, one catastrophic wildfire, and a typical assort-
ment of challenging life events, the only reason I had the courage to bring
this project to a conclusion is the good will and encouragement of so many
fine people. One of the underlying themes of this study is the way in which
communities govern our thoughts and assumptions; in the thanks I issue
below, you'll see an outline of the communities that have sustained me in my
work. Any strengths this study may have to offer are a credit to these people
and to the knowledge embedded in their communities that they shared with
me. The inevitable errors, misunderstandings, and deficits are the result
of my own limitations both as a scholar and as one particular individual
attempting to enter into others' particular communities.

I owe an enormous debt to John Witvliet and Betty Grit and all the other
staff at the Calvin Institute of Christian Worship (CICW) based at Calvin
College in Grand Rapids, Michigan. My experiences as a recipient of two
CICW Worship Renewal Grants provided the impetus for this study. CICW
then provided me office space, research privileges, and a wonderfully hospitable Christian intellectual community for two year-long sabbaticals. The
mental and physical space CICW afforded allowed each of those necessary
paradigm shifts to occur.

I owe a further debt to two Calvin Summer Seminars, one near the beginning of my research, in 2003, entitled "Art, Theology and Liturgy" and
led by Nicholas Wolterstorff, and the other nearer the end, in 2011, "Congregations and Social Change," led by Gerardo Marti. Professor Wolterstorff

and Professor Marti and my fellow participants provided necessary interdisciplinary perspectives as I sketched out and later refined the parameters of my inquiry.

My thinking was furthered in crucial ways by Westmont students, both as participants in our two Worship Renewal Grant projects and as students in successive versions of my "Art, Theology and Worship" class. I thank in particular the students in the last iteration of the course who read and commented on a draft of this book: Brandon Daniels, Benicia Grace, Barbara Pointer, Nikki Ramage, Katie Shara, Jessica Shuholm, and Rachel Urbano.

At the heart of this book, however, are all the people in Grand Rapids and Santa Barbara who took time to talk with me and respond to my thinking: Father Anton Frunze, Father John Winfrey, Father Andrew Lowe, Father Daniel Daly, Matushka Darya Carney, Kathleen Dunn, Dana Alexander, Dorothy Alexander, David Vander Laan, Kate Vander Laan, Patricia Hughes, Robert Czerew, Father Tom Simons, Father Stephen Dudek, John Knight, Michael Northup, Linda Ekstrom, Debra Nardin, Rev. Jack Roeda, Virginia Wieringa, Jim Fissel, Wendy Huizinga, Steve Caton, Laurie Gorden, Catherine Vlieger, David Wiltse, Dick and Marion De Vinney, Mark Loring, Tia Grass, Lori Vanden Bosch, Erica Sims Huff, Marianne Ruel Robins, Jon Lemmond, Cheri Larsen Hoeckley, Chris Hoeckley, Deborah Dunn, Susan Savage, Scott Anderson, Nathan Huff, and Meagan Stirling. Of these I single out for particular thanks Darya Carney and Linda Ekstrom, whose help and expertise within their respective Orthodox and Catholic contexts were invaluable.

Finally, I thank the editors who helped shape and polish this book: Tom Raabe and Alexander Bukovietski at Eerdmans for their work with the text and images, Lisa Stracks for her support as a friend and for her expertise as an astute reader and content editor. I've no doubt that without her help, this book would have been an additional year in the making and much less readable!

I dedicate this book, as is appropriate, to the congregations that fulfilled their baptismal vows by receiving me into Christ's church, welcoming me in love, praying for and encouraging me, and nurturing me in the faith: Calvin Christian Reformed Church, Grand Rapids; Second Christian Reformed Church, Grand Haven; Church of the Servant, Grand Rapids; Campus Chapel, Ann Arbor; the Chapel of the Resurrection, Valparaiso; and Saint Andrew's Presbyterian Church, Santa Barbara.

Learning by Doing

A Story

In the fall of 2002, a number of art students at Westmont College, a Christian liberal arts college in Santa Barbara, California, embarked on an adventure. Funded by a generous Worship Renewal Grant from the Calvin Institute of Christian Worship[1] and working under the direction of a prominent artist from Santa Barbara, three groups of student artists were tasked with developing works of art for the campus that represented the different ways we worship as a college community. One piece was to go somewhere near a residence hall and was to envision "life as worship." Another, destined for the library, was to portray "learning as worship." A third was to be for the gymnasium, where the Westmont community gathers three times a week for chapel services, and was to focus purely on corporate worship.

Those of us involved in the project knew we were in for some challenges. But as is the case with the best sort of learning, the true challenges were not the ones we expected. We had anticipated difficulty getting permission to work in and around the buildings. We had imagined having problems finding affordable technical experts to provide help with casting, welding, or earthscaping. We even predicted challenges in apportioning the actual physical labor of creating the pieces. None of these, in the end, was an issue.

---

1. This program was made possible through a Worship Renewal Grant from the Calvin Institute of Christian Worship, Grand Rapids, Michigan, with funds provided by Lilly Endowment, Inc.

Our major challenges arose on two unexpected fronts. First, this project required that the artists work creatively together — sharing, adjusting, and melding their ideas. This turned out to be a formidable obstacle. In retrospect, the student artists agreed that never before in their artistic training had they been required to work so closely with other artists. They had virtually no training for creative collaboration on this scale. Unlike music or theater students, visual artists are taught to work almost entirely alone. Our curricula, our teaching techniques, and our very idea of *art* all emphasize conceptual, technical, and, above all, creative independence. Our sense of what a painting or sculpture or installation is — indeed, our sense of what an *artist* is — is deeply bound up with the notion of individuality. This view has many advantages as well as disadvantages. Those who work alone enjoy the luxury of being able to work intuitively, and need not pause to articulate or verbalize their processes. They needn't be interrupted or distracted by requests to explain or justify their choices. They can follow, unhindered, the free-flowing dialogue between experience and process, between inquiry and materials. The effect of this is to allow the artistic process itself to remain largely mysterious and resistant to discussion. We don't always teach that it can be helpful to verbalize the underlying question or premise of a piece to others, to recount the discoveries made along the way. We don't sufficiently teach that in addition to developing one's own exploratory path, another artist — living or dead — may be able to enrich that path. We don't always teach the basic skills of listening, articulating, negotiating, and compromising that will serve our students as artists beyond college, where artistic freedoms are almost always in conversation with real-world limits, such as the terms of a contract, the interests of the market, or the requirements of a commission.

Our second challenge was even more daunting. In fact, it was nearly intractable. As we scouted locations, brainstormed, and sketched ideas, it gradually became clear that most of us had deep-seated assumptions that we didn't even know we had about art destined for religious uses. Even more shocking, we discovered that many of our assumptions were irreconcilable! Some assumed that art related to worship would of course be figurative. Others believed that any art related to worship would of course be abstract. Still others assumed that we would work only with the traditional symbols of the Christian faith. Some argued that the pieces would have to be two-dimensional because sculpture can lead to idolatry; others, that they should be three-dimensional for maximum impact. Some claimed that art for worship should be simple, in order to speak to the broadest number of people, while others held that art for worship should demonstrate the most sophisticated and most advanced work of the art department as a fitting offering to God. And the list could go on. One group, the one charged with developing a piece for the chapel space, nearly imploded. None of us predicted that this project would quickly escalate into a heated debate about our most deeply held, yet unexamined, convictions about what *kind* of art was suitable for worship, and we soon realized that few of us were prepared for this particular conversation.

The experience of this group illustrates the central problem that this book is meant to address. None of the artists participating in this project had any qualms about its legitimacy. All of them were artists and Christians, eager to put their talents to work for God's glory and for the good of our college community. As a group, we were not lacking in biblical or theological rationale for our intentions, nor were we lacking in historical or philosophical perspectives. What we were lacking was (1) a coherent communal framework for integrating these perspectives on the visual arts into a worshiping community, and (2) any actual experience in doing so. As a faculty, we at Westmont had evidently done a good job teaching our students that art matters, and therefore that it matters, in theory, for the church, too. But we had not done much with the "so now what?" questions that follow.

One would hope that at a Christian college we might have had a bit of practice thinking through these issues. But in truth, we had had no practice, and Westmont College does not seem unusual in this respect. I have taught at three Christian colleges, each rooted in a different segment of the Christian church, and have visited and observed visual art programs at many other Christian colleges. Dealing intentionally with the relationship between art, artists, and the church is not high on the current list of priorities for these institutions. We are much more intent on preparing our students for successful careers as artists beyond the church. Certainly, we do need to prepare our young artists to work in our culture at large. We do them no favors by ignoring what is happening in New York and Los Angeles, Basel and Beijing. But by ignoring the role of the arts and of artists in the church, are we sending out an unintentional message — that "real artists" don't work for churches, that working for churches is for failed, second-rate artists who can't make it in the "real world"? We only compound this negative message by repeating, with few countervailing positive examples, our habitual lamentations about the state of the visual arts in our churches.

> Congregations probably contribute to our society's arts arena more extensively than they contribute to either the social services arena or the political arena.
>
> — Mark Chaves,
> *Congregations in America*

This is an unfortunate state of affairs both for those of us who care about artists who are Christians and for those of us who care about the future of the visual arts in the church. As a Christian, I want my church to be equipped to use every God-given means to render praise, sanctify its members, and bear witness in the world to the God we worship. Therefore, as a professor teaching at a Christian liberal arts college working with the Christian artists of the future, I need to be prepared to point them to a role in the church, even if it is a role still fraught with challenges and difficulties.

These reasons are cause enough to write a book of this sort. Beyond these core commitments to artists and to the church, however, I, along with many others, believe that this is an auspicious moment for both the arts and the church in our culture. Right now, artists, pastors, and church members alike have more energy for and hospitality toward the arts than ever before. In the culture at large, the range of spiritual and religious questions being explored in the arts is equally impressive. New territories for both the arts and the church are rapidly opening up; if we don't wake up and pay careful attention, we run the risk of squandering a great opportunity through either timid inertia or thoughtless enthusiasm.

> One of the most important reasons that spirituality seems so pervasive in American culture is the publicity it receives because of its presence in the arts.
>
> — Robert Wuthnow, *All in Sync*

Lack of action would also be an act of supreme faithlessness to the many Christian artists and thinkers who have gone before us and who have helped to prepare this hospitable moment. It should give us hope to recognize that in the Protestant world, at least, much progress has been made in just one generation. As William Dyrness has pointed out, "Up until 1960, about the only book available for Christians was an exhaustive collection of materials by Cynthia Pearl Maus, *Christ and the Fine Arts*. This anthology of pictures, poetry, and even music centered on the life of Christ but did not provide critical or historical reflection. The 1960s, however, experienced a virtual explosion of books exploring this topic, many of them thoughtful and theologically sophisticated."[2] Happily, there are now hundreds of books and thousands of articles on this topic. And the pace of publishing and experimentation is only increasing.

Some of these studies focus on the necessary biblical and theological foundations for engaging in the arts and for integrating them into the life of the church. Others illuminate Christians' rich history in the arts — the glorious (the Sistine Chapel) as well as the painful (iconoclastic riots) and the problematic (the Precious Moments Chapel). Some take a more philosophical perspective by delineating how in our Western tradition

I would argue that what the developing art world is longing to discover in their multimedia, shock art exuberance is exactly the compelling and integrative experiences that the Christian faith offers. The exciting proliferation of media and styles, the collaborative world-embracing character of contemporary art may have set the stage perfectly for such holistic events; indeed, it has often echoed these events in exciting ways. The world in one sense is ready to see it; perhaps the church is open in new ways to provide it.

— William Dyrness, *Visual Faith*

we have come to think about art and how these ideas affect the role of the arts within the church. Perspectives from all these areas — theology, history, philosophy — are important and necessary. Each provides a crucial vantage point from which to understand our current location, and each deserves our careful attention.[3]

2. William Dyrness, *Visual Faith: Art, Theology, and Worship in Dialog* (Grand Rapids: Baker Academic, 2001), p. 66.

3. For example, Jeremy Begbie's *Voicing Creation's Praise* works from a theological framework; John Dillenberger's *The Visual Arts and Christianity in America* works from a historical framework; and Nicholas Wolterstorff's *Art in Action: Toward a Christian Aesthetic* works

This book, however, will not reiterate those important contributions. Rather, it concentrates on a piece of the puzzle that has been missing from the art-and-worship conversation: the crucial role of the varied *communities* that shape what we think about *art* and what we think about *church* in the first place. Rather than offering theological, philosophical, or historical perspectives, this study offers a more sociological approach, though theology, philosophy, and history can't — and shouldn't — be entirely absent. Its emphasis is on the human communities, both inside and outside our churches, that have shaped the dialogue between the visual arts and the church.

A Visual Metaphor

If you are reading this book, you probably already have a biblical and theological vision that motivates you and directs your desire to explore the place of the arts in Christian churches. Stories from Scripture and the powerful theological concepts of creation, redemption, incarnation, and Trinity make it clear to you how the arts matter and why your calling as an artist matters. You may feel that your journey is a lonely one and that you have too few fellow travelers, which is its own challenge. Nonetheless, you don't lack motivation or general direction. You know where you want to go and have a trusty biblical and theological passport in hand. Many of us also have a historical atlas that shows us where we've been. That atlas helps us see the fissures and ruptures that separate the past from the present, as well as the points of continuity that offer possible avenues for continued experimentation. From that historical atlas, we can draw lessons, ideas, and inspiration, as well as a roster of artistic ancestors to encourage us on our journey.

Very few of us, though, have a decent topographical map showing the hills, plains, mountains, and river valleys of our local geography. Those hills, plains, mountains, and river valleys exert tremendous influence over the actual path of our journey. This book, I hope, will work something like that topographical map, helping us to identify the most remarkable features of our local geography, showing us where barriers to exploration may exist,

---

from a philosophical framework. For an accessible book that introduces all these areas, see William Dyrness's *Visual Faith*.

Fig. 1. Chapel of the Good Shepherd, Saint Peter's Evangelical Lutheran Church, New York City. Designed by Louise Nevelson, 1977. PHOTOGRAPH COURTESY OF BEATRIZ CIFUENTEZ

making sense of the "path of least resistance" we are often encouraged to take, sparking ideas about how to best work with our local landscape, or even indicating where to consider serious earthscaping.

The major communities, the "topographical features" that will dominate this discussion, can be grouped into two larger affiliations. On the one hand is *the church,* and on the other hand is what we commonly refer to as *the art world.* On the surface, this may seem laughably obvious. Every Christian interested in the role of the arts in the church belongs both to a church and to some part of the art world. But a bit of probing reveals that these communities are not that simple. All of us have ideas about art we have learned from those who have gone before us. But we haven't all learned the same thing. We may all be committed to *art,* but what is meant by *art* differs from person to person and from community to community in important, if seemingly subtle, ways.

Additionally, if you are reading this book, you are also probably committed to integrating the visual arts into the life of your church. But again, your ideas about what that involves may be very different from those of another artist who has the same firm commitment. I'm not talking here about mere differences in taste. In fact, sometimes our arguments about taste are really masking much deeper and divergent core assumptions about the primary purposes of art, the role of the artist, and the relationship of those to what

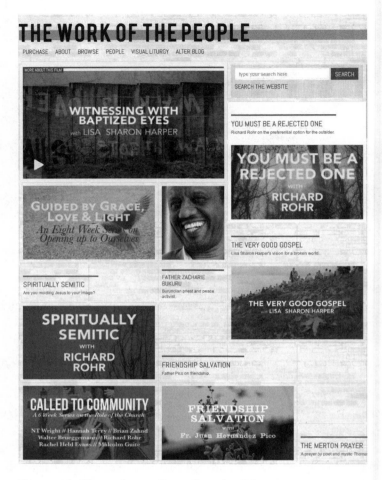

Fig. 2. workofthepeople.com. Screenshot taken July 6, 2016

happens in church. Just think about the different assumptions about art and its role in the church that lie on the one hand behind the commissioning and construction of the Chapel of the Good Shepherd, designed by Louise Nevelson for Saint Peter's Church in New York City (fig. 1),[4] and on the

4. Ann T. Foster, "Louise Nevelson's Worship Environment for St. Peter's Church: A Transformative Space," *Arts* 11, no. 2 (January 1, 1999): 24–27, and Amy Levin Weiss, "Breaking Boundaries: Louise Nevelson and the Erol Beker Chapel of the Good Shepherd," *Arts* 23, no. 3 (January 1, 2012): 38–48.

other behind the creation and marketing of the worship videos produced and sold by www.workofthepeople.com (fig. 2). Both represent a firm commitment to the importance of the arts for the church, but each is rooted in a different conversation about art and its role in the church. Thus, the very, very different results. A few words, then, on *the church* and *the art world* are in order here.

Ecclesiology

Christians share a common identity rooted in our love of the triune God and our desire to follow Christ's call. But our ideas of how we connect our love of Christ and our desire to serve God to our lives in the church can differ in important ways. The Jesuit theologian Avery Dulles sees five basic theological lenses through which churches typically understand themselves. Dulles's goal in his now-classic study *Models of the Church* was not so much to argue that a particular model was correct but more to name and describe a variety of models operative in the life and work of a range of churches. "The method of models or types," he wrote, "can have great value in helping people to get beyond the limitations of their own particular outlook, and to enter into fruitful conversation with others having a fundamentally different mentality."[5] Over the years, Dulles has refined and expanded his mod-

ECCLESIOLOGY: The doctrine and discussion about the church in relation to God, human history and Salvation.

— *Blackwell Encyclopedia of Modern Christian Thought*

CHURCH, *n,* 4a: The community or whole body of Christ's faithful people collectively; all who are spiritually united to Christ as "Head of the Church." More fully described as the Church Universal or Catholic. . . . 10. A congregation of Christians locally organized into a society for religious worship and spiritual purposes, under the direction of one set of spiritual office-bearers.

— *Oxford English Dictionary*

---

5. Avery Dulles, *Models of the Church* (Garden City, NY: Image Books, 1987), p. 12.

Fig. 3. Emerald Bay, Lake Tahoe. PHOTOGRAPH BY MICHAEL MARFELL, (ORIGINALLY POSTED TO FLICKR AS EMERALD BAY) [CC BY 2.0 (HTTP://CREATIVECOMMONS.ORG/LICENSES/BY/2.0)], VIA WIKIMEDIA COMMONS

els to include six: "institutional," "mystical communion," "sacrament," "herald," "servant," as well as his own proposed model, "community of disciples," with an eye to the scriptural warrant, heritage in the church, and the strengths and liabilities of each. The reader comes away with a renewed appreciation for the glorious richness as well as the glorious complexity of the mystery of the church. In my own thinking and research on the place of the visual arts in Christian churches and in Christian worship, I, like Dulles, have become attuned to the importance of a community's ecclesiology — that is, its theology of itself as a church, particularly with respect to unpacking the potential and actual roles for the arts in our churches.

The ecclesiastical element that came to the fore in my research concerns the ways in which any given congregation understands itself as "universal" and "local." The necessity to understand one's church as *both* universal and local is, as Gordon Lathrop calls it, an "essential tension" in our lives in the church. The church is always local: "it has no other existence. . . . It is always a local gathering of people with their leaders,

Fig. 4. The Gooseneck, Colorado River south of Moab, Utah. Canyonlands National Park.
PHOTOGRAPH BY JIM WARK

around the Scriptures and the sacraments, knowing Christ risen and *here*."[6] This local character of any church accords with definition 10 of the term "church" from the *Oxford English Dictionary*. Yet the church is also always universal, as in definition 4a. It is "in communion with all the churches of Christ, in every time and every place, and that what it celebrates is a Gospel which has universal significance, albeit expressed in local terms and ways."[7] Though all Christians would acknowledge this truth, we interpret the character of "universal" and "local" quite differently in our everyday, operative ecclesiologies and also, sometimes, tend to privilege one over the other in our regular patterns of worship and life. In Dulles's typology, for example, his first three types — institutional, mystical communion, and sacrament — tend to emphasize the universal, while his second three — herald, servant, and community of disciples — underscore the local character of the church.

6. Gordon Lathrop, "Worship: Local Yet Universal," in *Christian Worship: Unity in Cultural Diversity*, ed. Anita Stauffer (Geneva: Lutheran World Federation, 1996), p. 48.
7. Ibid., p. 49.

To return to the topographical metaphor used earlier, a given congregation's sense of itself as primarily universal or primarily local can be imagined as the land features on a topographical map — the mountains, hills, and plains. Where the universal character of the church looms large, we see prominent land features like mountains, canyons, and bluffs that channel the visual arts into deep, beautiful mountain lakes or spectacular river canyons. Lake Tahoe (fig. 3) and the Colorado River (fig. 4) come to mind as visual metaphors of strongly universalized ecclesiologies that, in turn, give very specific form to the artistic talents in their watershed. The waters of Lake Tahoe or of the Colorado River can't flow in just any direction. These waters can only go where the surrounding mountains and canyons allow them to go. In both cases, the geography itself reflects to varying degrees the accumulated effects of many years of water flowing in that direction. These mountain lakes and rivers are often breathtakingly gorgeous near their source. But sometimes, if there isn't enough water at the source, or if they aren't regularly replenished by rain or by springs, they are reduced to muddy puddles and trickles.

Our Art System

The ecclesiological conversation, however, contributes only half of our landscape. Not only do we inhabit churches with different operational ecclesiologies, we also inhabit different parts of what we commonly call "the art world." The philosopher Larry Shiner, in his book *The Invention of Art*, prefers the term "art system" to "art world" because it allows him to distinguish a number of different art worlds that are nonetheless all part of a greater whole — our art system. This is an extremely useful distinction. Too often the term "art world" is used in an exclusive way rather than in an inclusive way. It is assumed to mean a rather small set of A-list galleries in New York and Los Angeles and the contemporary artists, cutting-edge journals, prominent critics, and prestigious art schools that support them. A typical version of that definition is given by James Elkins, a prominent, prolific, and helpful critic of the current art scene: "I will be using *art world* to denote fine art together with its economic support, and usually — but undogmatically, and with exceptions — I will be excluding tourist art, children's art, religious art, commercial art, graphic design, and all other forms of art."[8] But after excluding all that, what remains is only a fraction of the big picture! While Elkins's definition does describe his commitments and serve his argument, it can't fully describe every artist's commitments or serve every artist's purposes. Nor, with its blanket elimination of "religious art" from the "art world," could it hope to serve our purposes.

Our North American art system is rich and varied. It embraces the art worlds of the weekend watercolorist, the graphic designer, the high school art teacher, and the woodworking aficionado — as well as the A-list gallery artist — and the multitudinous fans, friends, teachers, critics, and patrons who support them. It unites all those worlds around a basic, fundamental conviction that art is a manifestation of something profoundly human, something that at once expresses and nourishes individuality, community, creativity, and freedom. For participants in our art system, it follows logically that a failure to appreciate art is a defect of character; that depriving people of art (especially children) is a violation of their humanity; and that using art to persuade or communicate is possible, powerful, and potentially dangerous.

> An ART SYSTEM "[h]as a larger scope that includes the various art worlds and sub-worlds. . . . *Art worlds* are networks of artists, critics, audiences and others who share a common field of interest along with a commitment to certain values, practices, and institutions. An *art system* embraces the underlying concepts and ideals shared by various *art worlds* and by the culture at large, including those who only participate marginally in one of the art worlds."
>
> — Larry Shiner,
> *The Invention of Art*

While it is true that within this system, the A-list galleries and their supporters may have more national visibility and therefore more cultural clout than the millions of K-12 art educators, graphic designers, and weekend watercolorists, it is also true that those educators, designers, and hobbyists enjoy their own substantial

---

8. James Elkins, *On the Strange Place of Religion in Contemporary Art* (New York: Routledge, 2004), p. 4. Elkins acknowledges the internal tensions in the phrase "art world" but chooses to restrict it to the strata of art we think of as "fine art." I, too, acknowledge the tensions in my use of "art system" versus "art worlds" but must allow for multiple art worlds to address the situation in the church.

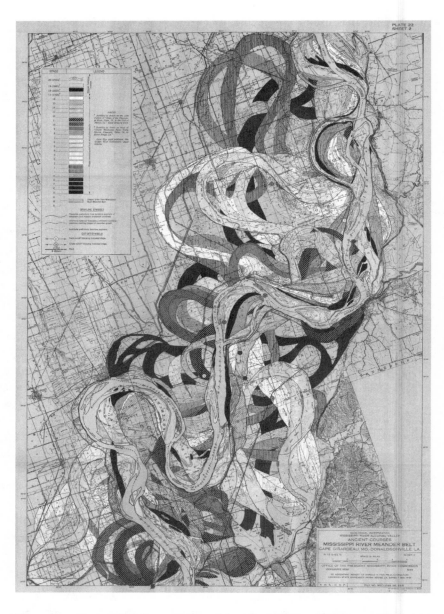

Fig. 5. Army Corps of Engineers Survey of the Alluvial Valley of the Lower Mississippi River. Harold N. Fisk, 1944.

social and economic power. Each of these art worlds within our art system has, as Shiner notes, "networks of artists, critics, audiences."[9] Art worlds are not abstract — they are concrete, communal, and regulated. They exist in physical structures, like the Los Angeles County Museum of Art. They exist in publications, like *Watercolor Magazine* and the *Journal of Art Education*. They exist in membership criteria, like those for the College Art Association and the American Institute of Graphic Arts. They exist in accreditation standards, like those maintained by the National Association of Schools of Art and Design. They exist in our local city art councils and in the halls of our state legislatures. More to the point, all these art worlds are represented in our churches by the varied artists and art lovers in our midst. While all are members of our common art system, we often belong to different art worlds within that system.

If ecclesiology can be imagined as land features (mountains, hills, plains), then our art system can be imagined as water features such as lakes, rivers, and streams. Where the ecclesiology is strongly universalized, the direction and flow of the arts will be determined by the land features. Artistic activity will be channeled into a pristine mountain lake or a deep canyon river. Where ecclesiology is understood as primarily local, the direction and flow of the arts might look more like the Mississippi River (fig. 5), where there is little keeping the water from flowing where it will across the land.

The Mississippi is a majestic and awe-inspiring river. It is an economic corridor. It is a reliable source of water for irrigation and consumption. It is the source of rich silt that renews farmland and protects the Gulf Coast shoreline. But the Mississippi is also prone to damaging floods, and it changes its course over time, leaving a trail of isolated oxbow lakes in its wake. It can be both bane and blessing. In churches with highly local ecclesiologies, the force of our art system and its attendant, sometimes conflicting, art worlds can be like the Mississippi. Its energy is impressive and its waters can bring great blessing. But the surrounding land features provide few external restraints to direct that energy into the most useful channels. At times, the river takes on a life of its own and significantly remaps the landscape. Some communities build dams, locks, and levees to try to harness the river for their own ends. Others, having been flooded once too often,

9. Larry Shiner, *The Invention of Art* (Chicago: University of Chicago Press, 2001), p. 11.

choose to move away from the river altogether, concluding that proximity is too dangerous despite the beauty and riches of the water.

Every metaphor has its breaking point, and I certainly don't want to push this one past its usefulness. Moreover, metaphors drawing on natural imagery run the serious risk of naturalizing phenomena that are essentially cultural — the result of human activity. In the real world, our art system and some elements of our ecclesiastical lives are just as much the product of human minds and hands as any dams, locks, and levees that we invent to attempt to control the flow of water through a landscape.

God ordained the church, but for good or ill we have given it its many shapes and forms. And the briefest survey of the arts around the world reminds us that our current twenty-first-century North American ideas about art are also extremely particular to our own place and time. Art and church are not abstract. Each takes on specific and varied forms that interact with one another in specific and varied ways. Particular churches resonate with particular art worlds for particular reasons. When it comes to understanding the role of the visual arts in your local church, you may find it helpful to consider the dominant ideas of church and the dominant forms of art at work in your congregation, as well as to recognize the ways in which these understandings have become embodied in living, breathing people, and in communities, institutions, and practices. How does your church understand its universal and local character? Which of the many art worlds in our larger art system are well represented in your church? Does the ecclesiology of your church shape the use of the arts? If so, how? If not, what does shape and direct the use of the arts? If you can't answer these questions now, my goal is that you will be better equipped to do so after reading this book.

Description and Discernment

This book has two goals. The first goal is description. I want to sketch a topographical map of the existing landscapes within which we work to provide all of us with helpful information about the localities we inhabit. To make this description as accurate and as vivid as possible, I've located it in a very specific area, western lower Michigan. After many months of corresponding with artists and churches across the nation and across the confessional spectrum, it became clear that the kinds of church-based art activities taking place in the greater Grand Rapids area were representative of church-based art activities taking place across the United States. Additionally, the Calvin Institute of Christian Worship, which has generously granted me the time and space for this study, is located in Grand Rapids. This physical proximity allowed me direct access to these worshiping communities. Certainly, not every particular activity can be found in West Michigan, so occasionally I've gone beyond this region to include something helpful to the discussion. My expectation, though, is that every reader will find in these descriptions family resemblances to the assumptions and activities that characterize the reader's own situation.

Part 1 of this book is largely aimed toward this descriptive goal, and its three chapters correspond to the three major families of Christian churches: Orthodox, Roman Catholic, and Protestant. For each, I discuss how notions of church and notions of art interact by examining the institutions and frameworks that have shaped each conversation. For the Orthodox and Roman Catholic discussions, the starting point is ecclesiology. Ecclesiology determines what currently can and can't happen with the visual arts. For the Protestant conversation, where the ecclesiology often — though not always — emphasizes the local over the universal, the starting point is generally one of the various art worlds within our art system. For Protestants, then, the discussion typically starts with "art" and then "goes to church." Though you may be interested only in the chapter that describes your own ecclesiastical family, I hope you will read the other chapters as well. Each of these major traditions demonstrates in different ways the power of art to bear witness to God in the church and in the world. Since the ecumenical movement of the 1960s, all these traditions have already learned much from one another. Yet we've also learned that not all forms of witness are appropriate or effective in all places. We need to appreciate what is currently possible given the contours of our local landscape before we can lay any more ambitious plans — plans that might actually require modifications of that landscape to be effective.

This brings me to the second purpose of this book: discernment. Discernment comes into play in two ways. First of all, as the noted art historian Michael Baxandall pointed out long ago, no act of description is entirely neutral. Every description is "a selective sharpener of attention."[10] Thus

10. Michael Baxandall, *Giotto and the Orators: Humanist Observers of Painting in Italy and*

my descriptions, like all others, are not neutral, but are meant to serve as "selective sharpeners of attention." Though I am an appreciative visitor to all the communities this book surveys, and though I have tried my best to be a fair and careful observer of landscapes that are not my own, I am sure that my underlying habits of looking and thinking seep through in ways I can't recognize. My own theological, historical, and social inclinations have been shaped by the Reformed tradition of Christianity, and some readers might notice this inflection from time to time. My hope, however, is that the perspective of a respectful, interested outsider may be of some use to the inhabitants of other landscapes and may be of help to clergy, laypeople, and artists trying to better understand their own situation.

Both the conversational questions posed at the end of each descriptive chapter and the second section of this book are intended to nurture the discernment we need to bring to our work with the visual arts in our churches. Description may be intrinsically interesting, but what does it tell us that is helpful for our work in our churches? What might we see more clearly, by way of contrast, that we might not have seen otherwise? How does this topographical map inform our sense of place, point to where we may want to go in the future, and equip us to get there? The shorter chapters of part 2 consider the themes and questions that emerge when we set the descriptive chapters side by side and compare them. What elements of your own ecclesial topography pop into relief when viewed alongside a different tradition? How do ideas of church emerge in worship, and how do they direct what the arts do (or don't do) in your congregation? How do the arts in your congregation mirror (or not) the dominant ideas of art drawn from culture at large? Part 2, without being prescriptive, attempts to draw some practical conclusions from what's been observed with the hope that, whatever the future brings for artists in the worshiping church, our work will be faithful, fruitful, and sustainable. Each of these criteria needs to be discerned at the local level. What is faithful, fruitful, and durable in one type of church can rarely be translated directly to another type of church. Faithfulness involves discerning what functions for art are compatible with your church's ecclesiology and current patterns of worship. Faithfulness also involves discerning what the

---

the Discovery of Pictorial Composition (1350–1450) (Oxford: Oxford University Press, 1971), p. 48.

highest ideals and hopes of your church are and working as faithful artists to change what may need to change for the flourishing of the church. Finally, faithfulness goes two ways. It also requires each church to be faithful to its artists, trusting them to work in and with the church for the good of all.

Fruitfulness requires honest and careful evaluation of what the arts are bringing to the church and of how the church is being blessed by them. Just having an arts program or arts ministry isn't enough. All arts activities need to be subject to the same prayerful, evaluative attention to which every other area of church life is subject. This is very difficult if artists don't enjoy the faithful support of their church. But if a church is faithful to its artists, an ongoing conversation about what is working or not, and why, is absolutely indispensable. Lastly, few people who are not themselves artists understand how costly and labor intensive work with the visual arts can be. If a church is to be faithful and fruitful in this area, it can't afford to abuse either its human or its material resources. A sustainable program needs to be integrated into the structure of the congregation so that it is not entirely dependent on (or at the disposal of) the good will, labor, and financial generosity of one or two people.

Audience

My focus in this study is on the visual arts — painting, sculpture, ceramics, textiles, digital media, installations, and, to some extent, architecture. Though the term "the arts" often includes music, drama, and dance, for the purposes of this study, "the arts" will generally refer to the visual arts. One reason for this focus is my own work in a studio art department and my concerns about the future of our emerging visual artists in the church. A second is more pragmatic: taking drama, dance, and music into account would make this a much larger and even more complex task. I am confident, though, that if your artistic involvement in the church is in drama, dance, or music, you will nonetheless find helpful parallels to your experiences in this account of the place of the visual arts in various Christian churches.

I also imagine that the majority of readers of this book will be Protestant. Protestant churches have had a vexed relationship with the visual arts going all the way back to the tumultuous days of the Reformation. That legacy is still with us. We often begin our stories about "art in the church" in the six-teenth century, recounting tales of the iconoclastic riots that swept through parts of Germany and the Low Countries with the advent of Zwinglian and Calvinist preaching. Even though historians have begun to revise our traditional ideas about iconoclasm and its effects, many Protestants still begin conversations about art in the church with this narrative of loss.[11] Many observers, and especially artists, lament the loss of visual literacy in our own Protestant traditions and look enviously at the church buildings and worship practices of our Catholic and Orthodox brothers and sisters for whom the visual arts are still very much a part of life in the church. From that perspective, there isn't much good news for Protestants when it comes to the visual arts.

But there is another side to this story. Contrary to the litany of lament we typically encounter in writing about the arts in Protestant churches, this survey proposes that Protestants may, at the moment, actually have more room to experiment and more room to make the visual arts a living part of the worshiping community than do many Catholic and Orthodox churches. While the challenges for Protestants remain very real, the opportunities are equally real.

To return to the story with which I opened, I'm grateful for the enthusi-asm with which my students embraced a project bringing together art and ideas about worship. The very fact that we had no arguments about the basic legitimacy of the project signals a huge advance in the relationship between the arts and Protestant Christianity. I imagine, though, that if we had had a better map of where each of us was coming from, we would not have been so surprised by the debates that arose, and the discussion itself would have been marked by more clarity, charity, and purpose. It is my sincere wish that this book will provide a resource for a clearer, more charitable, and more purposeful discussion about the place of the visual arts in your church.

---

11. For two examples of revisionist approaches to the "narrative of loss," see Paul Corby Finney's *Seeing beyond the Word: Visual Arts and the Calvinist Tradition* (Grand Rapids: Eerdmans, 1999) and William Dyrness's *Reformed Theology and Visual Culture: The Protes-tant Imagination from Calvin to Edwards* (Cambridge and New York: Cambridge University Press, 2004). For a secular discussion of the complexities of iconoclasm, see the catalogue for the *Iconoclash* exhibition, edited by Bruno Latour and Peter Weibel (Cambridge, MA: MIT Press, 2002).

Part One

DESCRIPTION

CHAPTER I

Miracles of Belief:
The Orthodox Covenant with Icons

We confess and proclaim our salvation in word and images.

— KONTAKION FOR
"THE TRIUMPH OF ORTHODOXY"

The last place one might expect to encounter Christians praying with icons is a theology classroom in a Calvinist school. John Calvin, after all, firmly rejected the usefulness of images for the purposes of worship. But such is the widespread fascination with icons across the Christian spectrum that students at Calvin College have shown interest in such an encounter. A theology professor's January-term course on iconography, cotaught with an area iconographer, has attracted its fair share of student interest, introducing students to practices associated with making and using icons and orienting students to the theology out of which they come. In my own Presbyterian congregation in Santa Barbara, amateur artists have taken to icon painting. The large Episcopal congregation in downtown Santa Barbara has offered icon-painting seminars.[1] You can probably think of similar examples from your own experience.

---

1. Throughout this study, I will use the verb "paint" rather than "write" to describe the activity of making an icon. "Icon writing" appears to be a neologism unique to the English-speaking Orthodox world. It is, according to David Coomler and Dr. John Yiannias, rooted in a narrowly literal translation into English of the Greek and Slavic terms *graphi* and *pisánie*,

What should we make of all this interest in icons? Curiosity about icons is in part the by-product of the rediscovery, over the last few decades of the twentieth century, of the Eastern Orthodox Christian tradition by non-Orthodox American Christians. Of all the varieties of Christianity in the United States, the Eastern Orthodox churches were until recently the least visible, least accessible, and most "exotic." But that has changed.[2]

The Context: Authorizing the Icon

Missions, Immigrants, and Converts

Orthodoxy arrived in North America in the eighteenth century with Greek settlers in Florida and Russian missionaries in Alaska. But these small Orthodox communities were the exception rather than the rule for patterns of immigration and mission in North America. Scholars estimate only fifty thousand Orthodox Christians in the United States at the turn of the twen-

---

which mean "depiction" and can indicate both writing and pictorial delineation. The earliest reference I've found to this debate comes from Coomler's *The Icon Handbook: A Guide to Understanding Icons and the Liturgy,* where he adds, in a terse aside on the use of "iconwriting" as a term, "though theological excuses are often made for use of the term, it is best avoided as an affectation" ([Springfield, IL: Templegate Publishers, 1995], p. 78). More recently, Yiannias, an art historian and Greek Orthodox Christian, has argued for the elimination of the term: "Not only does the expression do violence to English and sound just plain silly, but it can introduce notions without basis in the Greek texts — such as, that an icon is essentially a representation of words, as opposed to a representation of things that words represent. The theologically important fact that icons, which are pictorial, and Scripture, which is verbal, are nearly equivalent can be conveyed in other ways than by torturing English" (orthodoxhistory.org/2010/06/08/icons-are-not-written, accessed November 7, 2011). Over the course of the last decade, more and more North American iconographers have begun to use "painting" rather than "writing" to describe the process of creating an icon.

2. I am grateful for the time Grand Rapids–area Orthodox clergy spent with me in the early days of this project, helping me understand Orthodox theology, liturgy, and iconography: Father Anton Frunze, Father John Winfrey, Father Andrew Lowe, and Father Daniel Daly all took time to meet with me and guide me through their churches. More recently, Kathy Jo Broekstra at Holy Trinity Greek Orthodox Church was a hospitable and helpful tour guide. Special thanks go to iconographer Matushka Darya Carney, who has a special gift for helping a Calvinist understand Orthodoxy. Any errors or misunderstandings that remain are due to my shortcomings, not to their gracious efforts.

tieth century. By the end of the century, however, that number had climbed to at least 1.2 million (though some estimates go well beyond this number).[3] Some of this increase is due to immigration — especially intense around the middle of the century with the establishment of Communism in much of eastern and central Europe.[4] Even with these increased numbers, however, as a proportion of the overall population of the United States, Orthodox Christians remain a tiny minority. Immigration alone can't fully account for the growing awareness of Orthodoxy among American Christians at large.

Protestant and Catholic conversions to Orthodoxy have certainly helped increase awareness.[5] Perhaps the most spectacular example of this dynamic, as narrated by the now-Orthodox priest Peter Gillquist, occurred in 1987 in Southern California. Beginning in the late 1960s, a group of evangelical Christians based in Santa Barbara, most of whom had roots in the parachurch organization Campus Crusade for Christ, dedicated themselves to re-creating what they called "the New Testament church." Through study and prayer, over the course of about a decade, the community inched closer and closer to Eastern Orthodoxy. Resisting the idea of forming a new denomination, they first organized themselves as the New Covenant Apostolic

3. Estimated numbers of Orthodox Christians in the United States vary widely from study to study, ranging from 1.2 million to 6 million (David B. Barrett, ed., *World Christian Encyclopedia*, 2nd ed. [Oxford: Oxford University Press, 1999], p. 12); Mark Stokoe and Leonid Kishkousky estimate 2 million in *Orthodox Christians in North America (1794–1994)* (Syosset, NY: Orthodox Christian Publications, 1995), p. 86; Alexei Krindatch provides much more modest estimates: the 1.2 million figure comes from his *Atlas of American Orthodox Christian Churches* (Brookline, MA: Holy Cross Orthodox Press, 2011). Elsewhere, his estimates from a 2010 survey conducted by the Standing Conference of the Canonical Orthodox Bishops in the Americas (SCOBA) run to slightly less than 800,000 adherents and slightly more than 200,000 regular attenders (http://hirr.hartsem.edu/research/quick_question17 .html, accessed June 18, 2012).

4. Alexei Krindatch, "The Orthodox (Eastern Christian) Churches in the USA at the Beginning of a New Millennium" (2002). See particularly section 2, "The Development of the Orthodox Churches in USA during 20th Century: Premises, Trends and Challenges" (www.hartfordinstitute.org/research/orthodoxpaper.html, accessed October 14, 2011).

5. Technically, "reaffiliate" would be a better term to describe those who come to Orthodoxy from other Christian traditions, leaving "convert" as the proper descriptor for those who come to Christianity from non-Christian belief systems. But since "reaffiliate" is not a commonly used term, and since most Christians who come to Orthodoxy from Catholic or Protestant backgrounds self-identify as "converts," I will use the less precise, but also less awkward, term "convert."

Order. Further study convinced the community that an "order" can't really exist independently from a church; a few years later, the New Covenant communities reorganized as a denomination of sorts, the Evangelical Orthodox Church. In time, this formal identification with Orthodoxy led to a desire to be properly united to the Orthodox Church, and in the spring of 1987 seventeen Evangelical Orthodox congregations in Southern California officially joined the Antiochian Archdiocese of North America.[6] Peter Gillquist's journey, and that of his fellow travelers, brought Eastern Orthodoxy into the spotlight for many American evangelicals.

Then, in 1992, Frank Schaeffer, the son of prominent evangelical author Francis Schaeffer, joined the Orthodox Church. Subsequent affiliations have drawn further attention to Orthodoxy — Frederica Mathewes-Green, a Christian author and columnist, left the Episcopal Church for the Orthodox Church in 1993; Yale University church historian Jaroslav Pelikan, a prominent scholar in Lutheran circles, joined in 1998. Other, less publicly known figures, like Englishman Timothy Ware, now Metropolitan Kallistos Ware, also played important roles in raising the profile of Orthodox Christianity in the English-speaking world. Ware is the author of the best-selling general work on Orthodoxy in the English language, *The Orthodox Church.*[7] John Maddex, a former associate of Moody Radio, went on to found Ancient Faith Radio, which operates under the auspices of the Antiochian Orthodox Archdiocese of North America. Ancient Faith Radio has greatly increased the accessibility of Orthodoxy in North America and far beyond.

The real story, though, doesn't lie with this list of individuals. It lies with the large number of ordinary American Christians who have "traveled the road to Constantinople." Today, in congregations associated with the largest Orthodox body in the United States, the Orthodox Church in America, over 50 percent of the parishioners and nearly 60 percent of current and future priests are converts to Orthodoxy. Though numbers of noncradle Orthodox

6. This story is recounted in Peter Gillquist's *Becoming Orthodox: A Journey to the Ancient Christian Faith* (Ben Lomond, CA: Conciliar Press, 1992). For the story particular to Santa Barbara, see also the history of Saint Athanasius Church in Santa Barbara (http://www.stathanasius.org/site/content/38, accessed November 9, 2011).

7. Kallistos Ware's *The Orthodox Church* was first published in 1963, then revised in 1964 and 1993, and is distributed in the United States by Penguin Books. Kallistos Ware is also the author of *The Orthodox Way* (Crestwood, NY: St. Vladimir's Seminary Press, 1990), a basic introduction to Orthodox doctrine.

are smaller in the more ethnically oriented Greek Orthodox Church, they are still significant: 29 percent of parishioners, 14 percent of current priests, and 26 percent of seminarians were not born into Greek Orthodoxy.[8]

The Recovery of the Icon

One need not become Orthodox, however, to deepen one's appreciation for Eastern Christianity. On the scholarly level, the liturgical renewal movements of the late nineteenth and early twentieth centuries, which culminated in both the Catholic Church's Second Vatican Council and the midcentury ecumenical movement, were animated by renewed attention to patristics, that is, to the writings of the ancient church fathers at the core of Orthodox theology.[9] Returning to the primary sources that gave shape to all streams of the Christian faith fostered renewed attention to the riches of Eastern Christianity.

On the popular level, we need only note the avalanche of books on icons that has appeared over the last couple of decades to appreciate the level of interest and curiosity that now exists for this formerly obscure (in North America, at least) Christian art form.[10] Something has changed indeed when the former archbishop of Canterbury, Rowan Williams, publishes two books on praying with icons![11] But then again, Williams is himself a

8. Alexei Krindatch, *"American Orthodoxy" or "Orthodoxy in America"?* (Berkeley, CA: Patriarch Athenagoras Orthodox Institute, 2004), p. 8; Krindatch, *Evolving Visions of the Orthodox Priesthood in America* (Berkeley, CA: Patriarch Athenagoras Orthodox Institute, 2006), p. 6; Krindatch, *The Orthodox Church Today* (Berkeley, CA: Patriarch Athenagoras Orthodox Institute, 2008), pp. 6–11.

9. For a discussion of the relationship of the Orthodox churches to the liturgical movement, see chapter 10 in John R. K. Fenwick and Bryan D. Spinks, *Worship in Transition: The Liturgical Movement in the Twentieth Century* (New York: Continuum, 1995). pp. 95–103.

10. Interestingly, in the narratives of those who embrace Eastern Orthodoxy, the use of icons in worship can actually be, initially, at least, a source of consternation. See Amy Slagle's "Imagined Aesthetics: Constructions of Aesthetic Experience in Orthodox Christian Conversion Narratives," in *Aesthetics as a Religious Factor in Eastern and Western Christianity*, ed. Wil van den Bercken and Jonathan Sutton (Leuven: Peeters, 2005), pp. 53–63, and chapter 5, "Convert Perspectives on Eastern Orthodox Ritual," in Slagle's more recent book, *The Eastern Church in the Spiritual Marketplace: American Conversions to Orthodox Christianity* (De Kalb: Northern Illinois University Press, 2011), pp. 105–23.

11. Rowan Williams, *The Dwelling of the Light: Praying with Icons of Christ* (Grand Rapids: Eerdmans, 2004) and *Ponder These Things: Praying with Icons of the Virgin* (Brewster, MA: Paraclete Press, 2006).

Fig. 6. Icon of Christ, Monastery of Saint Catherine, Sinai. Sixth century.

child of the liturgical renewal movement. He studied patristics as a student, wrote his PhD thesis on the theology of twentieth-century Orthodox theologian Vladimir Lossky, and today serves as a patron for the Fellowship of Saint Alban and Saint Sergius, an Oxford-based organization dedicated to "fostering dialogue among Christians East and West."[12]

It was Vladimir Lossky, the subject of Williams's 1975 thesis, who helped make icons and their theological framework more easily accessible in the West. Lossky was one of many Russians who fled their homeland after the 1917 revolution and eventually settled in Paris. With his fellow expatriate, iconographer Leonid Ouspensky, Lossky published *The Meaning of Icons* in 1952, the first major study of icons available in English that took into account not only their artistic aspects but also their theological import.[13] This work, as one reviewer put it, "has done more than any other single book for the study and appreciation of icons in the twentieth century."[14]

Parallel to Lossky's work, Princeton art historian Kurt Weitzmann brought to light for the English-speaking world some of the oldest surviving icons we know of. Though it is hard to believe, the now familiar and beloved sixth-century icon of Christ from the Monastery of Saint Catherine (fig. 6) was not reproduced or properly catalogued until the mid-1950s when it was first included in a French study by a Greek scholar. It wasn't published in color in its restored state until Weitzmann's study of the Sinai icons was

---

12. Rowan Williams, "The Theology of Vladimir Nikolaievich Lossky: An Exposition and Critique" (DPhil thesis, University of Oxford, 1975). For the Fellowship of Saint Alban and Saint Sergius, see www.sobornost.org.

13. There were a handful of earlier publications: Nikodem Kondakov's *The Russian Icon* (Oxford: Clarendon, 1927), "the only serious and comprehensive discussion of the subject in English," was also deemed, by Alfred Barr Jr., the director of MOMA, to be "often misleading and irrelevant" (quoted from his introductory essay in *Russian Icons* [New York: American Russian Institute, 1931], p. 6). Barr's essay details essentially the same exhibition as the one on display at the Victoria and Albert Museum in 1928, which was also accompanied by a catalogue with a handful of scholarly entries (*Masterpieces of Russian Painting: Twenty Colour Plates and Forty-Three Monochrome Reproductions of Russian Icons and Frescoes from the XI to the XVIII Centuries* (London: Europa Publications, 1930).

14. Charles Lock, review of *Theology of the Icon*, by Leonid Ouspensky, *Canadian Slavonic Papers/Revue Canadienne des Slavistes* 37, no. 1/2 (March-June 1995): 226. Pavel Florensky's *Iconostasis*, trans. Donald Sheehan and Olga Andrejev (Crestwood, NY: St. Vladimir's Seminary Press, 1996), first published in Russian in 1922, has also been influential, but until recently, only among those who could read Russian. The full text was first translated into German in 1988, into French in 1992, and into English in 1996.

released in 1976.[15] The work of Ouspensky, Lossky, Weitzmann, and other scholars during the second half of the twentieth century began a renewal of the iconic tradition that continues to this day.

While immigrant Orthodox Christians always had access to the icons in their homes and churches, these icons varied in quality and sometimes in canonical correctness. The new scholarship on icons gave American Orthodox Christians a richer, fuller understanding of their own tradition. For non-Orthodox American Christians who had little or no regular access to actual icons, it made accessible a wealth of information about icons that was entirely new to them. Though the primary audience for all this new work was scholarly, popular interest soon caught up, which makes the late twentieth-century tidal wave of fascination with icons — branded by one irritated Mennonite as "iconitis" — a bit more comprehensible.[16]

Orthodox believers, though, would see more in all this than just the currents of research and scholarship bearing fruit. They would see the power of icons themselves at work.

Authorizing the Icon

Icons, as understood by the Orthodox, are no mere pictures. They are "windows to heaven," "sacred doorways," "the gospel in line and light," "theology

---

15. This icon, first catalogued by George and Maria Georgiou Soteriou in *Icones du Mont Sinai* (Athens: Institut Français d'Athènes, 1956–1958), received its first extensive discussion in English in 1967 in Manolis Chatzidakis and Gerry Walters's "An Encaustic Icon of Christ at Sinai," (*Art Bulletin* 19 [September 1967]): 197–208). Its first postrestoration, quality color reproduction was in Kurt Weitzmann's *The Monastery of Saint Catherine at Mount Sinai, the Icons* (Princeton: Princeton University Press, 1976). In his 1947 essay "Byzantine Scholarship and Art in America," *American Journal of Archaeology* 51 (Autumn 1947): 394–418, Weitzmann commented with respect to the biggest exhibition of Byzantine art on American soil thus far: "it must be admitted that there was not a single first-rate icon. . . . Considering the central position of icon painting in the orthodox world, this was perhaps the most serious lacuna in presenting a comprehensive picture of Byzantine culture" (p. 405). Contemporary readers can turn to *Holy Image, Hallowed Ground: Icons from Sinai*, ed. Robert Nelson and Kristen Collins (Los Angeles: J. Paul Getty Museum, 2006), for a summative discussion with excellent reproductions.

16. John M. Janzen, "Mennonite Icon — an Oxymoron," *Mennonite Life* 59 (March 2004), an online journal found at www.bethelks.edu/mennonitelife/2004Mar (accessed November 18, 2012).

in color." They do not represent; they make present. And what they make present are Christ and the fully perfected and transfigured saints in communion with Christ as well as the salvific events of the church's past *and* future. It comes as no surprise to an Orthodox Christian that anyone longing for hope, for beauty, for compassion, for the transcendent, would be drawn to icons. Icons, it is said, convert. There are even "iconic" instances of this effect. In my interviews with iconographers, I heard more than once how the exercise of painting an icon, even if done by a skeptical atheist, can result in conversion to faith. This is exactly the account given for Leonid Ouspensky's conversion in Paris in the 1930s.[17] The claim is not new. It's difficult to find a book on Orthodoxy that does not recount the story of the conversion of the Slavic Rus' people to Orthodox Christianity in 988, inspired by the splendid music and image-rich liturgy in Constantinople: "We knew not whether we were in heaven or on earth. For on earth there is no such splendor or such beauty, and we are at a loss how to describe it. We only know that God dwells there among men, and their service is fairer than the ceremonies of other nations. For we cannot forget that beauty. Every man, after tasting something sweet, is afterward unwilling to accept that which is bitter, and therefore we cannot dwell longer here."[18] The efficacy of icons as mediators of divine presence parallels many Protestant Christians' understanding of the power of inspired Scripture to convert readers to Christ.

Books on icons typically begin with a theological discussion that immediately transports us back over twelve hundred years. Unlike Protestant arguments about art in the church, which are typically located in the 1500s, and unlike Catholic arguments, which are located in mid-twentieth century, Orthodox arguments about art in the church were considered settled by the middle of the ninth century. A handful of foundational texts outline the basic contours of the argument: the writings of John of Damascus (c. 676–749); those of Theodore the Studite (759–826); and the pronouncements of the Seventh Ecumenical Council, which took place at Nicaea in 787 (also known

---

17. Patrick Doolan, *Recovering the Icon: The Life and Work of Leonid Ouspensky* (Crestwood, NY: St. Vladimir's Seminary Press, 2008), p. 12.

18. *The Russian Primary Chronicle: Laurentian Text*, trans. Samuel Hazzard Cross and Olgerd P. Sherbowitz-Wetzor (Cambridge, MA: Mediaeval Academy of America, 1953), p. 111. Whether apocryphal or not, the evident explanatory power of this story is telling in and of itself.

as the Second Council of Nicaea). These sources present the legitimacy of images as a matter of fundamental importance for Christian faith properly understood, that is, of a truly orthodox faith. According to this line of argumentation, to deny the possibility and legitimacy of an image of Christ — and by extension, his saints — is tantamount to denying the incarnation. Denying the incarnation invalidates the heart of Christian belief. Ouspensky, in explicating this intersection of image, theology, and orthodoxy, cites an additional historical source, the ancient Athanasian hymn sung in honor of the triumph of Orthodoxy:

> No one could describe the Word of the Father;
> but when he took flesh from you, O Theotokos [God-Bearer]
> he consented to be described,
> and restored the fallen image to its former state
> by uniting it to divine beauty.
> We confess and proclaim our salvation in word and images.[19]

This hymn contains the basic elements of the entire theological system upon which icons rest: Christ's divinity, as is the case with the Godhead, is indescribable; but Christ in his incarnation allowed himself to be circumscribed in flesh, which can be depicted; in becoming flesh and consenting to be so circumscribed, Christ effects our salvation by redeeming us in our flesh; and does so by uniting us to his own divine beauty. Ouspenksy glosses this hymn with a saying from the church fathers, "God became man so man might become God," thereby making explicit the analogy between the Orthodox understanding of icons and the Orthodox doctrine of *theosis* — the complete eschatological realization of all Christians into the full, divine likeness of Christ.[20] Icons are a crucial fulcrum in this economy of salvation by which the incarnate Christ makes manifest his eternal kingdom across space and time through the church's Spirit-led acts of worship, a kingdom envisioned and made present to worshipers, in turn, by icons.

It's not incidental that this authoritative, pithy formulation of the legiti-

19. Leonid Ouspensky, *Theology of the Icon*, trans. Anthony Gythiel, with selections translated by Elizabeth Meyendorff, 2 vols. (Crestwood, NY: St. Vladimir's Seminary Press, 1992), 1:151.

20. Ibid., 1:152.

macy of icons comes in the form of a hymn. Another hallmark of Orthodox theology, which is especially true of recent North American Orthodox theology, is an insistence that theology cannot be divorced from worship and that dogma finds its origin and its fullest expression in the liturgy. The Orthodox theologian Alexander Schmemann probably did more than anyone to call attention to the lived theology of the worshiping church.[21] Liturgy for Schmemann and for many who came after him is best viewed as the source of theology. Liturgy is "primary theology." Analytical, systematic attempts to understand the content of our faith — what we typically think of as theology — are actually, in this view, secondary to the rule of worship.[22] According to this *lex orandi, lex credendi* dynamic (the rule of prayer is the rule of belief), the theological content of Orthodox icons can never be properly understood apart from the worshiping church. William Dyrness's analysis of how ordinary Orthodox Christians discuss worship, liturgy, and icons bears this out entirely: "[T]he overarching relation that Orthodox believers sustain with icons is in the context of their corporate worship. . . . The visual practices that they learn before an image are inseparable from the worship practices that are appropriate in the liturgy. The response to one is of a piece with their response to the other. As a result, it is difficult to isolate the spiritual experience of the icon from the other elements of the liturgy."[23] In worship, icons are the material nexus of a set of intertwined convictions that, taken together, constitute the heart of Orthodox faith: incarnation (the ground of our salvation), *theosis* (the goal of our salvation), eschatology (the kingdom of God accomplished), and not least, ecclesiology (the communion through which God works to bring all this about). Therefore, as the ancient hymn proclaims, the Orthodox "confess and proclaim salvation in word and images." Since the ninth century, "the defense or condemnation

---

21. For the Jesuit scholar Robert Taft, Schmemann, with his insistence that we reverse our inherited relationship between theology and liturgy, "effected — perhaps unwittingly — a 'paradigm shift' in liturgical theology that created a veritable tsunami in its wake." Taft, "The Liturgical Enterprise Twenty-Five Years after Alexander Schmemann (1921–1983): The Man and His Heritage," *St. Vladimir's Theological Quarterly* 53, no. 2–3 (2009): 166.

22. David Fagerberg elaborates these categories as first- and second-order theologizing in *Theologia Prima: What Is Liturgical Theology?* (Mundelein, IL: Hillenbrand Books, 2004). pp. 80–81.

23. William Dyrness, *Senses of the Soul: Art and the Visual in Christian Worship* (Eugene, OR: Cascade Books, 2008), p. 60.

of the liturgical veneration of icons is . . . to be equated with the defense or denial of the Christian faith itself."[24] Thus "The Triumph of Orthodoxy," the yearly feast that celebrates the definitive reintroduction of images into the Eastern churches in 843. The hymn quoted above is sung every year on that Sunday.

Interestingly, the christological argument for the legitimacy of images at the heart of the eighth- and ninth-century defenses of icons did not emerge in earlier centuries, when christological controversies were at their height. Though some church fathers drew analogies to images and image making to illustrate their arguments, their focus was directly on the nature of Christ in relation to the Godhead.[25] What their analogies and illustrations show, however, is that images were in circulation among Christians in a number of forms in the centuries before the iconoclastic controversies erupted in the East. In his study of imagery in the church before iconoclasm, the art historian Ernst Kitzinger emphasizes that the church's official texts are rarely composed in moments of serene reflection but emerge in the wake of incidents and practices that have become problematic. This is especially true for religious images: "Explicit statements on the nature and function of images were mostly *ex post facto* rationalizations of developments which had already taken place."[26] Christian images were used to facilitate a variety of practices — from personal devotion in a home, to intercession for specific needs, to protection in wartime — for many, many years, sometimes for centuries, before such practices were given an explicit christological foundation.

While the Seventh Ecumenical Council pronounced images legitimate, it did not specify exactly how they were to be used. Henry Maguire has

24. Egon Sendler, *The Icon, Image of the Invisible: Elements of Theology, Aesthetics, and Technique*, trans. Fr. Steven Bigham (Redondo Beach, CA: Oakwood Publications, 1988), p. 40; first published as *L'icone: Image de l'invisible* (Paris: Editions Desclée De Brouwer, 1981).

25. Robin Jensen's *Face to Face: Portraits of the Divine in Early Christianity* (Minneapolis: Fortress, 2005) examines the analogies and examples drawn from art that theologians used to make their points about the nature of the Trinity and the nature of Christ. These instances, which are hardly dogmatic, probably did prepare the way for later, dogmatic formulations emphasizing the centrality of incarnation, the first of which appeared in 692 in the pronouncement of the Quinisext Council at Constantinople.

26. Ernst Kitzinger, "The Cult of Images before Iconoclasm," *Dumbarton Oaks Papers* 8 (1954): 86. More recently, Hans Belting's magisterial survey of cult images, *Likeness and Presence: A History of the Image before the Era of Art* (Chicago: University of Chicago Press, 1994), traverses the same territory in much more depth and detail.

detailed the ways in which some uses of Christian images were deemed improper in the wake of iconoclasm and were forbidden or curtailed. Images that used generic saints' visages in repeated patterns, for example, virtually disappeared, as they were associated with more magical, talismanic uses of holy imagery.[27] Written and visual evidence for the use of images in the Orthodox liturgy — in the ways in which they function today — is scant for several centuries. As one historian of Byzantine art put it, "Veneration of icons is one thing, their integration into the liturgy another, and the latter may have proceeded at a slower rate than one might be inclined to assume."[28] We know that shortly after the definitive end of iconoclasm in 843, Emperor Basil I built a new, centralized, domed church in the imperial palace and dedicated it to Mary, the mother of God. The sermon preached by Photius, the patriarch of Constantinople, at its dedication in 864 referenced an image of Christ surrounded by angels in the dome; an image of the Virgin Mary in the apse; and images of apostles and martyrs, prophets, and patriarchs on the upper walls of the nave.[29] But this arrangement was nothing particularly new. Versions of this schema adapted to various building formats — centralized or longitudinal — could have been seen in churches both East and West since the 500s.

Thomas Mathews points to the hanging of icons on chancel screens as the first step toward integrating icons into the liturgy, encouraging worshipers to "identify their veneration of the icons with their veneration of Christ" while simultaneously reducing the potential rivalry between icons and the sacrament as mediators of grace.[30] Textual sources from the eleventh and twelfth centuries describe the increasing practice of singling out particular saints (and thus their icons) for veneration on specific feast days, yet it still isn't clear how such a practice anchored the imagery in the liturgy.[31] The earliest visual evidence we have for more explicit *liturgical* use

27. Henry Maguire, *The Icons of Their Bodies: Saints and Their Images in Byzantium* (Princeton: Princeton University Press, 1996), pp. 100–145.

28. Nancy Sevcenko, "Icons in the Liturgy," *Dumbarton Oaks Papers* 45 (1991): 46.

29. Belting, *Likeness and Presence,* p. 165; Hugh Wybrew, "The Orthodox Liturgy: The Development of the Eucharistic Liturgy in the Byzantine Rite" (Crestwood, NY: St. Vladimir's Seminary Press, 1990), p. 107.

30. Thomas Mathews, "Early Icons of the Holy Monastery of Saint Catherine at Sinai," in Nelson and Collins, *Holy Image, Hallowed Ground*, p. 53.

31. Belting, *Likeness and Presence*, pp. 225–49. To this day, explicit mention of icons in

of icons comes from the fourteenth century and involves a processional image of the Virgin Mary that was likely introduced into the liturgy via the regular Friday prayers and processions in honor of the Virgin Mary's role in the defense of Constantinople against the Avars and Slavs in 626.[32] Also during the fourteenth century, the general arrangement of the iconostasis became regularized.[33] These developments in the imagery of the church reflect concurrent developments in architecture and liturgy that culminate in Orthodox worship as it is largely practiced today.

In a similar manner, the distinctive *look* of icons is rooted in the materials and stylistic conventions of late antique and early medieval art.[34] A preference for frontality; relatively flat rendering of static figures; nonnaturalistic backgrounds often covered in gold leaf; particular schema for faces, bodies, gestures; formulaic architectural settings — all these general traits undoubtedly came to be seen as of a piece with Orthodox sensibilities very early in the development of church tradition and required no explicit theological justifications until those conventions were challenged by new, Renaissance conventions from western Europe. At that point, the look of holy images, which had been taken for granted for hundreds of years, began to require explanation and defense. A Russian anthology of instructions, admonitions, and devotional passages for iconographers, for example, includes a 1690 interpolation of a fourteenth-century statement condemning "imaginative," overly elaborate icons painted in an alien style using contemporary hair and clothing. It also includes a statement by Joachim, patriarch of Moscow (1674–1690), on the need to reject the innovations of the "Latins and Germans, which are not similar to the originals . . . but are new creations done according to their

liturgical texts and rubrics is scant. One may find, for example, in the Matins liturgy, occasional instructions to sing a particular hymn *if* the corresponding icon is present, but other than that, icons are not mentioned in the rubrics.

32. Sevcenko, "Icons in the Liturgy," pp. 48–49.

33. Wybrew, "The Orthodox Liturgy," p. 147; Sevcenko, "Icons in the Liturgy," p. 45. Chancel screens with movable images, however, were in use long before the iconoclastic controversies, and after 843 were reintroduced in great variety. See Belting, *Likeness and Presence*, pp. 233–49.

34. See Georges Drobot, "Icons: Lines, Language, Colours, and History," in *Icons: Windows on Eternity*, ed. Gennadios Limouris, Faith and Order Paper 147 (Geneva: WCC Publications, 1990), pp. 160–69; Olga Popova, "Byzantine Icons of the 6th to 15th Centuries," in *A History of Icon Painting: Sources, Traditions, Present Day*, ed. Lilia Evseyeva (Moscow: Grand Holding Publishers, 2005), pp. 41–94.

own passions."[35] It wasn't until the early twentieth century that the formal properties of icons received a robust, positive apologetic along the lines of those articulated by Pavel Florensky in his *Iconostasis* of 1922 and by Ouspensky and Lossky in their 1952 book, *The Meaning of Icons*.[36]

In sum, images were present in Christian churches from at least the fourth century on. They then received a definitive, Orthodox theological justification in the eighth century and in the mid-ninth century; a satisfactory, basic stylistic vocabulary by the tenth and eleventh centuries; and a settled place in Orthodox worship by the fourteenth century.[37] In the ensuing centuries, icons gradually evolved in the eastern portion of the Christian world, along with the liturgy and the architecture of the church, to become the potent representatives of Orthodoxy they are today. Now, given the traditional, long-established relationship between icons and the entire liturgical edifice of Orthodox worship and theology, neither the pictorial content nor the pictorial form of an icon can be substantially changed without compromising the entire system.

This is a complex history, but no less rich, meaningful, or truthful for all its historicity. At the popular level, some Orthodox Christians are told — and want to believe — that their worship is unchanged from the very earliest days of the church and that their sacred images have always been much as they are today. But Orthodox theologians themselves do not believe these ahistorical claims to be accurate, necessary, or even helpful. While upholding the rich synthesis of belief and practice that Orthodoxy has come to offer, theologian Theodor Nikolaou states succinctly, "the absence of icons reduces the possibility for the faithful to experience liturgical life in its most complete form." He then continues: "This does not mean, of course, that the completion of the sacraments and in particular that of the sacrament of the holy Eucharist

35. S. T. Bolshakov, *An Icon Painter's Notebook: The Bolshakov Edition (An Anthology of Source Materials)*, trans. and ed. Gregory Melnick (Torrance, CA: Oakwood Publications, 1995), pp. 19–20. The exact origins of the anthology itself, published in 1903 in Russia by A. N. Uspensky, are unknown. Uspensky may have transcribed an existing collection or assembled the anthology himself. Nonetheless, the most recent excerpts included in Uspensky's anthology date to 1690.

36. Florensky, *Iconostasis*, pp. 99–112; for Ouspensky's analysis, see Leonid Ouspensky and Vladimir Lossky, *The Meaning of Icons*, 2nd ed. (Crestwood, NY: St. Vladimir's Seminary Press, 1999), pp. 37–41.

37. Drobot, "Icons," pp. 163–64.

is not possible without icons. . . . It is correct that icons are a desirable element where the fulfillment of the holy Liturgy is concerned, and have their organic place in the liturgical mystery. . . . The point of view that icons are 'necessary' to the fulfillment of the holy Liturgy also puts a misinterpretation upon the deeper meaning of the liturgical life of the church."[38]

Misinterpretation though it may be, the strong perception among many Orthodox and non-Orthodox alike that icons are "the expression of Orthodoxy as such" goes some way toward explaining the passion with which icons are discussed, analyzed, and debated among Orthodox Christians as well as the fascination they exert for many non-Orthodox Christians. If icons are more or less synonymous with Orthodoxy itself, then their creation, use, and treatment are a matter of the utmost importance. Used or painted improperly, icons might expose one to corruption or even to eternal judgment. Thus, for Paul Evdokimov, the author of a major twentieth-century treatise on icons, "a bad icon is an offence to God."[39] Thus, the story, recounted in the literature, of the seventeenth-century patriarch of Moscow, Nikon, who decreed that icons painted in too-Western a style be taken down, have the eyes gouged out of them, be paraded through the streets, and then burned.[40] Improperly painted icons are not bad art. They are something akin to blasphemy. At a minimum, respecting the theological and liturgical framework for icons, which has been securely in place for over half a millennium, helps us understand the proscriptions and prescriptions around their painting and use.

The Covenant with Icons

So, what constitutes an authoritative icon? The succinct answer to that question is: an icon *painted and used in prayerful obedience to tradition*. The iconographer and the worshiper inhabit the same sacred world; embrace

38. Theodor Nikolaou, "The Place of the Icon in the Liturgical Life of the Orthodox Church," *Greek Orthodox Theological Review* 35, no. 4 (1990): 327–28 and 332.

39. Paul Evdokimov, *The Art of the Icon: A Theology of Beauty* (Redondo Beach, CA: Oakwood Publications, 1990), p. 188. This book was first published in French in 1970.

40. The czar intervened to see that they were buried, rather than burned. Recounted in full in Boris Uspensky's *The Semiotics of the Russion Icon* (Lisse: Peter de Ridder Press, 1976), p. 22, as well as in David Coomler's *The Icon Handbook*, p. 75.

the same canons of worship and representation; and, in so doing, create, reinforce, and maintain a consistent "covenant with images." The phrase "covenant with images" was coined by art historian David Morgan in part to help scholars treat religious imagery with more nuance and sensitivity. For Morgan, covenants establish "a particular range of possibilities and codes of interpretation before the viewer is able to see what the image may reveal. The miracle of seeing what the image envisions does not happen without this covenant."[41] What Morgan calls a "miracle of seeing," Evdokimov calls a "miracle of belief."[42]

Though Morgan's phrase "covenant with images" would seem to restrict our analysis to the relationship between individuals and the images they are viewing, his explication of covenants makes clear that, fundamentally, covenants are social. They regulate interpretive communities — in this case, a holy community. Refocusing our analytical lens from the icons themselves to the community of Orthodox Christians who create and use them might be seen as a dilution of the claims icons make on us. Florensky, for example, was profoundly irritated by Western theologians who reduced icons to vessels of memory. For him, this psychologized the icon, reducing it to an entirely human, subjective phenomenon, thereby denying the ontological reality it embodies.[43] Were Florensky to weigh in here, he might say shifting our attention from the icon itself to its interpretive community is merely the substitution of sociology for psychology. But such an analytical move doesn't necessarily undermine the icon's ontological status. Instead, it clarifies how icons' authoritative claims are recognized, maintained, and promulgated by Orthodox Christians and, just as importantly, why these claims are so often refuted or misrepresented by non-Orthodox viewers who don't subscribe to this particular covenant. Focusing on the covenant with icons gives full weight to the beliefs and practices of Orthodox Christians, while also providing an account of them that makes sense to the non-Orthodox, even as the non-Orthodox may still decline participation in that covenant.

41. David Morgan, *The Sacred Gaze: Religious Visual Culture in Theory and Practice* (Berkeley: University of California Press, 2005), p. 76.

42. From Paul Evdokimov, *L'orthodoxie* (Paris: Desclée de Brower, 1979), p. 226, quoted by Ruud Welten, "Toward a Phenomenology of the Icon," in van den Bercken and Sutton, *Aesthetics as a Religious Factor in Eastern and Western Christianity*, p. 403.

43. Florensky, *Iconostasis*, p. 70.

Morgan describes a range of what he calls "external covenants" that governs the relationship between individuals and a community of viewers and a range of "representational covenants" that governs the mode in which the image is recognized. "[A]ny image might combine several covenants in its viewing and visual consumption. Indeed, the more contractual relations in place, the more secure the meaning ascribed to the image and the more confident the gaze that apprehends the image."[44] According to Morgan's categories, Orthodox icons enjoy a remarkably strong set of "contractual relations." They exemplify three of his four types of external relations: "communal," insofar as icons represent what the community holds true; "orthodox," insofar as icons represent what the community understands to be correct; and "authoritarian," insofar as icons are approved by ecclesial authority. Representationally, icons exemplify at least two of Morgan's five possible representational covenants: they are "exemplary," insofar as they represent ideal appearances, and "expressivist," insofar as they represent "the essence or spirit of a subject, not its accidental appearances."[45] ("Expressivist," as used by Morgan, should not be taken in its everyday sense as subjective, individual expression.) The degree to which some narrative icons (as opposed to icons of persons) function allegorically, and the degree to which all icons potentially initiate a deconstructive relationship to conventional, everyday vision — two more of Morgan's representational modes — could be debated. Icons definitively refute, however, the mimetic mode of address, which claims to conform to conventional, everyday vision. Together, the exemplary, expressivist, and adamantly antimimetic character of icons and the communal, orthodox, authoritarian relations they establish among viewers create a hermeneutical covenant through which the central truth of Orthodoxy — "Christ is in our midst!" — may be reliably, consistently envisioned.

The density of the Orthodox "covenant with images" helps us appreciate

44. Morgan, *The Sacred Gaze*, p. 107.

45. Ibid., p. 106. Ouspensky's characterization uses similar notions described somewhat differently. For Ouspensky, icons are profoundly "realistic" because they reveal a spiritual reality unlike anything to be found in the world around us. Analogously, he argues that icons cannot be understood as *ideal* because, for him, idealization is an exercise of the human imagination, bound to the forms of this world and therefore inherently subjective (Ouspensky and Lossky, *The Meaning of Icons*, p. 41). What remains the same, no matter the terms used, is the conviction that the world we see around us is incomplete and inferior compared to the divinely transfigured world revealed by icons.

the degree to which icons, as images *created and used in prayerful obedience to tradition*, are the fruit of a social compact that cannot be fully accounted for by the church's dogmatic statements about them alone. Those statements may provide a basic theological justification for holy images, but they don't come near to adequately explaining their liturgical role; their specific content; their particular formal properties; and the preferred materials and appropriate techniques, or spiritual protocols, for painting them and approving them for the use of the church — all of which are fundamental to an icon's authenticity and therefore to its efficacy for the believer. Nor can the documents alone explain the arguments and anxieties about specific icons that have continued to characterize Orthodoxy — the anxieties of Patriarch Nikon in seventeenth-century Russia as well as those of contemporary Orthodox Christians concerned about which icons are more or less legitimate. As is the case with the relationship between theology and liturgy, the Orthodox covenant with icons is sustained not just by beliefs but by a "thick" set of rites and practices. When those rites and practices depart from tradition, an icon ceases to be an icon and becomes at best merely "sacred art" and, at worst, an idol.

Created in Prayerful Obedience to Tradition

Superficially, it is easy to see that icons are a very traditional art form. The repertoire of subjects, the schema for representing them, the materials, and the techniques are nothing if not traditional. But to define icons as traditional according to these criteria would be to miss the heart of the matter. Father John McGuckin finishes his chapter on the Orthodox understanding of tradition with this arresting, but clarifying, observation: "The Western systematic tradition would probably have entitled such a chapter as this the 'doctrine of revelation.'"[46] Tradition, for Orthodox Christians, is not merely authoritative in a legalistic sense. It is, in the words of Father John Meyendorff, "the permanent presence of God in the community of the New

46. John Anthony McGuckin, *The Orthodox Church: An Introduction into Its History, Doctrine, and Spiritual Culture* (Oxford: Blackwell, 2008), p. 116. Vladimir Lossky provides an in-depth discussion of tradition in *In the Image and Likeness of God* (Crestwood, NY: St. Vladimir's Seminary Press, 1985), pp. 141–68.

Israel."[47] Tradition is the testimony of the Holy Spirit's work in the church, forming its worship, shaping its canonical Scripture, guiding its councils and their pronouncements, and inspiring its continued witness to the gospel: "Orthodoxy does not subscribe, either to the notion of the end of the age of revelation, or to the theory of the development of doctrine."[48] Because God does not change, and the gospel does not change, neither does the witness of the Holy Spirit through the church. "[R]evelation continues; in different modes and at different levels, but ever the same in so far as it is the direct energy of the Holy Spirit at work creating the vitality of the church."[49] In this framework, honoring tradition and submitting oneself to it are at once a means to holiness and the end of holiness. To fully inhabit Holy Tradition is to fully inhabit God's kingdom. While all Christians are called to live into Holy Tradition, those who paint icons do so in a particularly focused way to be able to properly apprehend and transmit that tradition through their icons. As was said of Lazarus, a sainted iconographer of the ninth century, he persisted "in asceticism and prayer so as to prepare himself to transcribe his inner contemplation onto the images that he painted."[50]

Content, style, materials, and techniques, then, are not merely traditional, in the sense of "old-fashioned" or "folkish," as many today might think. The elements of icon painting are traditional in the sense that they proclaim the tradition — "the permanent presence of God in the community of the New Israel." Like Scripture, the liturgy, and the creeds, icons are not the property of any one individual or any one local congregation. Like Scripture, the liturgy, and the creeds, icons are "canonical," submitting to the authority of the Spirit via church-confirmed content, methods, and patterns.[51] Even the choice of materials is bound by tradition.

---

47. John Meyendorff, *Living Tradition: Orthodox Witness in the Contemporary World* (Crestwood, NY: St. Vladimir's Seminary Press, 1978), p. 20.

48. McGuckin, *The Orthodox Church,* p. 116.

49. Ibid., p. 116.

50. *Le Synaxaire: Vie des saints de l'Eglise orthodoxe*, vol. 4 (Thessalonica: Editions To Perivoli tis Panagias, 1987), p. 578, as quoted in Steven Bigham, *Heroes of the Icon* (Torrance, CA: Oakwood Publications, 1998), p. 88.

51. This sentence captures, from an Orthodox perspective, one of the key differences between Orthodoxy on the one hand and Roman Catholicism and Protestantism on the other in describing Scripture as a manifestation of, rather than the font of, church tradition. "While Orthodoxy ascribes infallibility to the Scriptures as the Word of God, it does

Ideally, icons should be painted in egg tempera using natural pigments (though they may also be done in mosaic or fresco, and the very earliest icons were done in a wax-based medium known as encaustic). Though iconographers debate the merits of acrylic paint — and for durability, speed, and practicality, it might be the best choice for certain icons — most would view tempera as ideal.[52] Oil paint is seen as completely inappropriate because it is thought to invite a subjectivity and sensuality entirely at odds with the asceticism and spirituality of icons.[53] Icons should be painted on hard, wood surfaces, not pliable ones like stretched canvas, which, like oil paint, is thought to invite too much of the artist's own subjectivity and expression into the work.[54] Regarding subject matter, only saints and stories acknowledged by the church and embedded in its liturgical life should be represented. The depiction of these saints and stories must conform to meaningful representational patterns handed down by tradition: flatness, stasis, a certain treatment of light, certain approaches to color, particular treatments of anatomy and drapery, and a sense of atemporality created by the use of gold backgrounds and so-called inverse perspective.[55] Together,

---

not divorce them from the tradition. . . . Nor does Orthodoxy separate out Scripture from tradition in the manner of the Roman Catholic doctrine of the twin sources of revelation: tradition alongside Scripture. Scripture, for the Orthodox, is one of the purest manifestations of tradition. It is constitutively within sacred tradition, not apart from it" (McGuckin, *The Orthodox Church,* p. 101).

52. As Darya Carney put it, "we don't allow plastic in church, and acrylic is a form of plastic." Personal conversation, June 6, 2008.

53. There is a fascinating study to be written on the language of praise and criticism used to evaluate icons. The most common adjectives used to praise icons are "spiritual" and "beautiful." The next most common describe certain kinds of restraint attributed to icons: "ascetic," "sober," and "laconic." The most common negative evaluations represent lack of restraint: "sentimental," "sensual," and "subjective." One could also usefully analyze the use of evocative, ekphrastic writing as a form of analysis in much of the literature on icons.

54. Florensky provides a fascinating and extended discussion of the meaning of materials in his "Dialogue with Sophia Ivanova," in *Iconostasis,* especially pp. 100–113. While not all contemporary iconographers would agree with his entire analysis, his clear sense that materials have meaning is shared.

55. Florensky offered an early theological interpretation of space in Russian icons in his 1922 *Iconostasis.* Florensky's interpretation is the subject of critique and analysis in Clemena Antonova's *Space, Time, and Presence in the Icon: Seeing the World with the Eyes of God* (Farnham, UK: Ashgate, 2010). Erwin Panofsky's 1927 *Perspective as Symbolic Form* stimulated further Russian thought. See, for example, chapter 9, "Theories of Inversed Perspective," in Sendler's *The Icon,* pp. 135–48.

canonical subjects, portrayed canonically, proclaim a transcendent message in a consistent visual language that ideally can be received by all in whom the Spirit is at work, in all times and places.

The visual proclamation of tradition is a high calling. According to Ouspensky, "[t]he task of an iconographer has much in common with the task of a priest officiating."[56] Florensky writes, "Because they [iconographers] are raised in the ecclesiastical hierarchy above ordinary laypeople, they must therefore practice a greater humility, purity and piety, a profounder practice of fasting and prayer, and a more constant and deeper contact with their spiritual father. Thus the bishops consider their icon painters as people 'higher than the ordinary.'"[57]

Historically, most iconographers were monks; even today, many are monks or nuns or priests, and some historic iconographers have been designated saints.[58] All iconographers, ordained or not, aspire to a level of holy living necessary for the painting of icons. This involves receiving the blessing of one's bishop, participating regularly in the Divine Liturgy, fasting, and constant prayer.[59] Some iconographers talk of the process of painting an icon as "praying an icon." An eighteenth-century text from Mount Athos aptly demonstrates the degree to which Holy Tradition, worship, prayer, and iconography are intertwined and mutually reinforcing. The text, which contains a list of subjects and brief descriptions of how they should be painted, begins by describing the blessing the iconographer receives from his bishop: "[L]et there be a prayer on his [the iconographer's] behalf to the Lord Jesus Christ, and supplication before the icon of the Mother of God Hodegetria. When the priest gives the blessing . . . he should mark his head and say aloud 'We beseech thee, O Lord.'"[60] Then follows a prayer:

56. Ouspensky and Lossky, *The Meaning of Icons*, p. 43.

57. Florensky, *Iconostasis*, p. 90.

58. John Baggly, *Doors of Perception: Icons and Their Spiritual Significance* (Crestwood, NY: St. Vladimir's Seminary Press, 1988), pp. 54–55; Bigham, *Heroes of the Icon*, p. 84–102.

59. A variety of prayers may be used before and during the painting of an icon. Gennadios Limouris reproduces a common one here: "A Prayer Recited before Painting an Icon," in his *Icons: Windows on Eternity*, p. 159.

60. *The "Painter's Manual" of Dionysius of Fourna*, translated and with commentary by Paul Hetherington, codex gr. 708 in the Saltykov-Shchedrin State Public Library, Leningrad (Redondo Beach, CA: Oakwood Publications, 1989), p. 4.

Lord Jesus Christ our God, uncircumscribed in your divine nature, having become inexpressibly incarnate for the salvation of man from the last things by the Virgin Mother of God, Mary, has become worthy of circumscription. Who, having imprinted the sacred character of thy immaculate face on the holy veil, and through this healing of the illness of the governor Abgar and bringing about enlightenment of his soul into the full knowledge of our true God; and who, through the holy spirit brought wisdom to the holy apostle and evangelist Luke to depict the form of thy most innocent mother, who carried thee in her arms as a child and said "May the grace of Him who was born of me, through me be imparted to them"; the same, O God and master of all things, enlighten and bring wisdom to the soul and heart and mind of thy servant [*name*] and direct these hands for the irreproachable and excellent depiction of the form of thy person and of thy immaculate mother and of all thy saints, to thy glory and to the splendor and beautification of thy holy church, and the remission of the sins of those paying homage in regard to her and devoutly kissing and so bringing honour to the prototype; redeem him from all harm inflicted by the devil, as he diligently follows all the commands of the ministers of thy immaculate mother, of the holy and illustrious apostle and evangelist, Luke, and of all the saints, Amen.[61]

This instruction directs the priest to pray to Christ on behalf of the painter, then petition Mary before an icon of the *Hodegetria* type. The *Hodegetria,* which is Greek for "shows the way," is one of the most common and beloved depictions of the Virgin and is a type associated with the apostle-painter Saint Luke.[62] In an *Hodegetria* icon, Mary points to the infant Christ, the way of salvation, whom she holds in her arms. Mary, who bore Christ in her body and shows us the way to salvation through him, is the model for the iconographer, whose task is to do the same. The prayer that follows is thick with Holy Tradition: it contains the dogmatic language of both Theodore the Studite (uncircumscribed divine nature, becoming circumscribed in the incarnation) and John of Damascus (honor is passed to the prototype), the two most prolific defenders of icons from the eighth

61. Ibid., p. 4.
62. Belting speculates that the association of the *Hodegetria* type with Saint Luke emerged circa 600. See Belting, *Likeness and Presence,* pp. 57–59, for a summary of the sources on the question.

and seventh centuries, respectively; it recounts the story of Abgar and the "image made without hands" and the story of Saint Luke painting the Virgin to underscore the authoritative origins of icons; it gives a verbal representation of the *Hodegetria* ("May the grace of Him who was born of me . . ."); it specifies the proper subject matter for icons (Christ, Mary, the saints) and the purpose of their depiction (to glorify God, beautify the church, and aid in the remission of sin for those who honor Christ and his saints). Finally, it petitions Christ for physical, spiritual, and artistic sustenance for the iconographer in his work. A prayer like this demonstrates the extent to which Holy Tradition is both the form and the content of Orthodox worship.

To be trained as an icon painter is nothing less than to be discipled by and within Holy Tradition for the service of the church. Unlike priests, who attend seminaries and undergo a formal process of professional formation and then ordination, training as an iconographer — at least here in North America — remains less professionalized and much more personal. While Russia can boast a growing number of seminary-based programs in iconography, in North America there is currently no residential, academically based equivalent. Many iconographers begin as artists, some with conventional, academic training who then teach themselves the rudiments of icon painting through reading and practice. If they are serious about serving the church, they look to one or more experienced, master iconographers — acknowledged as such by the church's reception of their work — for further training, often through intense, short-term workshops. Knowledge about these workshops is conveyed by word of mouth, from parish to parish, or by newsletter; there is no established, central "clearinghouse" for information about iconography in the United States.[63] The iconographers who have worked in the Orthodox congregations of Grand Rapids show the variety of paths one may travel to become an iconographer in North America:

63. The jurisdictional complexity in the United States among Orthodox communities makes it difficult to maintain any one organization that would enjoy the endorsement of all Orthodox churches. Orthodoxwiki.org maintains a list of contemporary iconographers, but the criteria for inclusion are not clear, as a number of prominent iconographers (e.g., Athanasios [Tom] Clark, Father Patrick Doolan, Ksenia Pokrovsky) are not listed. For a time in the middle of the decade 2000–2009, it looked as if iconofile.com was hoping to function as a clearinghouse for iconographers in the United States, but the site is updated only sporadically.

- Constantine Youssis, an important iconographer of the Byzantine tradition working in the United States around midcentury, came from a family of iconographers and thus grew up in the profession.[64] He lived in Pennsylvania and was commissioned in the late 1970s to paint the icons at Holy Trinity Greek Orthodox Church.

- Athanasios (Tom) Clark, who painted the sanctuary icons for Saint George Antiochian Orthodox Church, attended Hellenic College in Boston but did not study art. He experienced a call to become an iconographer at the age of twenty-seven while traveling in Greece and apprenticed himself to a Greek iconographer, Kostas Tsilsavides, for four years.[65] Since then, he has worked extensively for the Greek Orthodox Archdiocese in America and for its churches.

- Father Theodore Koufos is based in Toronto and is undertaking the iconographic program for Saint Nicholas Antiochian Orthodox Church. Father Theodore studied art in college, earning a BA and an MFA, and taught art for three years. He then attended Holy Trinity Seminary in Jordanville, New York, where he was able to work under the supervision of two of Jordanville's iconographers. He has an extensive practice in the United States and Canada.

- Matushka Darya Carney, who is carrying out the iconographic program for her own parish, Saint Herman of Alaska, comes from a distinguished Russian Orthodox family. Her grandfather, Leonid Turkevich, was an early twentieth-century missionary to the United States who eventually became the head of the Russian Orthodox Church in America. Darya, his granddaughter, initially followed in the scientific footsteps of her father, Anthony, a physicist at the Uni-

---

64. Biographical details about Constantine Youssis are sparse, though he was clearly an important figure in American iconography, having created and executed programs for at least fifty-six Orthodox churches. Most notices of his work simply describe him as "the renowned iconographer Constantine Youssis." He is listed as an influence on younger iconographers. An entry for one of his icons now in the collection of the Jimmy Carter Presidential Library and Museum lists him as "a fourth-generation Byzantine Icon artist." (This note is included in the Center's "events page" maintained on Facebook: http://www.facebook.com/note.php?note_id=412814663703; accessed March 25, 2012.)

65. See the *Best of Times* newsletter of Shreveport, Louisiana, for a brief biographical sketch, at http://www.thebestoftimesnews.com/images/upload/468_April2011.pdf; accessed March 21, 2012.

versity of Chicago, and studied medicine. Eventually, however, she followed a vocation to iconography. After learning some of the basic principles of art at a community college in California, she studied first under the Russian iconographer Dmitri Andrejev and later under Father Patrick Doolan of Kelseyville, California.

Whatever the details of any one iconographer's specific path, all receive Holy Tradition as handed down, largely person to person, in a master-apprentice relationship that has its roots in the monastic history of the discipline. In Evdokimov's words, "[t]he essential elements of iconography are found in the direct teaching and oral transmission from a master to his disciples."[66] Secular training in art plays a useful role, but only for "technical value";[67] any emphasis on personal expression, invention, or novelty one might have acquired in art school must be severely tempered by obedience to tradition. The preference in the contemporary art world at large for work that raises questions, critiques society, or engages in a variety of deconstructive strategies must be rejected entirely. The notion of artistic autonomy — which remains at the heart of much contemporary art-world practice even as many artists see it as a myth to be deconstructed — must give way to prayerful obedience. True autonomy, in fact, is understood by Orthodox Christians to be possible *only* through prayerful submission — this is the path to the full realization of one's personhood in the image of Christ before the throne of God. Iconographers willingly submit their creative autonomy to the church's tradition to a degree unimaginable for most academically trained, contemporary artists.

Yet such submission does not foreclose the possibility of innovation. Nothing is more nonsensical to Orthodox iconographers than an opinion like that of Adolphe-Napoléon Didron, a nineteenth-century French scholar who discovered and published a late eighteenth-century collection of advice to iconographers, known as The "Painter's Manual" of Dionysius of Fourna. In his preface, he writes: "The Greek painter is the slave of the theologian. His work is the model for his successors, just as it is a copy

---

66. Evdokimov, *Art of the Icon*, p. 216.

67. Darya Carney, personal conversation, June 6, 2008. Though these are the words of one iconographer, it is easy to find many similar assessments in the writings of others.

of the works of his predecessors. The painter is bound by tradition as the animal is by instinct. He executes a figure as the swallow builds its nest, the bee its honeycomb. He is responsible for the execution alone, while invention and idea are the affair of his forefathers, the theologians, the Catholic Church."[68] Aside from the condescending comparison to animals and insects that simply follow "instinct," the actual content of Dionysius's manual makes very clear the degree to which such instructions do not diminish, much less obliterate, the painter's role. The bulk of the manual is devoted to extremely terse descriptions of the standard subjects of Orthodox iconography — stories from the Old Testament, stories from the Gospels, and images from Revelation, into which are interpolated events from the lives of Mary and of the martyrs of the church, and finally the calendar of saints. A typical entry, the "Hospitality of Abraham," for example, reads: "Houses, and three angels sitting at a table; in front of them is an ox's head on a platter with loaves and other vessels with food in them, and jugs of wine and cups. Abraham comes from the right holding a covered vessel and from the left Sarah brings another with a roast fowl."[69] One need only look at a handful of examples of the subject to see how individual painters varied their handling of the scene while remaining faithful to an immediately recognizable schema.[70] Composition, proportion, gesture, use of line and color, treatment of drapery and setting — all provide scope for creative interpretation, though in a more limited fashion than many contemporary artists would choose.

---

68. Adolphe-Napoléon Didron, as translated and quoted by Belting, *Likeness and Presence*, p. 18. Adolphe-Napoléon Didron, from the original preface to the first edition of the *Manuel d'iconographie chrétienne, grecque et latine, traduit du manuscrit byzantine, le guide de la peinture par P. Durand* (Paris: Imprimerie Royal, 1845), p. ix.

69. The *"Painter's Manual" of Dionysius of Fourna*, p. 20. This is an unusual and somewhat perplexing text. Hetherington's introduction provides a helpful discussion of the distinctive characteristics and possible motives and purposes of Dionysius's compilation.

70. We often overlook the extent to which artists painting for the church in western Europe, especially after the Council of Trent, were also expected to follow accepted schemata. In one famous incident, the Venetian painter Veronese was hauled before a church tribunal to account for a painting of the Last Supper that departed so radically from the established formula that he was forced to choose between altering the picture or changing the title to *Feast in the House of Levi*. For the trial documents, see Elizabeth Holt, *A Documentary History of Art*, vol. 2, *Michelangelo and the Mannerists* (New York: Doubleday, 1958), pp. 66–67.

Fig. 7. Andrei Rublev, *Holy Trinity*, Tretyakov Gallery, Moscow. Early fifteenth century.

Leonid Ouspensky was fond of proclaiming that "there are no rules."[71] Florensky insisted, "Church norms, even when very strictly observed, exercise almost no restraint upon the icon painter."[72] Florensky continues in praise of the most celebrated example of iconographic creativity, Andrei Rublev's *Holy Trinity* icon (fig. 7): "The iconic subject of three angels seated at a table existed within the canonically determined ecclesiastical art long

71. Doolan, *Recovering the Icon*, p. 97.
72. Florensky, *Iconostasis*, p. 83.

Fig. 8. **Viktor Vasnetsov,** *Mother of God,* **Vladimir Cathedral, Kiev. Late 1890s.**
PHOTOGRAPH BY GEORGE MITREVSKI

before St. Andrei. In this sense, he invented nothing new." Yet this icon
"shows in the most astonishing way this new vision of the Holy Trinity, a
new revelation shining through the veils of what are now the old and clearly
less significant forms."[73] At its most inspired, as with Rublev's *Trinity,* iconography illuminates Holy Tradition in fresh ways, which the church then
affirms as canonical.

Lack of what we might call genuine "canonical creativity" is actually
seen as a threat to the health of the church, a threat that reveals itself in
two mirror-image perversions of Holy Tradition. On the one hand is
"self-indulgent 'original' artistic fantasy" that distorts and disguises tradition.[74] Florensky compared the appearance of Viktor Vasnetsov's Western-
influenced *Mother of God* (c. 1895) in the apse of the Vladimir Cathedral in
Kiev (fig. 8) to substituting Ernest Renan's nineteenth-century biography
of Christ, *Vie de Jesus,* for the Gospels in worship.[75] Just as we don't mistake

73. Ibid., p. 84. For similar assessments, see also Evdokimov, *Art of the Icon,* pp. 213–17
and 243–57; Ouspensky and Lossky, *The Meaning of Icons,* pp. 200–205.
74. Doolan, describing Ouspensky's opinion, *Recovering the Icon,* p. 96.
75. Florensky, *Iconostasis,* p. 82.

humanist literature for Holy Scripture, we don't mistake humanist art for holy icons. Father Steven Bigham provides a different example of rogue creativity — an icon of the Virgin Mary and Joseph embracing, which copies a schema associated with Mary's parents, Anna and Joachim. The icon of Anna and Joachim embracing is meant, among other things, to teach that Mary was conceived naturally, through sexual union. Using the same schema for Mary and Joseph risks implying the same for the supernatural conception of Jesus. This is a theological mistake of the first order and a complete misappropriation of the church's pictorial tradition.[76]

At the opposite extreme, overly deferential reliance on established models is just as big a challenge in the eyes of many Orthodox. "Copying is undoubtedly an important part of contemporary icon painting but what we find is often not a creative re-working of old traditions, but repeats of famous icons with a disastrous loss of quality."[77] Uninspired copying results in "craft-work that is correct, but empty. Paralyzed and blinded by its fixed, hermetic 'method,' the new-Byzantine or neo-Russian icon satiates itself in self-reflection."[78] Even worse, it can lower iconography "to the common vulgarity of the everyday marketplace" in a desire to make money from the contemporary vogue for icons.[79]

Ideally, well-trained iconographers whose diligent work and constant prayer have opened them to the presence of the Holy Spirit will create fresh interpretations of traditional themes. Yet each of those fresh interpretations must resonate immediately with all that has come before (and, in time, with all that will come after). The church confirms such resonance with a bless-

76. Bigham, *Heroes of the Icon*, pp. 45–48.

77. Irena Yazykova, *A History of Icon Painting: Sources, Traditions, Present Day* (Moscow: Grand Holding Publishers, 2006), p. 244. Copying remains a valuable part of an iconographer's training, a method for internalizing forms. The *goal* of iconography as such, however, is not to execute literal copies.

78. Mahmoud Zibawi, *The Icon: Its Meaning and History* (Collegeville, MN: Liturgical Press, 1993), p. 151.

79. Constantine Kalokyris, *The Essence of Orthodox Iconography* (Brookline, MA: Holy Cross Orthodox Press, 1985), p. 100. For additional examples of these "mirrored" critiques, see Kalokyris, pp. 94–100; Yazykova, *History of Icon Painting*, pp. 244–45; and Bigham, *Heroes of the Icon*, pp. 43–48 and 59–61. For a more practical exposition, see "Iconography for the Twenty-First Century," a talk delivered at Sidney Sussex College, Cambridge, England, in 2005 by British iconographer Aidan Hart (http://www.aidanharticons.com/articles/Iconography%20for%2021st%20century.pdf, accessed September 22, 2011).

ing. These rituals are not elaborate and vary from region to region, but they may consist of a short prayer along the lines of this one, from the Greek Orthodox Archdiocese:

> O Lord our God, Who created us after Your own Image and Likeness; Who redeems us from our former corruption of the ancient curse through Your man befriending Christ, Who took upon Himself the form of a servant and became man; Who having taken upon Himself our likeness remade Your Saints of the first dispensation, and through Whom also we are refashioned in the Image of Your pure blessedness; Your Saints we venerate as being in Your Image and Likeness, and we adore and glorify You as our Creator; Wherefore we pray You, send forth Your blessing upon this Icon, and with the sprinkling of hallowed water bless and make holy this Icon unto Your glory, in honor and remembrance of Your Saint (N); And grant that this sanctification will be to all who venerate this Icon of Saint (N), and send up their prayer unto You standing before it; Through the grace and bounties and love of Your Only-Begotten Son, with Whom You are blessed together with Your All-Holy, Good and Life-creating Spirit; both now and ever, and unto ages of ages.
>
> *While Sprinkling cross fashion the Icon with Holy Water, the priest says*: Hallowed and blessed is this Icon of Saint (N) by the Grace of the Holy Spirit, through the sprinkling of Holy Water: in the Name of the Father (+), and of the Son and of the Holy Spirit: (+), Amen.[80]

As with the prayer that blesses the iconographer, this blessing for the icon instructs those present on the icon's meaning (a sign of our remaking in the image of Christ, as saints), underscoring what is proper to God (adoration and glorification), proper to the saints (honor, remembrance, veneration), and proper to the worshiper (his or her sanctification via the prayers to the triune God spoken before the icon). Sanctuary icons are formally consecrated in a public liturgy; one may bless personal and household icons with a short prayer or by laying them on the altar for a period of time.

---

80. This prayer can be found among the liturgical texts offered via the website of the Greek Orthodox Archdiocese of America, http://www.goarch.org/chapel/liturgical_texts/ icon_blessing (accessed March 20, 2012). See also George Galavaris, *The Icon in the Life of the Church: Doctrine, Liturgy, Devotion* (Leiden: Brill, 1981), p. 5, for comments on consecration.

Consecration does not "activate" or "animate" the image in any sense; that would endow the priest with a peculiar power that he does not have and should not claim. Consecration does confirm a particular image as in and of the church's tradition and therefore blessed to the use of the faithful.[81] Prayerful obedience to tradition allows icons, both in their making and in their use, to become a living medium for the work of the Spirit. In this sense, one might say that all true icons are essentially predetermined insofar as they exist in, of, and for the church.

Received in Prayerful Obedience to Tradition

Covenants join theory and practice. They require both ideological justification and a set of rites and practices that instantiate and propagate their justification. One of the hallmarks of any living tradition is its ability to sustain itself through processes that induct as they instruct. Anthropologists and sociologists call this "enculturation," "the process by which a person is inserted into his or her culture."[82] All Orthodox iconographers are deeply enculturated to the meaning and use of icons long before they become iconographers, through the practice of their faith. Such practices begin at the very start of one's life as an Orthodox Christian and continue every step of the way: at baptism and chrismation, one might be given an icon of John the Baptist, of Christ's baptism, or of one's name-saint; in the home, morning and evening prayers are said before household icons usually collected in one particular corner of the home; at marriage, a new couple receives icons for their home; at burial, the funeral procession is often led with icons of one's name-saint and the Virgin. All these icons and the prayers that accompany their use are the same icons and prayers the church uses for Divine Liturgy. This reciprocity creates continuity between personal devotion and public worship, each reinforcing the other, but with public liturgy as the key. As Archimandrite Vasileios of Stavronikita, the abbot of a prominent monas-

---

81. David Freedberg includes an extensive discussion of consecration rituals in chapter 5 of *The Power of Images: Studies in the History and Theory of Response* (Chicago: University of Chicago Press, 1989), and notes the sparseness (both in number and in character) of Christian rites in comparison to those of other religions.

82. Aylward Shorter, *Toward a Theology of Inculturation* (Maryknoll, NY: Orbis, 1988), p. 5.

tery on Mount Athos, remarked, iconography is "a script illegible to anyone who has not participated in the liturgy."[83]

In public worship, icons play a number of crucial roles. Orthodox Christians are fond of referring to the church building and the liturgy carried out in it as an "icon" of heaven. To worship in an Orthodox church is to step into a resonant, representational realm structured, animated, and amplified by "iconicity" at every level. At the structural level, specific "fixed" icons map the space of the church, defining the meaning of narthex, nave, dome, and sanctuary. Whenever it is possible, most Orthodox congregations choose to build their churches as domed, centralized spaces, based on the "perfect" forms of a square or circle, and oriented, that is, aligned, to the east, the direction of the rising sun. The entrance vestibule, or narthex, on the west side of the structure marks the dividing line between the earthly realm of everyday life and the transfigured realm of God's kingdom. In the earliest days of the church, Eastern as well as Latin, the narthex was reserved for penitents, those undergoing preparation for baptism, and for non-Christian observers, though it has been many years since this practice has been observed in most Orthodox churches. Some ceremonies (marriage, baptism) may still begin in the narthex. The imagery there often signals the transitional, liminal character of this space; at Holy Trinity Greek Orthodox Church in Grand Rapids, for example, two icons flank the main entrance to the nave, one of Jesus being brought to the temple as an infant and being received by Simeon and Anna, and the other of Mary being brought to the temple as a young girl by her parents, Joachim and Anna. These images define the narthex as an entrance to sacred space and help define the sanctuary beyond as the space in which Christ is recognized and in which worshipers dedicate themselves to him.

In leaving the narthex — which can be small, cramped, low-ceilinged, and, at the beginning and end of worship, very crowded — one enters the nave, a loftier, more open space. The dome over the nave marks the heavenly, cosmic realm above our earthly (albeit now sanctified) realm below and is almost always reserved for an image of the *Pantocrator* — the cosmic

---

83. Archimandrite Vasileios of Stavronikita, *Hymn of Entry: Liturgy and Life in the Orthodox Church*, trans. Elizabeth Briere (Crestwood, NY: St. Vladimir's Seminary Press, 1984), p. 81.

Christ, ruler of heaven and earth — represented by a large, half-length Christ holding the Gospels in his left hand and making a gesture of blessing with his right. The *Pantocrator* is one of the earliest schemas for the representation of Christ and dates back to at least the sixth century.[84] The *Pantocrator* is in turn typically ringed with saints and angels, apostles and martyrs, and supported in the four corners by images of the four Gospel writers, reflecting the description of heavenly worship found in the book of Revelation.

On the eastern side of the nave is the sanctuary — the holy of holies, containing the altar, where only clergy are permitted — framed by the iconostasis. If space permits, there may be a quarter-dome above the sanctuary, often reserved for an image of the Virgin and Child of the *Platytera* type. *Platytera*, literally "more spacious," is a shortened version of the phrase *Platytera ton ouranon*, "more spacious than the heavens." It is a poetic evocation of the mystery of the incarnation by which the infinite God was contained in Mary's womb, making her body more spacious than the heavens, evoking in turn the analogous, mystical way in which Christ meets us in the sacrament celebrated on the altar below the image.

The icons of the iconostasis perform the same interpretive task. Though the traditional schemata can vary from region to region and from era to era, and the taste for fewer, larger icons or a profusion of smaller icons differs among the various subcultures within Orthodoxy, one would typically find, on either side of the central doorway to the altar, an icon of Christ (on the right) and an icon of the God-bearing Virgin (on the left). The door itself might display icons of the annunciation or of the four Evangelists, emphasizing the good news of Christ's incarnation. Above the door, one often finds a "Mystical Supper." This is not a historical depiction of the Last Supper but rather an evocation of the ongoing communion we enjoy with Christ and his saints via the sacrament. Saints not present at the Last Supper might be found around the table in an icon of the Mystical Supper. Farther to

---

84. Early manifestations of the schema include the sixth-century encaustic icon of Christ from Sinai and the enthroned Christ included in the upper section of the sixth-century Coptic tapestry now in the holdings of the Cleveland Museum of Art. Mathews discusses the history and use of the *Pantocrator* for church domes in his essay "Psychological Dimensions in the Art of Eastern Christendom," in *Art and Religion: Faith, Form, and Reform*, ed. Osmund Overby (Columbia: Curators of the University of Missouri–Columbia, 1986), pp. 1–21.

the right and the left of the central doors, one might find John the Baptist and the patron saint of the church (a typically Byzantine arrangement), then archangels on the secondary doors to the sanctuary, and, above all this, further rows of saints and apostles. Non-Orthodox visitors to an Orthodox church often construe the physical existence of the iconostasis as a barrier between the worshiper and the holiness of Christ's presence among us. Orthodox tend to see it as just the opposite, as a representation of the bridge, that is, of Christ, Christ's church, and the church's holy tradition, that makes possible our salvation.

In addition to the large, mostly fixed icons of the dome, the sanctuary, and the iconostasis, smaller, movable icons of saints and stories help worshipers enact the many feasts and festivals of the Orthodox Christian calendar, thus sacralizing time as the fixed icons sacralize space. Movable icons are displayed on the appropriate feast day on a small stand where those entering the narthex or nave may honor them by lighting candles, crossing themselves, and kissing them (generally on a hand, as a kiss to the face of the icon would be presumptuous).[85] Together, all these icons, from the cosmic *Pantocrator* in the dome of the church to the humblest icon of a personal, patron saint in the home, enfold Orthodox Christians within a constant consciousness of the present reality of Christ's universal church, throughout all time and space. Though there are stylistic differences and varied organizational preferences from place to place and from era to era among Orthodox communities, these differences are a matter of degree, not substance. The interior of an Orthodox church should be immediately recognizable to an Orthodox believer as a resonant glimpse into an eternal reality that permeates our day-to-day existence and immediately received as an invitation to pray and render *ortho doxa*, that is, "right glory," to God in the company of the saints and angels.

As interest in and knowledge about icons grow outside of the Orthodox community, what many non-Orthodox continue to fail to appreciate is the systemic nature of what I've described here as the Orthodox covenant with icons. It is more than an appreciation for the visual or material

---

85. Ware, *The Orthodox Church*, p. 271, and McGuckin, *The Orthodox Church*, p. 357, describe some of the common ways in which Orthodox Christians interact with icons in worship.

component of worship.[86] It is more than a rich repertoire of didactic or inspirational imagery. It is these things, combined with habits of thought and practice, that create a shared world actualized in worship that unites all Orthodox Christians. English-speaking Christians are aware of the ways in which the locutions of the King James Bible have seeped into the English language and of how motifs, images, and topoi from Christian Scripture have permeated much of the West's literature. As is language, vision is cultural. Languages shape what we say and how we say it; images shape what we see and how we see it. More importantly, images shape what we imagine. In interviews with Orthodox Christians, William Dyrness found a consistent appreciation for the ways in which Orthodox worship as a whole — including its icons — shapes, directs, and even disciplines the imagination of worshipers.[87] From time to time, the Western Church recognized this as well and sought to regulate the production of images destined for worship or devotion. In sixteenth- and seventeenth-century Spain, for instance, the church understood how depictions of saints' mystical encounters with God could become templates for ordinary Christians' mystical experiences and evolved a more or less consistent visual vocabulary for the depiction of such encounters. The language of pictures became the medium for religious experience. The church affirmed — but also informed — mystical experience, thereby reducing the risk to individual and community alike that such potentially unruly encounters would head off into heretical territory.[88]

The Western Church's attention to images, however — both Catholic and Protestant, as we shall see — can hardly be called consistent in comparison to the Orthodox treatment. Though there are myriad images, there is no universal, recognizable visual system to aid our apprehension of the reality of our faith or guide attempts to envision a sanctified cosmos. Orthodox Christians, by way of contrast, inhabit a shared visual system and a visualized theology that have the potential to shape a uniquely "Orthodox

86. At the popular level, many Protestant Christians are drawn to icons as an affirmation of art or as an appreciation for the material aspects of experience. These notions represent a misunderstanding of icons, which eschew entirely the notion of "art" as defined in the West.

87. Dyrness, *Senses of the Soul*, pp. 58–61.

88. Victor Stoichita, *Visionary Experience in the Golden Age of Spanish Art* (London: Reaktion Books, 1995), pp. 24–26.

imagination."[89] All Christians, for example, affirm the words of the Apostles' Creed, "I believe in the communion of saints," but of all Christians, the Orthodox engage this reality most seriously and systematically, mystically communing alongside the saints and joining them in the eternal Divine Liturgy.

The Discussion:
Tensions within the Orthodox Covenant with Icons

As David Morgan describes them, "[c]ovenants are necessary whenever people must operate on trust."[90] This is no less true of the Orthodox covenant with icons than with, say, the covenant assumed to operate between photojournalists and the viewers of their images in newspapers, in magazines, and on the six o'clock news. For photojournalism to function, we need to trust that the images we see meet the same standards of journalistic reporting that apply to the verbal accounts that accompany them.[91] For icons to function, Orthodox worshipers need to trust that they truthfully mediate Holy Tradition. Clergy and iconographers in turn must trust that ordinary Orthodox worshipers are submitting themselves appropriately to Holy Tradition in their reception and use of icons, neither overestimating nor underestimating their place in Christian life. Above all, Orthodox Christians must trust that the Holy Spirit is working in and through these images, as in the prayers and worship of the church, toward believers' salvation and

89. The term "Catholic imagination" was popularized by Andrew Greeley in his 2000 book by that title, itself a riff on David Tracy's 1981 *Analogical Imagination: Christian Theology and the Culture of Pluralism* (New York: Crossroad, 1981). Interestingly, there is no comparable literature on the "Orthodox imagination." Though there are many scholars of Russian art and literature who point to Orthodox Christianity as a profound influence, perhaps the phrase is avoided due to a general reluctance among Orthodox Christians to associate human imagination with the worship by the church in general — and with icons in particular. Anthony Ugolnik comes closest to making the case for an Orthodox imagination in his 1989 *The Illuminating Icon* (Grand Rapids: Eerdmans, 1989), especially in pp. 42–85 and 86–124.

90. Morgan, *The Sacred Gaze*, p. 76.

91. For an example of what can happen when the photojournalistic "covenant with images" is breached, see Cheryl Johnston's essay, "Digital Deception," *American Journalism Review* 25, no. 4 (May 2003): 10–11, which discusses the edited photo by *Los Angeles Times* photographer Brian Walski, which ran on the front page of the *Times* on March 30, 2003.

sanctification. At any of these points, trust can be disturbed. Any widely shared covenant will, from time to time, find itself exposed, examined, and contested. Most of the time, these disturbances are minor and the ambiguities introduced are tolerable within the overall security and clarity provided by the covenant. But sometimes the disturbances are too large to tolerate and can create very real challenges.

Icon/Idol

Historically, the chief pressure point of the Orthodox covenant with icons is signaled by the church's continual reiteration of one of the covenant's foundational elements: "the honor given the image is rendered to the prototype." This formulation was first put in place by Basil of Caesarea in the mid-fourth century as part of his argument regarding the nature of the Trinity.[92] Constant emphasis on the honor rendered to the *subject matter* of the icon protects the church from the charge of inappropriate attention paid to the *object* as such, which would constitute idolatry. This was the chief concern of the theologians who provided the dogmatic justification for icons in the seventh and eighth centuries, and it remains a point of emphasis today. Icon veneration, Father John McGuckin points out (somewhat testily), "is not some form of magical worship of an idol. . . . The Orthodox are not so dim in their faith as to mistake bowing down before a dumb idol for the veneration of Christ."[93] Evdokimov emphasizes the degree to which "[t]he icon does not have any existence in itself. It is participation and a 'guiding image.' It leads to the prototype, to the person represented, announces his

92. "For the Son is in the Father and the Father in the Son; since such as is the latter, such is the former, and such as is the former, such is the latter; and herein is the Unity. So that according to the distinction of Persons, both are one and one, and according to the community of Nature, one. How, then, if one and one, are there not two Gods? Because we speak of a king, and of the king's image, and not of two kings. The majesty is not cloven in two, nor the glory divided. The sovereignty and authority over us is one, and so the doxology ascribed by us is not plural but one; *because the honour paid to the image passes on to the prototype.* Now what in the one case the image is by reason of imitation, that in the other case the Son is by nature; and as in works of art the likeness is dependent on the form, so in the case of the divine and uncompounded nature the union consists in the communion of the Godhead" (emphasis mine). Basil the Great, *On the Holy Spirit* (Crestwood, NY: St. Vladimir's Seminary Press, 1980), chap. 18, par. 45.

93. McGuckin, *The Orthodox Church,* p. 355.

presence, and witnesses to his coming. The presence in no way incarnates itself in the icon, but the icon is nonetheless a center from which the divine energies radiate out."[94]

At stake here is a carefully articulated theory about how icons manifest "presence." They do so *through*, not *in*, the material properties of the image. Yet for all the emphasis on this distinction and for all the careful argumentation to support it, other Orthodox authors write about icons in ways that raise doubts as to whether the distinction between image and prototype is always properly maintained: "While every icon, in virtue of its sacramental nature, is 'miraculous,' in certain icons the presence of God is manifested more tangibly, and the prayers of the Church can accumulate in them and be 'capitalized' with greater density."[95] An instance of just such a phenomenon occurred in December of 1986, in Chicago, where an icon of the Virgin *Hodegetria* at Saint Nicholas Albanian Orthodox Church began to weep, attracting pilgrims from around the world. In one account, a flower that the priest had touched to the icon subsequently healed the hospitalized son of two of those pilgrims. The congregation refers to itself with due humility as "specially blessed" by the icon and sees it as "a treasure that God has entrusted to us" even as it is at pains to emphasize God's intent to bless all through this miraculous image.[96] Such accounts tip the locus of spiritual agency much further toward the material image than toward the healing love of Christ manifest through the Virgin and available to all who ask in faith.

For Protestant Christians in particular, these kinds of interactions with icons are very hard to understand. The analogy often made by Orthodox Christians in trying to help Protestants understand phenomena like wonder-working icons is that of saints. We all know people who seem espe-

---

94. Evdokimov, *Art of the Icon*, p. 196.

95. Gennadios Limouris, "The Apocalyptic Character and Dimension of the Icon in the Life of the Orthodox Church," *Greek Orthodox Theological Review* 33, no. 3 (1988): 257.

96. The phrases are taken from the web page Saint Nicholas Albanian Orthodox Church maintains on the miraculous image: http://stnicholasalbanianchicago.org/blessedvirgin .html. The *Chicago Tribune* covered the story within days of the initial occurrence: http:// articles.chicagotribune.com/1986-12-12/news/8604030109_1_parishioners-icon-virgin -mary. For the account of healing via an icon-touched flower, see the coverage in *People* magazine of January 19, 1987: http://www.people.com/people/archive/article/0,,20095456 ,00.html. All sources accessed April 9, 2012.

cially wise, especially close to God, and to whom we go for counsel, advice, and help. If some people are especially blessed for God's service, so too are some icons. We might consider books in this same way. While not equal to Scripture, a handful of books written by Christians are deemed by many Protestants particularly inspired. For example, many evangelical Christians look on the works of C. S. Lewis in this way. Such books seem especially blessed, especially efficacious in teaching and encouraging the faithful, and especially illuminating of the ways of God. While such analogies might help some Protestants gain a better sense of why wonder-working icons "make sense" to Orthodox Christians, the analogies don't really address the fundamental *distinctions* Protestants are likely to think must be drawn: the difference between people and pictures of people, or the difference between human-authored texts — no matter how inspired — and canonical Scripture. These differences are more central to Protestants' understanding of how God interacts with the world than the continuum of truth, presence, and tradition that the Orthodox experience as part of the mystery of faith.[97]

The Orthodox are by no means alone in having to work hard to teach, maintain, and observe proper interactions with images. Catholics and Protestants are not exempt from this challenge and must manage with far fewer tools than the Orthodox have to hand! Part of what led David Morgan to formulate the notion of a "covenant with images" was his interest in Protestants' interaction with a wide variety of religious images in entirely unexamined ways, occasionally attributing similarly miraculous properties to them (for example, the range of religious functions and miraculous deeds attributed to reproductions of Warner Sallman's famous *Head of Christ*).[98]

Admittedly, our contemporary environment is very different from the late Roman world where all manner of cult images and objects were regularly believed to have their own supernatural agency. Father McGuckin is right to insist that Orthodox worshipers are not "dim" people who regularly

97. For a lovely example of the range of interests people take to a wonder-working icon, see the *Grand Rapids Press* article by Juanita Westby, covering the visit of the Kursk Icon to Grand Rapids in March of 2004: "Russian History Buffs Join Faithful for View of Rare Icon," *Grand Rapids Press*, March 11, 2004, p. A1.

98. David Morgan, ed., *Icons of American Protestantism: The Art of Warner Sallman* (New Haven: Yale University Press, 1996), pp. 29–30, and David Morgan, *Visual Piety: A History and Theory of Popular Religious Images* (Berkeley: University of California Press, 1998), pp. 124–51.

attribute to the icon itself the agency of the figure represented. But the fact remains, that "[w]ithout its theological, exegetical norm, the icon is always fundamentally in danger of becoming an idol."[99] Proper instruction in the role and use of icons is essential, which is why Orthodox prayers, songs, and liturgies reiterate and instantiate the terms of their covenant so often in worship.

Icon/Eucharist

A second source of ambiguity concerns the status of the holy presence manifest through the icon, relative to the status of the holy presence manifest in the Eucharist.[100] Some Orthodox writers seem to elide icons with sacrament. Others are more careful to distinguish between the two. Theodor Nikolaou is emphatic in stating that icons are not sacraments and are not necessary for the exercise of the sacraments, but that their absence nonetheless "reduces the possibility for the faithful to experience liturgical life in its most complete form."[101] Likewise, Evdokimov states bluntly, "We can never say that 'the icon of Christ is Christ' as we say 'this bread is the body of Christ.' This would obviously be idolatry. The icon is an image which witnesses to a presence in a very specific way: it allows a prayerful communion with the glorified nature of Christ; it is, however, not a Eucharistic communion, that is, substantial."[102]

Other Orthodox, however, when speaking of icons, gravitate toward lyrical language one might also use to speak of the Eucharist. Here is Archimandrite Vasileios of Stavronikita, on Mount Athos, on the ways in which the icon is "Grace incarnate, a presence and an offering of life and holiness": "You stand before the icon with fear, yearning and joy. You stand before it. You venerate it. You receive life. You suck from it, you drink it in. You feed insatiably on it. What nourishes you now can never be exhausted."[103] And

---

99. Welten, "Toward a Phenomenology," p. 398.

100. These are ambiguities that exist in and around the Orthodox covenant for Orthodox Christians. Non-Orthodox will have a different set of questions and tensions to address, such as the relationship between icons and Scripture.

101. Nikolaou, "Place of the Icon," p. 332.

102. Evdokimov, *Art of the Icon*, p. 195.

103. Vasileios, *Hymn of Entry*, pp. 89, 90.

from Ouspensky (who, more generally, like most Orthodox, compares icons to Scripture but whose language sometimes shades into the sacramental): "liturgic art is not only our offering to God, but also God's descent into our midst, one of the forms in which is accomplished the meeting of God with man, of grace with nature, eternity with time."[104] Even Catholic icon enthusiasts occasionally blur the distinction. Basil Lefchick urges every Roman Catholic congregation to display an icon of Christ, "so that the Incarnation of the Word of God is shown to be real."[105] For most Catholics, that language would be most closely associated with the Eucharist; for most Protestants, with the witness of Scripture.

In part, like the tension between icon and idol, the tension between icon and Eucharist may be largely an "insider/outsider" problem. But even if we grant that this latter tension looms larger for non-Orthodox than for Orthodox, it's still a real tension. One of the iconographers I met with stated, "historically, there's been a danger here, yes. But it's no longer really a problem."[106] I've been assured that Archimandrite Vasileios and Leonid Ouspensky have always been entirely aware of the difference between the Eucharist and icons and are completely correct in their overall theological framework for understanding icons. In this view, the passages I've used as examples of the potential tension between icons and the Eucharist are better understood as examples of a particularly passionate, ekphrastic style of writing about icons. This style characterizes much of the literature written by Orthodox Christians about icons; rather than giving a sober analysis of the properties of an icon, it seeks instead to capture the sense of communion one might enjoy via the icon.

As is the case with the icon/idol tension, the regulative role of Orthodox worship is key to maintaining the proper place for icons relative to the Eucharist. In worship, it's absolutely clear that icons and Eucharist are different entities. Icons are one of a range of ways in which God's presence is made known to his people: Scripture, sacraments, relics, icons, and

104. Ouspensky and Lossky, *The Meaning of Icons*, p. 36.

105. Basil Lefchick, "The Resurgence of Icons: Why Now?" *Environment and Art Newsletter* 14 (September 2001): 103.

106. Darya Carney, personal conversation, June 26, 2013. I am especially indebted to Matushka Darya Carney for her helpful comments and corrections in this section. Remaining errors or misconceptions are due to my limitations.

the saints — both past and present — all manifest, in varying ways, the life-giving presence of "God with us." Orthodoxy has never insisted on carefully delineating and patrolling a given set of sacraments, though it generally acknowledges seven, among which two, baptism and Eucharist, are preeminent. Orthodoxy is more comfortable with the language of "mysteries of faith" than with specific lists of sacraments and accepts a range of "greater" and "lesser" mysteries. Most Orthodox would acknowledge that sacraments belong to the greater mysteries and icons to the lesser, but the continuity among all these mysteries receives more attention than the differences.[107] Nonetheless, inattention to the key difference between icons and the Eucharist in particular — that of material consubstantiality — could lead, in an Orthodox context, to the more fundamental challenge discussed above, that of collapsing image and prototype into one another, transforming the icon, as Evdokimov says, into an idol.

Mass-Produced Icons

A third source of tension within the Orthodox covenant with icons concerns the propriety of mass-produced icons. Unlike the previous two tensions (icon/idol, icon/Eucharist), which are real but less acute for Orthodox Christians than for non-Orthodox Christians, this tension is more lively for Orthodox Christians than for the non-Orthodox, who often can't fully appreciate the ways in which mass reproduction can distort the Orthodox covenant with icons. Even before mechanical production had become rampant, industrial-scale, assembly-line production of hand-painted icons in certain regions of Russia was already common.[108] It's estimated that by 1857, residents of the village of Kholuy, one of three villages particularly associated with the icon trade, produced from 1.5 to 2 million crude but hand-painted icons a year.[109] Chromolithography and,

107. Ware, *The Orthodox Church*, pp. 274–77; McGuckin, *The Orthodox Church*, pp. 277–82 and 354–57.

108. In his autobiography, Maxim Gorky recounts the workings of such an icon factory, writing, "Some evil genius had divided the work into a long series of actions, bereft of beauty and incapable of arousing any love for the business, or interest in it" (Maxim Gorky, *In the World*, trans. G. Foakes [New York: Century Co., 1917], p. 330).

109. Oleg Tarasov, *Icon and Devotion: Sacred Spaces in Imperial Russia*, trans. and ed. Robin Milner-Gulland (London: Reaktion Books, 2002), pp. 52–57.

later, photographic reproduction intensified the challenge. By the turn of the twentieth century, an entire industry had arisen in Russia purveying inexpensive printed tin and cardboard icons. The situation was seen as so dire in 1903 that a government commission attempted to ban the mechanical reproduction of icons altogether.[110] A covenant that had been established when hand production was the norm for *all* images was now confronted by technologies that allowed the mass reproduction of select images. Leonid Ouspensky, it is said, was hesitant to allow his icons to be photographically reproduced, fearing that the photographs, mounted on wood, would soon be viewed as adequate substitutes for painted icons.[111] His concerns were not unfounded.

Mass production disrupts the Orthodox covenant in a number of ways. Mechanically reproduced icons are not made of the same meaningful materials used in the creation of painted icons. This renders them incapable of conveying the restraint and sobriety communicated through medium and surface. More problematic, mass reproduction distances the icon from the virtuous life and prayerful practices of the iconographer who works in and for a particular community.[112] This is not the same "dilution of aura" that plagues the work of fine art in the age of mechanical reproduction — as Walter Benjamin so famously argued — but is a substantial weakening of the *communal* and *authoritarian* aspect of the Orthodox covenant with icons. While the imagery itself remains "orthodox" insofar as the subject matter is copied from previously sanctioned icons, the processes through which icons are authorized for communal use are distanced and diluted, and thus the intensely interpersonal character of icons suffers a grave loss.

Imagine a future where Orthodox Christians relied entirely on reproduc-

---

110. Robert L. Nichols, "The Icon and the Machine in Russia's Religious Renaissance," in *Christianity and the Arts in Russia*, ed. William C. Brumfield and Milos M. Velimirovic (Cambridge: Cambridge University Press, 1991), p. 141.

111. In recent years, the ability to project icons on screens has added yet another wrinkle to the question of mechanical reproduction. Is an immaterial, digitally projected icon still an icon? Is it problematic that projected icons appear and disappear with the push of a computer key? Is a projected icon better than no icon at all for churches with limited means? Interview with Darya Carney, June 6, 2008.

112. On the other hand, some mass-produced icons are manufactured in monasteries and blessed by monks before shipping, and therefore enjoy some proximity to a prayerful, virtuous hand.

Fig. 9. Saint John Chrysostom Russian Orthodox Church; the large icons on the bottom row are printed. PHOTOGRAPH BY AUTHOR

tions of existing icons. One immediate consequence would be the establishment of a sort of canon within the canon of popular, oft-reproduced icons. In turn-of-the-century Russia, in fact, the repertoire of mass-produced icons had already been reduced by economic selection to the point that some Orthodox were unable to acquire an inexpensive icon of their name-saint.[113] Churches might still exercise some creativity in the choice and placement of available images, but they would no longer be working with a living iconographer who would be praying and painting Holy Tradition in their midst. The particular character of individual congregations would be harder to represent — and perhaps even harder to identify. The diminished role of the iconographer would in turn weaken the reciprocity that sustains the relationship between prayerful creation and prayerful reception of icons. Without adequate reciprocity, the repetition of existing icons restricts the creative, local appropriation and renewal of Holy Tradition. Eventually,

113. Nichols, "Icon and the Machine," p. 139.

a living tradition could lapse into a traditionalism that serves the aims of commerce rather than the needs of the worshiping church.

Reservations duly noted, it is nonetheless the case that mass-reproduced icons are everywhere — in homes, in cars, in workplaces, in churches, and even in iconostases! In Grand Rapids, for example, both Saint John Chrysostom Russian Orthodox Church and Saint George Antiochian Orthodox Church still display printed, paper icons on their iconostases — at Saint George in the uppermost level of the iconostasis and at Saint John Chrysostom for the full-length icons of the lower level. The cardboard icons at Saint John Chrysostom (fig. 9) came from Odessa, probably purchased as a prepackaged set, and demonstrate the effects of mass production and mass marketing. John the Baptist — a standard saint for Russian churches — appears where one would typically see Saint John Chrysostom, the patron saint of this congregation. These paper icons, for both churches now nearly one hundred years old, date to the earliest days of each congregation and were all that could be afforded at the time. Connecting an early twentieth-century immigrant community to its European roots, over the years, the printed icons have been sanctified by the prayers and worship of the church. While openly acknowledged as inferior to painted icons, they are also not seen as entirely unsuitable simply because they are printed; instead, they keep each congregation physically connected to its immigrant roots.

Icons and "Style"

The cardboard icons at Saint John Chrysostom, with their robin's-egg-blue backgrounds, sweetly naturalistic faces, and convincingly modeled forms, expose yet another tension in the Orthodox covenant. Both internally within Orthodoxy and externally between Orthodox and non-Orthodox Christians, the relationship between Holy Tradition and a certain understanding of "style" is key to many debates. Unfortunately, it's also quite difficult to address because of a deep sense among Orthodox Christians that there is no peculiarly "Orthodox" style. Style for many Orthodox Christians is something that characterizes Western art, but not icons. Because art exists in specific places and cultures, at particular points in time, such specificities of culture, time, and place will manifest themselves as style. Icons, however, are not art. For Orthodox Christians, icons do not exist in ordinary time and in everyday space in the way that art does. Therefore icons have no real style in the way we ordinarily use that term, only canonicity. On the question of style, Ouspensky writes, "One can speak of style in scientific analysis, in historical or archaeological studies, but to use this idea in the Church to characterize its art is as absurd as discussing the 'style' in which the Creed or the Great Canon of St. Andrew of Crete is written. It is clearly a meaningless statement. In the Church there is only one criterion: Orthodoxy. Is an image Orthodox or not? Does it correspond to the teaching of the Church or not? Style as such is never an issue in worship."[114] Father Steven Bigham, with a little more nuance, makes a distinction between the oft-acknowledged parade of styles, properly speaking — Renaissance, baroque, rococo, neo-classical, etc. — that characterizes Western art and canonical iconography:

> It is often said that the Christian Church has not produced or adopted any particular, specific, artistic style and that it is open to all tastes, to all manners of representing the events and people of salvation history. . . . Has not Vatican II said it very well? . . . "The Church has not adopted any particular style of art as her very own; she has admitted styles from every period according to the natural talents and circumstances of peoples, and the needs of the various rites." . . . This point of view seems so obvious and reasonable that few people would even imagine anything else.
>
> I would nonetheless like to set out the opposite point of view: during the first 1000 years of its history, the Church did create images, either of people or of events of salvation history, which express her theological vision. As the Church through bitter disputes formulated the verbal and conceptual language of its faith, it also developed an artistic vocabulary and language that expressed the same faith, but this time in colors, lines, and forms. This historical development, this creative process, resulted in what is called canonical iconography. . . . It is not that the iconic tradition of the Orthodox

114. Ouspensky, *Theology of the Icon*, 1:12. Similar claims are made for liturgical chant: "The liturgical singing of the Orthodox Church constitutes an autonomous realm that is guided by its own aesthetic laws and standards" (Johann Gardener, *Russian Church Singing*, vol. 1 of *Orthodox Worship and Hymnography*, trans. Vladimir Morosan [Crestwood, NY: St. Vladimir's Seminary Press, 1980], p. 62). Morosan extends this view, using a variety of terms that could be equally used for the analysis of icons, in his article "Liturgical Singing or Sacred Music? Understanding the Aesthetic of the New Russian Choral School," in Brumfield and Velimirovic, *Christianity and the Arts in Russia*, pp. 124–30.

Church has not known various "styles." We can certainly identify different manners of making images and we can identify their specific period and country. . . . But the Orthodox Church claims that there is a universal, canonical iconography that is expressed by each of these historical and geographical "styles."[115]

There is a "universal, canonical iconography," with a distinctive "artistic vocabulary and language," that is manifest in a variety of manners or styles throughout the church's history. Yet what distinguishes one canonical Orthodox manner from another seems very minute compared to what distinguishes one artistic style (conventionally understood) from another. The difference between Byzantine icons and Russian icons is, we might say, the difference between two dialects of a mother tongue. Italian Renaissance art, Spanish baroque art, and French impressionist art, however, are speaking entirely different languages one from another.

Here's a thought experiment to help clarify what is at stake: Imagine a claim arguing that Italian Renaissance art is the only truly appropriate form for Christian art. Of course — the argument goes — we can distinguish Florentine from Sienese, and fourteenth-century from fifteenth- and sixteenth-century variants of this form, but essentially, Renaissance art is not a style. It is simply correct. Northern European approaches, sixteenth-century mannerist approaches, seventeenth-century baroque approaches are all degrees of degenerate deviation from a fundamental correctness rather than licit developments in their own right. Modern abstraction and non-Western stylization are of course entirely out of the question. (One can, in fact, trace a version of this claim through the art of Christian western Europe through the mid-nineteenth century, and a marked preference for Renaissance naturalism is still common today among ordinary Western Christians.) For Orthodoxy, rather than the Italian Renaissance, it is the art of early medieval Byzantium that defines fundamentally correct form, and it is out of this early medieval Byzantine representational mode that all licit regional variants evolve.

The challenge for Orthodox Christians then becomes discerning exactly

115. Steven Bigham, "The Icon: Sign of Unity or Division?" *Ecumenism* 176 (Winter 2009–2010): 5–6.

where Orthodox "canonical iconography" ends and disruptive, problematic deviations begin. Saint John Chrysostom's printed icons date from well before the mid-twentieth-century recovery of the iconic tradition. Their style reflects the Westernized Russian tastes of the turn of the twentieth century, yet they are clearly considered canonical enough for the worshipers at Saint John Chrysostom. Father Andrew Lowe describes them as a form of "soft iconography," similar to nineteenth-century devotional images. "They look like the kind of thing you would find on prayer cards. But Russians are very comfortable with western-style icons."[116] Non-Russian Orthodox Christians or Orthodox Christians who didn't grow up around such imagery might be less comfortable.

In late seventeenth-, eighteenth-, and nineteenth-century Russia, iconographers began to employ modeling and shading to create a sense of mass and volume in their figures. They began to use blue, sky-like backgrounds and cast shadows that indicated this-worldly light sources, as well as oil paints to create rich textures and details and to enhance lavish ornamentation borrowed from Western manuscript decoration. Entire pictorial schemas were borrowed from Catholic Dutch and German engravings.[117] Recently, scholars have sought to track the shifts in theology that gave rise to such stylistic alterations.[118] But given the theology and liturgical function of icons as articulated today — after the twentieth-century recovery of the icon — as thresholds of an ideal, spiritual, transfigured realm beyond our visible world, such illusionistic, "Western" pictorial devices undermine the profoundly nonnaturalistic mode of address that forms a core part of the Orthodox covenant with images.

Russian, Ukrainian, and Belarusian Orthodox Christians are sometimes ambivalent themselves in their assessment of such Westernized icons. On the one hand, these are *their* icons, deeply bound to local, national, and sometimes immigrant identity, yet such icons also have the potential to undermine the entire tradition. At what point does the degree of Western-

---

116. Interviews with Father Andrew Lowe, June 5, 2008, and June 12, 2013.

117. See Natalia Komashko, "Ukrainian Icon Painting" and "Belarussian Icons," pp. 191–202, and Mikhail Krasilin, "Russian Icons of the 18th to Early 20th Centuries," pp. 211–30, all in Evseyeva, *A History of Icon Painting.* See also Tarasov's *Icon and Devotion* for an examination of the theological shifts represented by such stylistic changes.

118. For one extended analysis, see Tarasov, *Icon and Devotion,* pp. 207–300.

ization tip the image from the category of icon into that of mere picture? At what point is the icon's otherworldly liturgical presence destroyed by this-worldly naturalism? Writing of the Westernization of Ukrainian icon painting in the eighteenth century, Natalia Komashko deems appropriate a sort of "Ukrainian Baroque" where "[t]he combination of the painterly manner with traditional iconography and a conventional artistic language is so harmonious that the icon does not lose its role as a devotional image."[119] But she also condemns later eighteenth-century icons that "departed from the principles of Ukrainian Baroque and became fully pictorial, with re-alistic treatment of space and volume," all the while proposing that these developments were nonetheless to be expected, because of the presence of Western artists in Kiev, many of whom also worked as portrait paint-ers.[120] Similarly, with respect to developments in Belarus, she praises mid-seventeenth-century icons where "in spite of the new pictorial devices, they still observe a measure of conventional artistic language that does not allow icons to be turned into purely pictorial works" but describes other devel-opments more negatively: "Elements of the landscape became artistically self-sufficient"; "there was an interest in complicated architectural-spatial construction"; "pictorial devices in the painting of faces made them concrete and recognizable, close to the portrait"; "[d]etails from everyday life also appeared."[121] In the end, she maintains that eighteenth-century Belarusian iconography was in "a gradual decline," resulting in the eventual "collapse of the whole icon painting system."[122]

The legacy of the seventeenth-century Russian iconographer Simon Ushakov is a prime example of the ambivalent place of Westernized icons. Ouspensky does not mince words: "The link with Tradition is broken. Church art becomes secularized under the influence of the nascent secular realistic art, whose father is the famous iconographer Simon Ushakov."[123] Engelina Smirnova, though, sees Ushakov as a renewer of tradition along-side Patriarch Nikon (who, we remember, publicly defaced and destroyed

119. Komashko, "Ukrainian Icon Painting," p. 195.

120. Ibid., p. 196. Hence the recommendation that iconographers not paint anything other than icons. See Uspensky, *Semiotics*, p. 23n20.

121. Komashko, "Belarussian Icons," pp. 201–2.

122. Ibid., p. 202.

123. Ouspensky and Lossky, *The Meaning of Icons*, p. 48.

overly Westernized icons), arguing, "[I]t would be wrong to regard these innovations simply as a step toward realist art of the Western European type."[124] Florensky mentions Ushakov in passing as an iconographer whose work merited special recognition by the church.[125] Krasilin says Ushakov "eroded the traditions of mediaeval icon painting,"[126] yet he attributes to Ushakov's followers the ability to create "images, following the compromise stylistics of Simon Ushakov," and later describes one of those followers as a "fine master [who] remained true to the artistic concepts of Ushakov" and therefore was traditional enough to fall out of fashion with the court at Saint Petersburg, which preferred more Westernized work.[127]

For all this ambivalence about how to assess and what to do with actual Westernized icons inherited from the past, current consensus clearly eschews such experiments as an option for contemporary iconographers. The challenge for today's icon painters is to recover and renew the iconographic tradition as it existed before its seventeenth-century Westernization, while avoiding the ossification of traditionalism.

Tradition/Traditions

Debates about style and canonicity go beyond the issue of Westernization. They've also played an often-unacknowledged role in another Orthodox argument about icons. A half-century ago, as the iconographic tradition was being recovered and rearticulated in the West, debates arose that turned on the distinction between, as the Orthodox put it, "Tradition and traditions." Meyendorff writes, "The one Holy Tradition, which constitutes the self-identity of the Church through the ages and is the organic and visible expression of the life of the Spirit in the Church, is not to be confused with the inevitable, often creative and positive, sometimes sinful, and always relative accumulation of human traditions in the historical church."[128] Differing opinions on how to distinguish Holy Tradition from its local instantiations

---

124. Engelina Smirnova, "Mediaeval Russian Icons: 11th–17th Centuries," in Evseyeva, *A History of Icon Painting,* pp. 121–64, here p. 164.

125. Florensky, *Iconostasis,* p. 90.

126. Krasilin, "Russian Icons," p. 211.

127. Ibid., pp. 213 and 215.

128. Meyendorff, *Living Tradition,* p. 21.

have sometimes manifested themselves in marked championing of particular national or regional styles. Ouspensky claimed late-medieval Russian icons as the *summa* of the iconographic tradition, "outstanding among all the ramifications of Orthodox iconography. It was indeed given to Russia to produce that perfection of the pictorial language of the icon, which revealed with such great force the depth of meaning of the liturgic image, its spirituality."[129] The Greek iconographer Photios Kontoglou, however, rated these same Russian icons "a light parody of Byzantine."[130] Given the Orthodox sense that Holy Tradition does not change or develop, but rather renews itself through the guidance of the Holy Spirit in each new context, any claim that this or that iconic tradition represents the height of development is, technically speaking, incoherent.

On a purely human level, though, such claims are perfectly understandable, especially when made by exiles and immigrants eager to retain some identification with their culture of origin. Most of us, after all, love best what we know best, and know best what we love best. Parochial claims for the superiority of one's own tradition are surely not limited to Orthodox discussions of icons. Debates about the superiority of one or another iconic style have been, nonetheless, a source of contention among some Orthodox and a point of confusion for non-Orthodox seeking to understand icons. Happily, this sort of intramural sniping about the relative perfections of Byzantine or Russian or Cretan icons belongs largely to the past. Contemporary iconographers feel free to draw on all the various "manners" (to use Bigham's term) as appropriate, to serve the needs of specific worshiping communities.

The mere existence of varied, licit, local manners, however, raises a deeper, more puzzling question for many like me who appreciate the Orthodox covenant with images but do not fully inhabit it. The tension here operates between, on the one hand, assent to the fundamental requirement that icons must be nonillusionistic to properly function as images that "depict the world in its transfigured state, that is, as transparent to uncreated light, as grace bearing,"[131] and the realization, on the other hand, that there

129. Ouspensky and Lossky, *The Meaning of Icons*, p. 45.

130. As quoted in Constantine Cavarnos's review of Ouspensky and Lossky's *The Meaning of Icons*, in *Speculum* 32, no. 3 (July 1957): 599.

131. This is how Aidan Hart described the fundamental requirement for icons in his lecture entitled "Iconography for the Twenty-First Century."

are many, many nonillusionistic, nonarbitrary, indigenous artistic idioms from all around the globe that might appropriately accomplish this goal — in addition to the one developed in the early Byzantine world and adapted for use within the church and subsequently institutionalized and globalized as canonical for Orthodox Christians.

Icons and Inculturation

Essentially, this is a question of inculturation.[132] Anscar Chupungco describes inculturation as the "process of reciprocal assimilation between Christianity and culture and the resulting interior transformation of culture on the one hand, and the rooting of Christianity in culture on the other."[133] What does it mean, then, for Orthodox Christians to claim the indigenous visual idiom of late Roman and early medieval Byzantine Christians (and a handful of later, regional variants of that idiom) as the best and only possible expression of canonical iconography? The conviction that iconography has no real style, only canonicity, makes this question puzzling to those within the Orthodox covenant with icons. When form and content have become so inextricably bound up in one particular visual vocabulary, it becomes impossible to imagine that anything that doesn't "look like an icon" could be appropriately iconic. From outside the Orthodox covenant, however, the promulgation of one particular stylistic mode inherited from one place and era seems the visual equivalent of the Catholic Church's long-held

132. Aylward Shorter's *Toward a Theology of Inculturation* is a widely used introduction to the topic from a Catholic perspective. Shorter uses "inculturation" to describe the "continuous dialogue between faith and culture" but acknowledges that the term "interculturation" may actually be preferable, as it foregrounds the reciprocity that should characterize the encounter between cultures: "It is also the case that Christianity is transformed by culture, not in a way that falsifies the message, but in the way in which the message is formulated and interpreted anew" (pp. 11–14). Lesslie Newbigin prefers the term "contextualization" to capture this dynamic, as it "suggests the placing of the gospel in the total context of a culture at a particular moment, a moment that is shaped by the past and looks to the future." See his *Foolishness to the Greeks: The Gospel and Western Culture* (Grand Rapids: Eerdmans, 1986), p. 2. Nonetheless, the dominant term in most recent studies of worship and culture is "inculturation."

133. Anscar Chupungco, *Liturgical Inculturation: Sacramentals, Religiosity, and Catechesis* (Collegeville, MN: Liturgical Press, 1992), p. 29.

conviction that Latin, the indigenous language of one segment of the late Roman and early medieval Western Church, was the only proper language for the Mass.

Orthodox theologians present Orthodoxy as extraordinarily open to local cultures. Two exemplary moments in Orthodox history loom large in these discussions: the Byzantine mission to the Slavs in the ninth and tenth centuries and the early nineteenth-century Russian mission in Alaska. Both of these historical moments are presented as laudable examples of inculturation where the Gospels, catechisms, prayers, and hymns of the church were translated into a variety of local tongues as quickly as was feasible and where indigenous clergy were cultivated very early on.[134] Given the horrible missteps that have characterized so much Christian missionary activity throughout history, and given the durability of Orthodoxy among these now-Christian peoples, the posture of openness seen to characterize Orthodoxy is remarkable, laudable, and apparently effective. Yet it's also true that most contemporary missiologists see linguistic translation, and even the translation of key symbols of the faith into local, "dynamic equivalents," as only the beginning of inculturation, not the end.[135] In Orthodox contexts, translation has not extended to the visual language of icons. Icons may depict a variety of human body and facial types in the portrayal of various saints, but not, it seems, using any local visual syntax — even if, as with the native peoples of Alaska, the local idiom is itself appropriately nonillusionistic and nonarbitrary. In Fern Wallace's pictorial documenta-

---

134. *The Russian Primary Chronicle*, pp. 62–63, gives an interesting account of the Slavic mission, including a fascinating vignette where the Roman pope intervenes to defend the translation of Scripture into languages other than Hebrew, Greek, and Latin. In Alaska, the Lord's Prayer was translated into Alutiiq and Tlingit using Latin script as early as 1816. Other key translations were published using Cyrillic script beginning in the 1840s. All Saints of North America Orthodox Church of Hamilton, Ontario (OCA), maintains a digital archive of Alaskan native Orthodox texts at http://www.asna.ca/alaska/#research (consulted March 13, 2012). For typical comments on the Alaska mission, see, for example, Schmemann's introduction to Constance Tarasar and John Erickson's *Orthodox America, 1794–1976: Development of the Orthodox Church in America* (Syosset, NY: Orthodox Church in America Department of History and Archives, 1975); and on the Slavic mission, John Meyendorff's "The Orthodox Church and Mission: Past and Present Perspectives," *St. Vladimir's Theological Quarterly* 16, no. 2 (1972): 59–71.

135. Peter Schineller, SJ, *A Handbook on Inculturation* (Maryknoll, NY: Orbis, 1990), pp. 15–16.

tion of the Alaskan mission, for example, the icons on view are all Russian. Many are even in the nineteenth-century Westernized, Russian style found so problematic today (even more so in this missionary context, showing, as they do, the holy figures as light-eyed, pale-skinned people). According to Wallace, the most valued icon in Alaska is a thoroughly Westernized version of the Theotokos of Kazan, an icon associated for centuries with the Russian empire.[136]

In an influential speech on Orthodoxy and mission given in 1964, Father Anastasios Yannoulatos formulated two goals of Orthodox outreach as "incarnation of the Logos of God into the language and customs of a country" and the "growth of an indigenous church which will sanctify and endorse the people's personality."[137] The challenge for the non-Orthodox viewer of icons is reconciling such Orthodox openness to what is local and native with its marked insistence on the canonicity of only one particular representational mode for its icons. The vast missiological and anthropological literature on inculturation testifies to the richness and complexity of these issues. It may very well be the case that native Alaskan converts to Orthodoxy associated their own representational idiom with religious practices and beliefs that they wanted to reject. They also seem to have quite successfully maintained a great deal of continuity with native forms of sociality, ritual, and domestic representation as compatible with Orthodox identity.[138] Ethnographers have noted that Orthodoxy is so indigenized among some native Alaskans that they claim they've always been Orthodox.[139] But the question still stands: Can prayerful obedience to tradition ever result in what we might call, for lack of a better term, canonical yet indigenous icons?

136. Fern Wallace, *The Flame of the Candle: A Pictorial History of the Russian Orthodox Churches in Alaska* (Chilliwack, BC: Saints Kyril and Methody Society, 1974), pp. 16–17.

137. Anastasios Yannoulatos, "Discovering the Orthodox Missionary Ethos," *St. Vladimir's Theological Quarterly* 8 (1964): 139–48.

138. Sergei Kan, *Memory Eternal: Tlingit Culture and Russian Orthodox Christianity* (Seattle: University of Washington Press, 1999); Sergei Kan, "Russian Orthodox Brotherhoods among the Tlingit: Missionary Goals and Native Response," *Ethnohistory* 32 (Summer 1985): 196–222; Lydia Black, *Russians in Alaska* (Fairbanks: University of Alaska Press, 2004); Robert R. Rathburn, "The Russian Orthodox Church as a Native Institution among the Koniag Eskimo of Kodiak Island," *Arctic Anthropology* 18 (1981): 12–22.

139. For the claim of original Orthodoxy, see Medeia Csoba DeHass, "Daily Negotiation of Traditions in a Russian Orthodox Sugpaiq Village in Alaska," *Ethnology* 46 (Summer 2007): 209–10.

Inculturation and Ecclesiology

Given the liturgical theology embodied in icons — their role in making present an eschatological reality that seemingly erases earthly distinctions of space and time — it is highly unlikely that indigenous icons will ever emerge. Among Orthodox Christians, there is not only little perceived need for such a thing, but the entire notion, viewed from within the Orthodox covenant, probably seems nonsensical. Orthodox Christians view any changes to the worshiping life of the church with extreme skepticism — and for them, this is a good thing. Peter Galadza explains, "Belief, then, is embodied, 'incarnated,' in liturgy. Worship does not only express faith, it *is* the faith in a certain sense."[140] He continues: "[I]n the medieval west, the 'gaze that saves' focused on the consecrated host. In the East the object of 'viewing' has remained the total worship event. People, images and gestures are all included in a 'gaze' that authentically 'mediates salvation,' for what is 'seen' at Orthodox liturgy is the heavenly city. . . . That is why it is so difficult to change this liturgy. For how can one 'remodel' the heavenly city?"[141] He adds, "[i]f a reform of Byzantine worship is ever to take place it will have to be preceded by a tempering of the identification between seen and unseen, the signified and its sign."[142]

Remodel the heavenly city, indeed. This observation turns the whole question of inculturation on its head. For Orthodox Christians, the primary purpose of worship is not to inculturate the gospel into our native cultures, but rather to inculturate *us* into God's kingdom. The primary purpose of worship is not local, but universal. Ideally, increasingly conformed to the image and likeness of Christ, in whom "there is no East or West, in Him no North and South," our this-worldly distinctions of time and place *should* drop away. And while the visual, musical, and poetic shape of the liturgy might be tinged with our human finitude and fragility, the liturgy remains, nonetheless, a gift from God, not a human creation. And gifts from God are not to be tampered with lightly.

Orthodox discussions of mission — the arena of church life where the

---

140. Peter Galadza, "Restoring the Icon: Reflections on the Reform of Byzantine Worship," *Worship* 65 (1991): 240.

141. Ibid., p. 242.

142. Ibid., p. 241.

challenges of inculturation are most easily recognized — talk much more of worship than of culture. A favored Orthodox phrase for mission is "the liturgy after the Liturgy." For Kallistos Ware, "the most important missionary witness we have is the Divine Liturgy, the Eucharistic worship of the Orthodox Church. . . . And therefore, to those who show an interest in Orthodoxy, I say, 'Come and see. Come to the liturgy.'"[143] John Meyendorff is confident that in terms of witness and mission, "the serene immutability of Orthodox worship, the sort of passive immunity which has been shown so far by the masses of Orthodox people . . . will prove to have been ultimately an effective witness."[144] A Romanian Orthodox priest states, "[P]eople are sanctified by participating through the liturgy in the thankful and joyful witness of salvation. In the liturgy, not only human culture and society but also the whole cosmos is transfigured in the divine light of God. In this sense, there is a strong positive relationship between the church and evangelized local and national cultures."[145]

In bringing people into communion with Christ, that is, in bringing them to worship, the Orthodox Church does not so much seek to inculturate the gospel into a variety of local idioms. Rather, it seeks to inculturate all those local idioms into God's universal kingdom, a kingdom that erases all boundaries of time and space. Fundamentally, worship is where the next world breaks into ours. Not vice versa.

143. David Neff, "The Fullness and the Center: Bishop Kallistos Ware on Evangelism, Evangelicals and the Orthodox Church," *Christianity Today* 55 (July 2011): 40. Later in this same essay, however, Ware does exhort Orthodox Christians to involve themselves more intentionally in mission, while pointing out to non-Orthodox Christians the historical challenges that Orthodoxy has had to face, namely, Communism, that most other Christians have not had to deal with.

144. Meyendorff, "Orthodox Church and Mission," p. 62.

145. Gheorghe Petraru, "Missionary Theology in the Theological University Education of the Romanian Orthodox Church," *International Review of Mission* 95 (July 2006): 383–89.

CHAPTER 2

Celebrating the Paschal Mystery:
Art and Worship in the Catholic Church

*The liturgical environment isn't the artistic play-
ground for even the most gifted of artisans. It is
the sacred space in which liturgy is celebrated so
that the paschal mystery of Jesus Christ unfolds.*

— JOYCE ANN ZIMMERMAN[1]

While visiting West Michigan during the course of my sabbatical, I had
occasion to attend an ecumenical worship service sponsored by a number
of churches in northern Ottawa County. Saint Mary's Catholic Church in
Spring Lake was the host congregation (fig. 10). After the service, as people
mingled in the parish hall, I asked some of the Protestant attendees what
they thought of the sanctuary. Most had never been inside Saint Mary's,
despite years, sometimes a lifetime, of living nearby. Everyone thought the
space looked surprisingly "Protestant." They did not see what they had expected — the rich decoration, paintings, statues, shrines, and other imagery
they stereotypically associated with Catholic worship.

Saint Mary's church building was dedicated in 1966. It is a large rectangle, with the altar in the center of the long side. Four banks of pews radiate

1. Joyce Ann Zimmerman, *The Ministry of Liturgical Environment* (Collegeville, MN:
Liturgical Press, 2004), p. ix.

Fig. 10. Saint Mary's Catholic Church, Spring Lake, Michigan. PHOTOGRAPH BY AUTHOR

outward from the altar in a large sweeping crescent. A large, modernist mosaic of the risen Christ covers the wall behind the altar and the pulpit. To the side, on the left, there is a smaller, more naturalistic mosaic of the Virgin. To the right, a large organ console holds pride of place. Running along the elegant slope of the open, cathedral-style ceiling, rows of clerestory windows provide dramatic lighting that draws worshipers' attention to the area around the altar. The entire space is bright, open, harmonious, and airy. The accent is on the character of the space as a whole — not on any one or two of its constituent parts. With the exception of the mosaic of the Virgin and a series of small, modernist enamels of the Stations of the Cross that run along the side walls, from the pews, Saint Mary's looks more midcentury modern than it looks specifically Catholic. That may be why so many of the Protestant visitors I spoke to thought the space looked very much like their own more or less midcentury modern churches — Methodist, Reformed, Lutheran, or Congregational. Merely *looking* at the space would not reveal much of its specifically Catholic character. One would need to join the Saint Mary's congregation in worship to see its Catholic character in action.

The goal of this chapter is to help readers better understand why a space like Saint Mary's looks like it does and how the Catholic Church has come to value the role and place of the visual arts in worship in particular ways. Art is a vital element of Catholic life and worship, but if you ask an American Catholic about "art and the church," you probably won't hear the same sorts of comments about the topic you would hear from Protestants. You are unlikely to hear about a church art gallery, much less an installation linked to a sermon series, or video projections or even banners — those lowest common denominators of church art! After a somewhat perplexed pause, what you are likely to hear about is "liturgy."

On the one hand, in the local congregation, a lot of what we might identify as art is likely on view in the sanctuary (the mosaics and enamels at Saint Mary's, for example), but it isn't really recognized as such. In a recent study of Christians' actual uses for and understandings of art and images in worship, William Dyrness writes that for his Catholic respondents, "images, the liturgy and the drama of the Mass are inseparable — in fact there was a general reticence on the part of many to single out images, or even the visual element in general for comment."[2] These responses may come as a surprise to some Protestants who still imagine that Catholic churches are mysterious, dim spaces, crowded with all kinds of paintings, statues, shrines, and candles — and that those paintings and statues sometimes look to be more the object than the vehicle of Catholic worship. That stereotype is misguided on a number of counts. It is true that art plays a vital role in Catholic worship in distinctive and important ways. It is so important, in fact, that many aspects of it are carefully channeled and supervised, and it would be quite unusual for a group of artists in a Catholic parish to form, as some Protestant churches do, a worship arts committee or a visual arts team to "add a visual element to worship."

On the other hand, ask a Catholic *artist* about "art and the church," and you are likely to get a pause and then an earful of lament on the dubious quality of the modern and contemporary galleries at the Vatican! The two poles of these responses are instructive. Ask ordinary Catholics about "the arts in your church," and they are likely to comment on worship and the

2. William Dyrness, *Senses of the Soul: Art and the Visual in Christian Worship* (Eugene, OR: Cascade Books, 2008), p. 75.

liturgy. Ask Catholic *artists* about "the arts in your church," and they often leap directly over their local context to that symbol of the Catholic Church as a whole — the Vatican. This points us to Catholic Christians' strong sense of being part of a much larger communion, and also to Catholic artists' lack of connection *as artists* to their local parish. Artists in the pew seem to find themselves stranded between their local parish, where there may be little call for them to exercise their talents, and the worldwide Roman Catholic Church, which clearly does welcome the arts but on such a scale and at such a distance that it's not clear how the individual artist can connect. This is not to say that there is no interest in the Catholic community in connecting local artists to their parishes. Rather, it is to point out that there are some structural realities in the Catholic communion that inhibit such connections.

Why is this? To appreciate the way in which the arts function in the Catholic Church, we'll have to unpack a bit of history and come to understand more fully how Roman Catholic concepts of the nature of the church and the centrality of liturgy contextualize an understanding of art's place in the worshiping church. For Catholics, all of this is very old news. For Protestant readers, though, my hope is that this discussion of the arts in the Roman Catholic Church, as our discussion of the role of icons in Orthodox worship, will provide fresh perspectives from which to examine the basic assumptions about art and worship that shape the ways in which we construct the relationship between art and worship.

The Context: The Church as an Institution

The papacy is, of course, the most prominent symbol, readily visible to Catholics and non-Catholics alike, of the institutional structure of the Roman Catholic Church. Avery Dulles, in his typology of ecclesial models, includes institution as his first model, a model that understands the church primarily via its structure, a hierarchical authority organized according to divine warrant.[3] But what many people outside the Catholic community may not fully appreciate is the pastoral role and function of this institu-

3. Avery Dulles, *Models of the Church* (Garden City, NY: Image Books, 1987), pp. 26–38.

tional church at every level, from the parish, through the diocese, to the archdiocese, to national conferences, to the Vatican. American Protestants who belong to congregationally organized churches, and whose sense of congregational independence and autonomy has become an invisible norm in church life, may never have paused to consider the benefits (as opposed to the hindrances) of a well-organized institutional structure. At a nuts-and-bolts level, this means that in a Catholic parish, unless a situation is absolutely unprecedented, there are very likely helpful and authoritative resources already to hand that have been thoughtfully created by experts in the field and carefully vetted for parish usefulness. These resources might exist at the level of the regional diocese. They might come from a national council of bishops (in the United States, this is the USCCB, the United States Conference of Catholic Bishops). They might come from a Catholic publishing house like Liturgy Training Publications in Chicago; from a Catholic seminary or monastery like Saint John's Abbey in Collegeville, Minnesota, which sponsors Liturgical Press; or from the Vatican itself. Only rarely would members of a Catholic parish need to begin a discussion on a matter of worship or church life from scratch. There is very little need to reinvent the wheel.

In the arts, this means that over the years the Catholic Church has developed a set of documents, some global and some regional in scope, that seeks to guide individual congregations in understanding and designing the spaces and objects used for corporate worship. Read any Catholic book or article on the visual arts and worship, and you will see these texts cited throughout. In the United States, one can even turn to a handy compendium assembled by Mark Boyer, *The Liturgical Environment: What the Documents Say.*[4] At the same time, this pattern of arranging institutional life means that any arts-related activities will happen within the parameters envisioned and mapped out by these documents. The freewheeling experimentation with the arts happening in many Protestant settings today is difficult, if not impossible, to imagine in the Roman Catholic Church, given its institutional structures, documents, and traditions.[5]

---

4. Mark Boyer, *The Liturgical Environment: What the Documents Say*, 2nd ed. (Collegeville, MN: Liturgical Press, 2004).

5. This is not to say that there has been no experimentation in Catholic worship. After

The fundamental document that has guided all Roman Catholic conversations about art and worship throughout the entire world during the past fifty years is not in fact about art. It is about worship. This is the *Constitution on the Sacred Liturgy*. It was the first document released by the enormously important Second Vatican Council (1962–1965). In the conclusion to his brief 1964 commentary on the *Constitution*, Rev. Dr. Gerard Sloyan wrote:

> One hesitates to estimate what the impact of this first document to emerge from the Second Vatican Council will be. It does not come out of the blue but as the fruit of liturgical and biblical movements that are now seventy or eighty years old in the Church. It could not have been framed by the Council Fathers apart from the contributions made to Christian life and thought by their Anglican and Protestant brothers. Surely our common concern with them over the Bible as the great prayer book of Christians and over meaningful rites and forms will bring us even closer together than in the past. Yet none of the hoped for benefits to the Roman Church that is our mother, or to all the communions of Christendom, will flow unless there is an openness to the teaching of the bishops contained in this constitution. This means that hard study lies ahead for all of us; a willingness to be converted, to be changed by the Spirit's action; a desire to come close to Jesus in *His* way — the way of the incarnation and the sacraments — rather than to cleave to familiar religious patterns that are more a thing of us than of Him.[6]

The themes sounded by Father Sloyan when the *Constitution* was first promulgated continue to resonate to this day. Thirty years later, in 1993, Father Sloyan and forty-three other Catholic clergy and scholars signed a statement underscoring the pivotal importance this document has played in the Roman Catholic Church:

Vatican II, in fact, before additional interpretive documents were developed, there was so much experimentation in the format and structure of the liturgy that a reaction soon set in.

6. *The Constitution on the Sacred Liturgy of the Second Vatican Council and The Motu Proprio of Pope Paul VI with a Commentary by Gerard S. Sloyan* (Glen Rock, NJ: Paulist, 1964), p. 28; hereafter *Constitution*. The *Constitution* was promulgated in Latin as *Sacrosanctum Concilium* on December 4, 1963. An English translation was released that same day by the United States bishops' press. That text was the one used for the Paulist Press edition cited here.

We affirm the blessings given to the universal church and the churches in the USA stemming from the vision of *Sacrosanctum Concilium,* the reform it launched and the renewal it anticipated. Among the blessings experienced by the Catholic Christian community are:

- The vernacular liturgical texts and their revision now underway
- Richer fare at the table of God's word
- New appreciation and creativity in the areas of ritual music and art
- New insight into the formative power of liturgical space
- An explosion of lay ministries
- Recovery of the essential dimension of Christian Initiation, reconciliation, care of the sick
- Experiencing the heightened power of Sunday, feasts and seasons.

All of these blessings have begun to open in us the central conviction that the liturgy is, at its heart, the day by day and Sunday by Sunday work of the body of Christ gathered in its local assembly.[7]

Though the *Constitution* itself is only forty-six pages long in its English translation, the impact of this document within the Roman Catholic Church and far beyond cannot be overstated. As the liturgical historian Edward Foley put it, "written for Roman Catholics, this document became pivotal in the reform of worship throughout the Christian churches."[8] It is indeed true that the conversation about worship crystallized in and inspired by the *Constitution* spilled over confessional boundaries to impact nearly every corner of the Christian world. This is a theme to which we will return.

The Church as the Body of Christ

For non-Catholics, considering the *Constitution on the Sacred Liturgy* is instructive. It demonstrates two fundamental aspects of the Roman Catholic Church that shape the ways in which the arts are understood and used in

7. "Thirty Years after *The Constitution on the Sacred Liturgy,*" *Worship* 68 (March 1994): 165.

8. Edward Foley, *From Age to Age: How Christians Celebrated the Eucharist* (Chicago: Liturgy Training Publications, 1991), p. 142.

Catholic settings. First, in its genesis and refinement in a church council, in its promulgation by a pope (Paul VI), in its judicial status as an official document, and in its not-uncontroversial pastoral application at the parish level, the *Constitution* reminds us of the majesty and force of the Roman Catholic understanding of "church." In part, this understanding of church asks us to appreciate its institutional structure and operation. But in part, this understanding of church is also theological. And the institutional and the theological are mutually interdependent.

In the words of the Catholic *Catechism,* "The Church is the People that God gathers in the whole world. She exists in local communities and is made real as a liturgical, above all a Eucharistic, assembly. She draws her life from the word and the Body of Christ and so herself becomes Christ's Body."[9] And, "It is in the Church that Christ fulfills and reveals his own mystery as the purpose of God's plan: 'to unite all things in him.'"[10] Father Sloyan quotes the nineteenth-century theologian J. A. Moehler: "The Church is the permanent incarnation of the Son of God," and then adds, "There is no way held out to us to enter into the life of God except through personal contact with Jesus in His sacraments."[11] As Mark Noll and Carolyn Nystrom recently summarized, "For Catholics, the church is central, an axis on which all of life pivots," and "If Christ and his church are one, then a great deal of Catholic doctrine simply follows naturally."[12]

For many Protestants, especially those who have spent most of their Christian lives in independent churches, this view of the church as universal *and* as a worldwide institution requires an imaginative effort. But it is an imaginative effort worth making to be able to understand the role of the arts in Catholic worship and to benefit from the rich resources available in this tradition. Rather than engage in a necessarily truncated — and

9. United States Catholic Conference, *Catechism of the Catholic Church*, 2nd ed. (Vatican City: Libreria Editrice Vaticana; Washington, DC: United States Catholic Conference, 2000), par. 752; hereafter *Catechism*.

10. Ibid., par. 772.

11. *Constitution*, pp. 14–15.

12. Mark A. Noll and Carolyn Nystrom, *Is the Reformation Over? An Evangelical Assessment of Contemporary Roman Catholicism* (Grand Rapids: Baker Academic; Bletchley, UK: Paternoster, 2005), pp. 150, 147. See also Geoffrey Wainwright's discussion of "fundamental ecclesiology" in *Is the Reformation Over? Catholics and Protestants at the Turn of the Millennium* (Milwaukee: Marquette University Press, 2000), pp. 61–65.

very likely distracting — discussion of differences in Catholic and Protestant understandings of "the church," I will simply note that these differences exist and are significant.[13] From a Protestant congregational perspective, a church is often imagined as a group of people, a voluntary association, who worship God together, who disciple one another, and who individually and as a community bear witness to God's deeds. Using Avery Dulles's taxonomy, these churches understand themselves primarily as "herald," tasked with proclaiming the gospel message and helping their members grow in faith. The individual precedes the church. For Catholics, it is the other way around: the church as the body of Christ (Dulles's "mystical communion" type) constitutes us fully as individuals and as a people. Any sympathetic account of the arts in Catholic worship requires a grasp of the absolute centrality of the church in both its theological and its institutional dimensions.

Having established something of the structural and theological realities that undergird the use of the arts in Catholic worship, we ask, what specifically does the *Constitution* say about art? Actually, not much. In the 1964 English edition, chapter 7, "Sacred Art and Sacred Furnishings," takes up only three pages. Father Sloyan remarks, "The chapter on sacred art and furnishings cannot be called a strong one."[14] Beginning with an affirmation of the arts as "among the noblest activities of man's genius" and as "by their very nature . . . oriented toward the infinite beauty of God," the *Constitution* singles out properties like "worthiness," "dignity," "nobility," and "moderation" as appropriate for art that serves the liturgy.[15] Articles 124, 125, and 126 address art most specifically.

> 124. Ordinaries,[16] by the encouragement and favor they show to art which is truly sacred, should strive after noble beauty rather than mere sumptuous display. This principle is to apply also in the matter of sacred vestments and ornaments.

13. For two fascinating, accessible, and complementary discussions of the liveliest divergences between Catholic and Protestant ecclesiology, see Noll and Nystrom's *Is the Reformation Over?* and William Shea's *The Lion and the Lamb: Evangelicals and Catholics in America* (Oxford: Oxford University Press, 2004).

14. *Constitution*, p. 27.

15. Ibid., par. 122. Official Catholic documents are organized by numbered paragraphs. References to these documents point readers to the relevant paragraph.

16. An "ordinary" is a member of the clergy with jurisdiction over a specified territory, such as a diocese.

Let bishops carefully remove from the house of God and from other sacred places those works of artists which are repugnant to faith, morals, and Christian piety, and which offend true religious sense either by depraved forms or by lack of artistic worth, mediocrity and pretense.

And when churches are to be built, let great care be taken that they be suitable for the celebration of liturgical services and for the active participation of the faithful.

125. The practice of placing sacred images in churches so that they may be venerated by the faithful is to be maintained. Nevertheless their number should be moderate and their relative positions should reflect right order. For otherwise they may create confusion among the Christian people and foster devotion of doubtful orthodoxy.

126. When passing judgment on works of art, local ordinaries shall give a hearing to the diocesan commission on sacred art and, if needed, also to others who are especially expert. . . .[17]

The *Constitution on the Sacred Liturgy* is a binding church document. Yet when it was issued, some of its directives needed to be carried out at regional and national levels. Still others required the revision of liturgical materials or the creation of new ones that had yet to take place.[18] *Environment and Art in Catholic Worship,* published in 1978 by the Bishops' Committee on Liturgy of the United States Conference of Catholic Bishops, represented this further working out of the directives and implications of the *Constitution* for a specific national setting. Insofar as *Environment and Art* is based on the *Constitution,* it is authoritative. But as a commentary and expansion of the *Constitution,* much of it is pastoral and speculative in nature, and at fifty spaciously printed, paperback-sized pages, it is very readable. The introduction states that the goal of *Environment and Art* is to offer "principles to guide rather than blueprints to follow," because, as the *Constitution* so clearly stated: "The Church has not adopted any particular style of art as her

17. *Constitution,* pars 124–126. In the United States, some dioceses enjoy a dedicated commission for questions regarding art for worship. Other dioceses use subcommittees or ad hoc committees convened under the auspices of their Diocesan Liturgical Commissions.

18. Ibid., p. 12.

very own; it has admitted styles from every period according to the natural talents and circumstances of peoples, and the needs of the various rites. . . . The art of our own days, coming from every race and region, shall also be given free scope in the Church, provided that it adorns the sacred buildings and holy rites with due reverence and honor."[19] *Environment and Art*, then, was intended to set forth some general principles that could be used in applying the directives set out in the *Constitution on the Sacred Liturgy* in the context of the Catholic Church in the United States. These principles are derived from the needs of the liturgy.

Liturgy: The Heart of the Church

For some Protestant readers, the Catholic (as well as the Orthodox) emphasis on liturgy might be vexing. Does one really need liturgy to worship God? Christians asking this question might think of themselves as belonging to a "nonliturgical" tradition that dispenses with formalized ritual. Yet even the most so-called nonliturgical worship, informal in style, follows a liturgy — that is, a pattern — however loose, of entering, praying, singing, proclaiming, receiving, giving, and sending. The Catholic understanding of liturgy, like its understanding of church, is at once structural and theological. In the Catholic Church, liturgy is the pattern of the church's actions through which the gospel is most fully represented, proclaimed, enacted, and appropriated. Liturgy, in particular the eucharistic liturgy, is rooted in and a manifestation of the great mystery of the faith, that is, Christ's incarnation. Liturgy is to the church as breath is to the body. Again, from the Catholic *Catechism*: "Christ's work in the liturgy is sacramental: because his mystery of salvation is made present there by the power of his Holy Spirit; because his Body, which is the Church, is like a sacrament (sign and instrument) in which the Holy Spirit dispenses the mystery of salvation; and because through her liturgical actions the pilgrim Church already par-

---

19. *Environment and Art in Catholic Worship* (Washington, DC: United States Catholic Conference, 1978), par. 8. This is the exact passage quoted by Father Steven Bigham to argue from an Orthodox perspective that the church actually *has* developed a unique manner, a distinctive "universal, canonical iconography" (Bigham, "The Icon: Sign of Unity or Division?" *Ecumenism* 176 [Winter 2009–2010]: 5–6).

ticipates, as by a foretaste, in the heavenly liturgy."[20] This is stated in more anthropological terms by Edward Foley: "Worship has the power to shape and change our belief. More than any official proclamation or systematic treatise, the liturgy announces who we are and who we are to become in Christ. Liturgy, therefore, is the bedrock upon which we build our theologies of God, church and salvation."[21] With this expansive understanding of all that is encompassed in the liturgy, we can begin to appreciate the seriousness of Joyce Zimmerman's statement, used at the opening of this chapter, that the liturgical environment is no artistic playground, even for the most talented of artists.

Environment and Art frames its discussion of art within this understanding of the liturgy. After opening sections on worship and the church, the document discusses the space in which the church celebrates the liturgy; the physical actions of the liturgy (gestures, postures, and processions); and finally, liturgical furnishings and liturgical objects. The guiding principles that emerge in this discussion include the engagement of the whole person, "body, mind, senses, imagination, emotions, memory";[22] hospitality; mystery; simplicity; rich and full use of symbols, "especially the fundamental ones of bread and wine, water, oil, the laying on of hands" (15); a dynamic that is at once personal and communal; quality, that is, "the hand stamp of the artist, the honesty and care that went into an object's making" (20); appropriateness, that is, the ability to "bear the weight of mystery, awe, reverence, and wonder which the liturgical action expresses" as well as the ability to "clearly serve (and not interrupt) ritual action which has its own structure, rhythm and movement" (21); contemporaneity, that is, "the work of artists of our time and place" (33); and beauty, which, "admittedly difficult to define . . . is related to our sense of the numinous, the holy" (34). The section on "images," the category into which would fall many kinds of art currently being experimented with in Protestant settings, conveys a clear sense of ambivalence about any art not directly in service to the liturgy: "[T]he attempt to recover a solid grasp of Church and faith and rites involves the rejection of certain embellishments which have in the course of

20. *Catechism,* par. 1111.

21. Foley, *From Age to Age,* p. vii.

22. *Environment and Art,* par. 5. Parenthetical numbers in the following text refer to paragraphs in *Environment and Art.*

history become hindrances. In many areas of religious practice, this means a simplifying and refocusing on primary symbols. In building, this effort has resulted in more austere interiors, with fewer objects on the walls and in corners" (99). Ideally, such images "should be introduced into the liturgical space upon consultation with an art consultant" and "must take into account the current renewed emphasis on the action of the assembly. If instead of serving and aiding that action, they threaten or compete with it, then they are unsuitable" (98). In sum, worship spaces should be simple; images should not threaten or compete with worship. Clearly, less is more. This section of *Environment and Art* contains a faint, reproving echo of the conditions that created the stereotype of image-laden Catholic worship and, as such, carries to some Catholic ears a tinge of Protestant visual asceticism.[23] Yet today, ironically, some forms of Protestant worship are more likely to be image driven in ways that do, perhaps, on occasion "threaten and compete with worship."

For twenty-two years, *Environment and Art in Catholic Worship* was the nonbinding yet highly influential pastoral statement on how the visual arts related to worship in the Catholic Church in the United States. Using simple and, at times, poetic and evocative language, it triggered a nationwide discussion in the Catholic Church and beyond about what kinds of spaces and what kinds of objects were best suited for use in worship. It is unlikely that the publication of a third document, *Built of Living Stones: Art, Architecture, and Worship*, in 2000, which expands, supersedes, and replaces *Environment and Art*, will significantly change the direction established by *Environment and Art*.[24]

23. It is also fair to point out, however, that this also echoes the decrees on art of the Council of Trent, issued December 4, 1563 (symbolically, the *Constitution* was issued December 4, 1963, four hundred years later, to the day): "[I]mages shall not be painted and adorned with a seductive charm, or the celebration of saints and the visitation of relics be perverted by the people into boisterous festivities and drunkenness, as if the festivals in honor of the saints are to be celebrated with revelry and with no sense of decency. Finally, such zeal and care should be exhibited by the bishops with regard to these things that nothing may appear that is disorderly or unbecoming and confusedly arranged, nothing that is profane, nothing disrespectful, since holiness becometh the house of God. That these things may be the more faithfully observed, the holy council decrees that no one is permitted to erect or cause to be erected in any place or church, howsoever exempt, any unusual image unless it has been approved by the bishop . . ." (*Canons and Decrees of the Council of Trent*, trans. H. J. Schroeder [Saint Louis and London: Herder, 1941], pp. 216–17).

24. United States Catholic Conference, *Built of Living Stones: Art, Architecture, and*

However authoritative and pastorally motivated these documents are, it would be a mistake to assume that their interpretation and implementation have been without controversy. For some conservative Catholics, harmful changes to the liturgy itself stem from improper interpretation of the *Constitution on the Sacred Liturgy*.[25] For critics of *Environment and Art*, the opinion of Charles Wilson, the founder of the traditionalist Saint Joseph Foundation, is representative: "*Environment and Art* is known to most faithful Catholics as the driving force behind the needless and devastating renovation of countless old parish churches and the hideous design of thousands of new ones."[26] *Built of Living Stones* has also come in for its share of criticism from both the reformist and the traditionalist wings within the Catholic Church.[27] Catholic readers probably have firsthand experience with the painfully visceral arguments that erupted over church renovations and building projects. Scanning the polemics on *Environment and Art* and

---

Worship (Washington, DC: United States Catholic Conference, 2000). This document can also be read online at www.ajdiocese.org/sites/default/files/Built%20of%20Living%20 Stones.pdf. *Built of Living Stones* was written to flesh out and further define aspects of the design process that *Environment and Art* was never meant to address. With eighty densely printed, 8½ x 11 inch pages and with considerably more detail, *Built of Living Stones* discusses the parts of a church and their meaning and function, specific celebrations and rites that the space must enable and support, and the particular ritual furnishings necessary. It even maps out the design process from the creation of a master plan and the hiring of design consultants to the role of the parish and financial considerations.

25. The late French archbishop Marcel Lefebvre is probably the most well-known traditionalist critic of Vatican II in general and of the revisions to the liturgy in particular. Even reform-minded leaders in the Catholic Church were sometimes taken aback by some of the experimental liturgies that followed in the wake of Vatican II. Andrew Greeley opened a 1970 essay in the *Critic* with the provocative hyperbole, "Now we have the pot Mass." This essay, "Come Blow Your Mind with Me," is reprinted in the book by the same name (Garden City, NY: Doubleday, 1970), which collects thirteen essays by Greeley, all of which give some insight into the challenges faced, from within and without, by the Catholic Church after Vatican II.

26. Charles Wilson, "U.S. Bishops' New Art and Architecture Document," *AD2000* 13, no. 6 (July 2000): 8.

27. For traditionalists, *Built of Living Stones* does not represent any clear rejection of *Environment and Art*; for reformists, its more directive tone and its interest in the role of the clergy represent potential restrictions. See, for example, the discussion recorded in *Ministry and Liturgy* 27, no. 2 (March 2000): 8–10, as well as the article in *AD2000* cited above. For the views of Richard Vosko, probably the most influential voice in Catholicism regarding the liturgical environment, see his "*Built of Living Stones*: Seven Years Later," *Liturgical Ministry* 17 (Spring 2008): 85–91.

Built of Living Stones is as disheartening as scanning the Protestant polemics on church music — though, tellingly, what is assumed to be "modern" in Catholicism is thought to be problematically elitist, and in the Protestant case, problematically popular!

Nonetheless, for our purposes, the inevitable controversies that accompany any change (or lack thereof) in a large institution like the Roman Catholic Church are of less importance than what we can learn from this brief excursus on the key documents that have shaped discussions of art and worship in the Catholic context. First, these documents, even as contested, present a theological *and* institutional demonstration of Catholic ecclesiology. Second, these documents clarify the fundamentally liturgical parameters within which the arts are asked to serve. These two points are uncontroversial and central to an understanding of art in the Catholic Church.

How, then, do these fundamental traits take concrete form in the arts of the worshiping Catholic Church? I will venture one primary fact and four resulting consequences that describe, to my outsider's eye, the current contours of the conversation on the visual arts in the Catholic Church. The primary point is this: given the Catholic commitment to the liturgical embodiment of the church, discussions of the visual arts have been purposefully channeled toward an emphasis on worship space, liturgical furnishings, and a defined number of liturgical objects — processional crosses, candlesticks, tabernacles, ambos, liturgical books, vessels, vestments, and the like. This statement will be self-evident to a Catholic reader.

The consequences of this point, however, may be less self-evident. First, this channeling process has resulted in a rich, accessible, and influential literature on the place and role of such objects and the development of extremely valuable resources for local parishes. Second, this literature has had an impact far beyond the Catholic Church and remains a great gift to all Christian churches should they wish to make use of it. Third, an unintended consequence, perhaps, of this channeling has been a corresponding lack of institutional interest in or robust attention to other ways in which the visual arts enter into Catholic worship — especially in, but not limited to, the area of devotional art. While wonderful resources are available for parishes who want to examine the material aspects of the liturgy, there are few corresponding materials to help a parish think through and learn from thorny, fascinating questions raised by the nonliturgical art in their spaces. This has become a pressing issue.[28] Finally, for good or ill, due to the increasing regulation of the arts in worship, the realm of liturgical art is becoming professionalized, with the result that few Catholics who are visual artists are explicitly invited to use their skills directly in their own parish, much less to form a visual arts committee or worship arts team to serve in the life and worship of their local congregation. Given the parameters laid out above, such a notion may be nearly unthinkable.

Environment and Art for the Liturgy

Channeling the uses of the visual arts toward attention to worship space, liturgical furnishings, and liturgical objects was certainly codified by the Second Vatican Council, but that conclave was by no means the first expression of this direction. Already in the early decades of the twentieth century, in Europe and in the United States, various Catholic organizations had been asking larger and deeper questions about worship and the nature of the church. In part, these questions were motivated by new biblical and historical scholarship arising from within the church. In part, they were motivated by changes in society at large. The response to these impulses, both from within and from without, is now called the "liturgical movement." Though the roots of the liturgical movement were in Catholic religious orders (especially the Benedictine and Dominican communities) in France, Belgium, and Germany and can be traced as far back as the seventeenth century, the movement's modern instantiation began around 1910. By the 1920s and 1930s, the movement had spread far beyond the religious orders — and beyond Catholicism and beyond Europe.

    Looking back, we clearly see a set of interrelated concerns that animated the liturgical movement. At the heart of everything lay a deep desire to express the identity of Christ's church through worship. This involved using

---

28. In 2002, the Vatican published the *Directory on Popular Piety and the Liturgy: Principles and Guidelines*, which brought into the mainstream the ongoing conversation about the proper relationship between devotional activities and the public liturgy of the church. The collection of essays edited by Peter C. Phan, *Directory on Popular Piety and the Liturgy: Principles and Guidelines — a Commentary* (Collegeville, MN: Liturgical Press, 2005), takes up that conversation. Interestingly, though both documents are important for understanding the issues at stake concerning devotional practice, neither document pays particular attention to the actual physical images and objects associated with these practices.

vernacular languages, recovering the role of the Word in liturgy, revisiting sacramental practice, and emphasizing the priority of corporate worship rather than individual devotion.[29] In the United States, one of its most telling manifestations was the formation in 1928 of the Liturgical Arts Society. The initial impetus for the society came from two directions: from American Benedictines, who were inspired by their European brothers and eager to transfer these new approaches to the United States, and from architects who were eager for a more intentional forum within which to think about what constituted good design for Catholic churches. Both constituencies were deeply committed to the material expression of new ideas about worship. The society's mission, "to devise ways and means for improving the standards of taste, craftsmanship, and liturgical correctness in the practice of Catholic art in the United States," is itself a succinct demonstration of how, in the wake of the liturgical movement, "Catholic art" came largely to be understood as "liturgical art." In perusing the issues of the society's journal, *Liturgical Arts* (published from 1931 to 1972), we can take that one step further and notice that liturgical art became essentially defined as architecture, liturgical furniture, and liturgical objects.[30]

In the decades after Vatican II, this channel, this pattern of thinking, was institutionalized. *The Constitution on the Sacred Liturgy* legislated that every Catholic diocese create, or cooperate with a neighboring diocese to create, a commission for liturgical art.[31] This Vatican mandate created a demand for

---

29. For a general introduction to the liturgical movement in several Christian confessions, see John Fenwick and Bryan Spinks's *Worship in Transition: The Liturgical Movement in the Twentieth Century* (New York: Continuum, 1995). For Fenwick and Spinks's summary of common themes, see pp. 5–12. For an introduction to the roots of the movement, see James Crichton's *Lights in the Darkness: Forerunners of the Liturgical Movement* (Collegeville, MN: Liturgical Press, 1996). For an early analysis of the progress of the liturgical movement in the Catholic Church, see George Devine, *Liturgical Renewal: An Agonizing Reappraisal* (New York: Alba House, 1973).

30. For a wonderful discussion of the history and importance of the Liturgical Arts Society, see Susan J. White's *Art, Architecture, and Liturgical Reform: The Liturgical Arts Society, 1928–1972* (New York: Pueblo Publishing Co., 1990). See p. viii for the mission of the society in particular.

31. *Constitution*, article 46. Pope Paul VI's *Motu Proprio "Sacram Liturgam,"* published in Latin on February 14, 1964, reiterates the desire that every diocese, insofar as possible, create commissions on sacred art and music. This process has had its complications, however, and has not taken shape uniformly across the American Catholic Church (John J. M. Foster,

educational resources that could be used to guide and teach local parishes. Clergy, architects, and artists who had been affiliated with the liturgical movement now had an officially sanctioned avenue in which to work. As Father Foley observed, the liturgical movement "was not an exclusively Roman Catholic phenomenon. It did, however, first become systematic within the Roman Catholic church."[32] Catholic publishing houses and diocesan presses went to work. A steady stream of accessible yet theologically rich resources on liturgical art and architecture began to roll off the presses.[33]

But how does all this work itself out at the parish level? What is the local face of the Catholic conversation about art and worship? Given the channeling of the Catholic conversation I've just described, it isn't a surprise to discover that, today, Catholic discussions about the arts and worship typically arise when a church building needs renovation or a parish decides to build a new facility. I say "today" because one of the important lessons learned in the Catholic Church after the Second Vatican Council is that any change probably requires more preparation and education than one might first anticipate. Two examples from the Diocese of Grand Rapids will help us appreciate both the opportunities and the challenges that Catholic parishes faced in implementing the changes in liturgy and liturgical space recommended by Vatican II.

The Parish of Saint Francis de Sales, Muskegon, Michigan

The design of Saint Francis de Sales in Muskegon (figs. 11–12) actually predates Vatican II. Father Louis LaPres, who came to the parish in 1955, had long been interested in liturgical renewal, and his contacts with peers connected to the Benedictine Abbey of Saint John in Collegeville, Minnesota, sowed the seeds of a grand idea: a new church for his new (established 1948), fast-growing parish, to be designed by Marcel Breuer, the same architect

"Diocesan Commissions for Liturgy, Music and Art: An Endangered Species?" *Worship* 71, no. 2 [March 1997]: 124–45).

    32. Foley, *From Age to Age*, p. 142.

    33. The major sources for this literature are Liturgy Training Publications (Archdiocese of Chicago; www.ltp.org), Liturgical Press (Saint John's Abbey, Collegeville, MN; www.litpress.org), and Resource Publications (www.rpinet.com), as well as the United States Conference of Catholic Bishops (www.usccbpublishing.org).

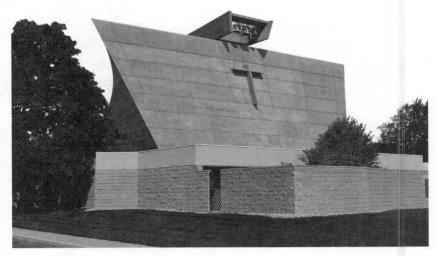

Fig. 11. East façade of Saint Francis de Sales Catholic Church, Muskegon, Michigan. Architect Marcel Breuer. PHOTOGRAPH BY DAVID M. VERSLUIS

who had designed the new abbey church at Collegeville. At midcentury, Breuer was one of a handful of internationally renowned modern architects working in the United States. It was ambitious indeed for Father LaPres to imagine a Breuer-designed church for his young, working-class parish. But visiting Collegeville in the spring of 1958, just as construction of the abbey church was beginning, and meeting with Frank Kacmarcik, professor of art at Saint John's University and a leading light among those interested in liturgical renewal, convinced Father LaPres that new understandings of worship, incarnated in new forms, were essential to the full expression of the church in the modern world.[34]

34. This summary account of the genesis of Saint Francis de Sales, Muskegon, is drawn from the excellent parish history written by Monica Schwind, OP, *In God's Own Time: St. Francis de Sales Parish, Muskegon, Michigan* (Muskegon, MI: Saint Francis de Sales Parish, 1997). Chapter 5, "Building for the Ages" (pp. 59–80), provides the most detail on the construction of the church. For the role of Collegeville in the liturgical movement, see also Robert L. Tuzik, ed., *How Firm a Foundation: Leaders of the Liturgical Movement* (Chicago: Liturgy Training Publications, 1990), and R. Kevin Seasoltz, OSB, "From the Bauhaus to the House of God's People: Frank Kacmarcik's Contribution to Church Art and Architecture," *U.S. Catholic Historian* 15, no. 1 (Winter 1997): 105–22.

Fig. 12. Nave of Saint Francis de Sales Catholic Church, Muskegon, Michigan. PHOTO-
GRAPH BY DAVID M. VERSLUIS

Incredibly, the parish leadership seems to have been quite enthusiastic about the possibility of a leading modernist architect designing an avant-garde church for their parish. Father LaPres impressed on his parish the fact that for hundreds of years, the Catholic Church had been the source of architectural innovation.[35] As narrated by Father LaPres, though, the key argument may have been as much economic as theological: "If you have a lot of money to spend you can hire the usual type of 'church' architect, but if you have limited funds then you must look for the highest type of professional competence."[36] LaPres later recounted that his own argument was quoted back to him as building expenses piled up!

Designed in 1961, the new church included many elements that would become common after Vatican II: an altar that allowed the priest to face

35. Interview with Father Thomas Simons, May 22, 2007.
36. This argument was actually made by Maurice Lavanoux, editor of *Liturgical Arts* journal, at meetings of the National Liturgical Convention in 1958. The argument was repeated by Frank Kacmarcik and by Father Hoogeterp (another Saint Francis priest) at the parish meeting when it was decided to commission Breuer as architect (Schwind, *In God's Own Time,* p. 64).

the assembly, a prominent pulpit, a chapel for the reserved host set apart from the altar, a minimum of secondary images, a large baptismal font in the church narthex, and a reconciliation chapel rather than confessional booths. All these elements were rendered in the ultimate modernist building material: fourteen thousand tons of reinforced concrete, encasing the space between trapezoidal front and back walls — the one an inversion of the other — and connected by hyperbolic paraboloid side walls.

The church is impressive. And from the very beginning, it put the parish on the map.[37] But it also presented challenges. As the walls were being poured, a church newsletter, *Domus Dei,* sought to keep the parish informed, drawing on materials generated by the Catholic Church in Germany (where rebuilding in the wake of World War II inspired a lot of new thinking about the church). Later, the newsletter was able to draw on materials emerging from Vatican II. But even as, in the words of Sister Monica Schwind, the building process was for many "a formative educational and spiritual experience," others in the parish were less enthusiastic: "The new church and rectory, while nationally and artistically significant, were controversial both in design and function."[38] Throughout the late 1960s and into the mid-1970s, tensions over the liturgical changes necessitated by the building and over the financial burden of debt management plagued the congregation. It wasn't until 1973 that finances stabilized to the point where the congregation could regularly meet all its obligations. Extraordinary expenses for the finishing, repair, and refurbishment of the structure continue to this day.[39] When Father Simons arrived at Saint Francis in 1994, he observed that "much of the last thirty years of this parish's identity was related to the physical and artistic character of its church building. I've said to people, 'We don't need any more building; we need people-building and that is my primary consideration.'"[40]

In retrospect, the building of Saint Francis was a grand experiment, by and large successful, but an experiment, nonetheless. A new, growing parish filled with young energetic families embraced an audacious plan presented

37. See Schwind, *In God's Own Time,* appendix E, p. 150, for a bibliography of articles and essays on the church.

38. Ibid., pp. 68, 84.

39. Ibid., pp. 87–88; conversation with Father Simons, May 22, 2007.

40. Ibid., p. 118.

to them by a trusted leader and then, over successive decades, had to figure out how to pay for it, how to live with it, and, eventually, how to make it their own. Father Simons himself has done much to recontextualize the building as the product of "people building." In commissioning a parish history (rather than a history of the Breuer church) in honor of the fiftieth anniversary of the parish, he's made it clear that the church building is a product of, not the cause of, parish life. The history itself begins, "A parish is at once a local church, an institution of the diocese, and member of the universal People of God. Parish history is, therefore, both local history and salvation history."[41]

Parish of Saint Sebastian, Byron Center, Michigan

Today, over fifty years after the *Constitution*'s mandate, the materials available to local parishes are much more extensive and the institutional process for building or renovation is more clearly defined than they were when Saint Francis de Sales was built. In Grand Rapids, for example, a local parish will start by getting a copy of *A House of Prayer: Building and Renovation Guidelines*. This pamphlet was written by the Liturgical Art and Environment Commission of the diocese and is promulgated by the bishop of Grand Rapids. It governs all building and renovation projects in the diocese. The foreword to *A House of Prayer* distills the essence of the themes from the *Constitution* and from *Environment and Art*:

> While there are many professional and technical considerations when undertaking such a process, this work must also be guided by values taken from areas such as theology, ecclesiology and liturgy. . . . It is the Church that gives shape to a church. A church building should be designed to enable the Christians who gather there to clearly understand that they come as a united community to worship God who in turn, calls the people to loving service of the human family. . . . All aspects of the church building (its size, materials, furnishings, lighting and sound systems, accessibility, etc.) are to serve the people and encourage them to deepen their faith. . . . The church building reflects this spirit when it is characterized by simplicity and beauty.

41. Ibid., p. 2.

Fig. 13. The new Saint Sebastian Catholic Church, Byron Center, Michigan. PHOTOGRAPH
BY LAUREN VANDEN BOSCH

These qualities are realized, not by sumptuous display and artificiality, but
through essential form, honest materials and works of art that are worthy
expressions of faith.[42]

After reiterating that the focus of building should always be on worship, the
document outlines a typical process of parish self-study, liturgical education,
consultation, and design.

This was where the parish of Saint Sebastian in Byron Center, Michigan, began. The parish was established in 1852; until recently, its members worshiped
in a brick, turn-of-the-century "little country church." Though full of charm
and memories, the building had grown too small for the parish. The lack of
space for fellowship and for education programs was especially pressing — they
even had to resort to an outdoor deck next to the church for after-church cof-
fee, an obviously unsatisfactory solution, given Michigan winters! In 2001, the

42. Liturgical Art and Environment Commission, Diocese of Grand Rapids, Michigan,
A House of Prayer: Building and Renovation Guidelines (1998).

Fig. 14. Interior view of Saint Sebastian Catholic Church, Byron Center, Michigan.
PHOTOGRAPH BY AUTHOR

parish formed an exploratory committee to evaluate their ministry and their facilities. They began with *A House of Prayer* and *Built of Living Stones.* After the parish concluded that they did in fact want to build a new facility rather than add to their present building, the Diocese of Grand Rapids recommended that they embark on a more formal process of liturgical education and formation. This was guided by a consultant from the diocesan Liturgical Art and Environment Committee. Working with their consultant, the parishioners and building committee members at Saint Sebastian delved into a six-month study of the meaning of the liturgy and how the liturgy is expressed in movement, ritual, sacrament, and space. This process was crucial for developing the ideas they brought to the design of their new building (figs. 13–14).

For example, because their old building had been so small and crowded and had been located directly on the street (as so many older churches are), and because the placement of the liturgical furnishings limited movement inside the sanctuary, the members of Saint Sebastian realized that they had lost touch entirely with the "processional" character of Catholic worship. This sense of procession has been created both outside and inside the new building. Outside of the church, as people leave their cars, a path channels them toward the main doors and the entrance of the building. The direction and convergence of their movement embody how worship gathers us together and constitutes us as the assembly, that is, the body of Christ. Inside the church, worshipers pass into a spacious narthex and continue past a large baptistery as they enter the sanctuary. The baptistery is aligned with the cross over the altar. Passing the font, and seeing the cross, worshipers are reminded every time they enter the nave that it is through baptism that they have died and risen with Christ, and thus entered into his holy body, the church.

The consultation and education process identified another less liturgical, but equally significant, concern: the members of Saint Sebastian wanted to retain the sense that they worshiped in a "little country church." They wanted their new building to connect them visibly to their Catholic history, their rural roots, and their sense of small-town intimacy. Neither a generic big-box structure nor a tour de force set piece would express their identity. Architecturally, the new building honors this by using functional structural principles drawn from Gothic architecture — pointed arches, buttresses, and a cruciform layout — but executed in contemporary materials. The pointed arches and buttresses do some of the same work they would do in a medieval church, but they are made of reinforced concrete and topped with spectacular, exposed wooden trusses. The finished building honors a Catholic heritage, yet it is not in any sense neo-Gothic in style.

The members of Saint Sebastian are justly pleased with their new building. There was very little friction about the decision and design process, in part because of the steady attention paid along the way to a deeper conversation about the meaning and purpose of worship. Though not every planning process in every parish goes this smoothly, the experience of Saint Sebastian is representative of what can happen in Catholic parishes wishing to build from scratch. To concentrate only on the buildings as the result of such a process would miss the point. The point is how well the new buildings embody and serve the parish's worship.

Resources for All Congregations

A danger, especially for non-Catholics, when describing such a mapped-out, formal process is to fail to see "the church" at work within all the institutional protocols. And so far, this has been a very institutional, document-driven description of how the Catholic conversation on the arts in worship has come to be the way it is. But through all of this, I hope that the profoundly pastoral issues at stake have remained visible. In the documents with which I began this section and in the resources that have been spilling from Catholic presses over the last decades, the paramount desire is that all Catholics come to understand and experience public worship as the central activity through which we most fully represent, encounter, and bear witness to the incarnate and risen Christ.

The best testimony to the pastoral power of the Catholic Church in discussions of worship and the arts may be a glance at the impact it has had on other Christian churches. Not surprisingly, a major contribution is in the arena of church architecture. In *An Architecture of Immanence*, Mark A. Torgerson traces the histories of the liturgical movement, the twentieth-century ecumenical movement, and certain strands of thought within modernist architecture to argue that all these converged to elevate a particular modernist architectural vocabulary in midcentury church architecture. The role of the Catholic Church is pivotal. Torgerson's appendix reprints sections from six documents, ranging from 1947 to 1978, that exercised great influence on ecclesiastical architecture. All of them are from the Catholic Church. As he points out, "The size and influence of the Catholic Church in Europe and the United States facilitated a wide distribution of these materials. Citations from these sources and references to these texts in bibliographies appeared in both Protestant and Catholic publications for many decades."[43]

By 1970, most of the major American Protestant denominations had generated a study of liturgy and architecture based on the principles of liturgical renewal first systematized by the Catholic Church.[44] The creation of the Revised Common Lectionary, for example, now used in many English-speaking Christian churches, both Catholic and Protestant, began with revisions to the Catholic lectionary after Vatican II. This, in turn, has stimulated the recovery of the liturgical year in many Protestant

---

43. Mark A. Torgerson, *An Architecture of Immanence: Architecture for Worship and Ministry Today* (Grand Rapids: Eerdmans, 2007), p. 229.

44. Ibid., p. 229. For Protestant publications, see Torgerson's chronological bibliography.

communions. As Emily Brink and John D. Witvliet recently summarized, the liturgical movement "has led Methodists and Presbyterians to sing their Eucharistic prayers, evangelicals to observe Advent and Lent, and . . . Episcopalians to nurture congregational participation in liturgical music and psalmody."[45]

Catholic liturgical renewal has also created a broader interest in Christian churches in general in the sacraments and in the objects used for the sacraments — baptismal fonts, communion tables, cups, pitchers, and plates.[46] The emerging field of liturgical consulting has its roots in Catholic diocesan commissions for liturgical art, yet it is attracting interest among Protestants. Programs like Catholic Theological Union's Institute for Liturgical Consultants and organizations like the Association of Consultants for Liturgical Space (ACLS) and the National Alliance for Liturgical Artists (NALA), while predominantly Catholic, are open to all Christians. Any Christian congregation that wishes to think more intentionally about worship space and liturgical art is more than welcome to avail itself of their services.[47]

---

45. Emily Brink and John D. Witvliet, "Music in Reformed Churches Worldwide," in *Christian Worship in Reformed Churches Past and Present*, ed. Lukas Vischer (Grand Rapids: Eerdmans, 2003), p. 333.

46. For a nice summary of the ways in which liturgical renewal has shaped Protestant worship, see Fred Anderson's "Protestant Worship Today," *Theology Today* 43, no. 1 (April 1986): 63–74. Anderson is right to point out that liturgical renewal predated Vatican II. Yet he does acknowledge that structurally, the major organizations, especially the North American Academy of Liturgy, are primarily Catholic in origin and membership and have been a major force in disseminating scholarship and materials.

47. Liturgical consulting is an emerging field. The Institute for Liturgical Consultants at the Catholic Theological Union (CTU) in Chicago is cosponsored by the CTU, the Chicago Archdiocesan Office for Divine Worship, and Liturgy Training Publications. It is open to Catholics and non-Catholics who have a desire to serve as liturgical consultants and have a professional background in art, architecture, or liturgy. ACLS (www.liturgical-consultants .org) is "a voluntary membership organization of professionals dedicated to the creation of beautiful worship spaces for faith communities." NALA (www.liturgicalartists.com) "was founded by a group of liturgical artists and professionals, in response to the need for a coalition dedicated to the production and promotion of the highest quality art for churches, mosques and synagogues." These last two organizations are endorsed by the Federation of Diocesan Liturgical Commissions (www.fdlc.org), the national organization for local diocesan liturgical commissions.

The Discussion: Beyond Liturgical Art?

If there is any downside to the Catholic channeling of attention to worship space, liturgical furnishings, and liturgical objects, it is the lack of corresponding attention to all the other ways in which the visual arts serve in Catholic worship and life. Certainly, Catholics have not been alone in decrying, downplaying, or ignoring the role that extraliturgical images and objects play in religious life. The vacuum here is all the more noticeable, though, because Catholicism boasts a venerable and still robust visual culture that until recently was generally assumed to be part and parcel of being Catholic.[48]

The "venerable" part of that visual culture is the stuff of traditional art history — the illuminated Gospels, the carved portals and bronze doors, the breviaries and missals, the altarpieces for the church and the household, the carved statues of Christ and the saints, the fresco cycles, and stained glass. The "still robust" part is the stuff of material culture or visual studies: the plaster saints, the prayer cards, the rosaries, the pilgrimage souvenirs, the *milagros* and *ex-votos*, the household shrines and the front-yard Madonnas. And lest we too complacently assume that these two lists break down neatly into "high" and "low" art forms, we note that both the masses and the cultural elites in just about every time and place have availed themselves of most of the items for most of the

---

48. In academic circles, there is now a wealth of literature on the relationship between visual culture and religious practice, both Protestant and Catholic. Foundational texts in this area would include Colleen McDannell's *Material Christianity: Religion and Popular Culture in America* (New Haven: Yale University Press, 1995), one of the earliest works to focus primarily on mass-produced religious imagery. The works of David Morgan serve as a thorough introduction to the area: *Visual Piety: A History and Theory of Popular Religious Images* (Berkeley: University of California Press, 1998); *Protestants and Pictures: Religion, Visual Culture, and the Age of American Mass Production* (Oxford: Oxford University Press, 1999); *The Sacred Gaze: Religious Visual Culture in Theory and Practice* (Berkeley: University of California Press, 2005); the edited volume *Icons of American Protestantism: The Art of Warner Sallman* (New Haven: Yale University Press, 1996); and, edited with Sally M. Promey, *The Visual Culture of American Religions* (Berkeley: University of California Press, 2001). The appearance of an academic journal in 2005, *Material Religion*, ushered the topic into the mainstream of academic inquiry. In addition, Betty Spackman's *A Profound Weakness: Christians and Kitsch* (Carlisle, UK: Piquant, 2005) is a lavishly illustrated treatment of a number of core questions regarding belief and practice that popular art raises.

purposes in these lists — even though styles, media, and patterns of patronage might have varied.

There is a discernible pattern of thinking in many of the currently available Catholic resources that goes something like this: if it doesn't fall into the category of "liturgical art," then it is "devotional art"; if it is devotional art, then it is liturgically problematic; and if it is liturgically problematic, then it's also very likely to be aesthetically problematic.[49] Sometimes arguments over liturgical correctness have served to justify the expulsion of artworks that are perfectly appropriate but not to the taste of a reigning elite. This has led, in the words of the Vatican's own *Directory on Popular Piety and the Liturgy*, to "unjustified criticism of the piety of the common people in the name of a presumed 'purity' of faith."[50] Too easily, many kinds of art that aren't the direct focus of documents like *Environment and Art* and *Built of Living Stones* have come to be seen as liturgically problematic at best, and as kitsch at worst. Either way, there are very few tools in the available Catholic literature to help a parish wade through the minefield of issues surrounding art beyond the liturgy.

49. For a recent example of exactly this line of thought, see the "Like Living Stones" essays by David Philippart in *Environment and Art Letter* 15, no. 2–7 (2002). "In the church building, works of art serve two different acts of worship: liturgy and devotion. Both are necessary for the full Christian life. The primary works of art for liturgy . . . do not draw attention to themselves, but evoke full, conscious, and active participation in the sacramental act being undertaken. Art for devotion is a bit different. To a certain extent, art for devotion does draw attention to itself. It invites the viewer — alone or in a group — to gaze and to contemplate, to look through and beyond the physical rendering to the mystery (most often the person) to which it points. The image for devotion may indeed evoke an action, a physical response — lighting a candle, placing a flower, giving a kiss or a loving touch. But this response is individual and spontaneous, not necessarily shared and therefore not governed by rubric. That's why the best place for art for devotion is in shrines, more intimate places apart from altar and ambo" (David Philippart, "Art for Devotion," *Environment and Art Letter* 15, no. 6 [2002]: 78). It follows quite logically that the next installation of this column is entitled "Quality" and quotes Thomas Merton as having observed, "To like bad sacred art, and feel one is helped by it in prayer, can be a symptom of real spiritual disorders." Helpfully, he also quotes Frank Burch Brown, "Given that one goal of the Christian life is to care for one's neighbor as one's self, one dimension of that care is to be careful in criticism" (David Philippart, "Quality," *Environment and Art Letter* 15, no. 7 [2002]: 110).

50. *Directory on Popular Piety and the Liturgy: Principles and Guidelines* (Strathfield, Australia: St. Pauls Publications, 2002), par. 1.

Liturgical Art "versus" Devotional Art

In the Catholic Church, one of the main outcomes of liturgical renewal was a concerted focus on worship as a corporate activity. This is clearly expressed in the section of the *Constitution on the Sacred Liturgy* entitled "The Promotion of Liturgical Instruction and Active Participation": "Mother Church earnestly desired that all the faithful should be led to that full, conscious, and active participation in liturgical celebrations which is demanded by the nature of the liturgy. Such participation by the Christian people as 'a chosen race, a royal priesthood, a holy nation, a redeemed people' . . . is their right and duty by reason of their baptism. In the restoration and promotion of the sacred liturgy, this full and active participation by all the people is the aim to be considered before all else."[51] Gerard Sloyan summarizes this in his commentary on the *Constitution* with the clear statement: "liturgical functions are in *no* sense private functions."[52] But what is meant by "private functions"? Non-Catholics might be a bit bewildered at the assumed context or foil against which this discussion of "full, conscious, and active participation" is playing out.

By "private functions," Father Sloyan is referring to a range of devotional practices that had, until Vatican II, been more or less carried out in conjunction with the public liturgy by many worshiping Catholics. These would include adoration of the consecrated host, veneration of a specific saint, or use of the rosary. Such activities evolved over time in part because in earlier periods of Catholic history the laity were excluded from full, active participation in the liturgy. Such devotions were to some extent substitutes for corporate worship.[53] With the new focus after Vatican II on full participation of the gathered assembly, these devotional activities were discouraged during the liturgy, and

51. *Constitution,* par. 14.
52. Ibid., p. 16.
53. For a brief introduction to these developments in the history of the Catholic Church, see Marcel Metzger's *History of the Liturgy: The Major Stages* (Collegeville, MN: Liturgical Press, 1997), pp. 122–38. He concludes his discussion of devotions by noting that "devotions fundamentally differ from the liturgy in their origins, in the way they are structured, and in their forms of expression. Whereas the liturgy is the present celebration by Christ, in his Church, of the mystery of the New Covenant, devotions are personal prayers, and even if they are practiced in common, they never will be anything more than the juxtaposition of individual acts" (p. 135).

most of the objects associated with them were ushered out of the sanctuary. As Anscar Chupungco describes it, "In an effort, which was truly praiseworthy, to direct the attention of the faithful to the liturgy as the summit and fount of Christian life, liturgists and pastors zealously banned popular devotions during liturgical celebrations."[54] The tabernacle for the reserved host (a receptacle for the consecrated bread, available for ministry to the elderly and the sick or dying, as well as for devotional adoration) was moved from the main altar to an adjacent space; side altars dedicated to particular saints were moved to less obtrusive locations in the sanctuary or taken out of the sanctuary altogether. Use of the local language, of congregational responses, and of congregational singing also made the rosary and all other popular devotions both more difficult and liturgically superfluous during Sunday Mass.[55]

None of this in and of itself, of course, prohibited such devotional activities *tout court*. According to the *Constitution,* "Popular devotions of the Christian people are to be highly commended, provided they accord with the laws and norms of the Church."[56] *Built of Living Stones* emphasizes that "Sacred images are important not only in liturgical prayer but also in devotional prayer because they are sacramentals that help the faithful to focus their attention and their prayer."[57] Devotional activities were to be encour-

---

54. Anscar Chupungco, *Liturgical Inculturation: Sacramentals, Religiosity, and Catechesis* (Collegeville, MN: Liturgical Press, 1992), p. 96.

55. *Built of Living Stones* discusses the purpose and location of the tabernacle in paragraphs 70–80, and images of saints in paragraphs 135–138. Throughout, the concern is that "[D]evotions should be so drawn up that they harmonize with the liturgical seasons, accord with the sacred liturgy, are in some fashion derived from it, and lead the people to it, since, in fact, the liturgy by its very nature far surpasses any of them" (*Constitution,* par. 13). In *Built of Living Stones,* the burden is on the church to make sure that devotions "ensure that they enhance and reinforce rather than compete with the liturgical life of the community" (*Built of Living Stones,* par. 131).

56. *Constitution,* par. 13.

57. *Built of Living Stones,* par. 131. Official teaching on these practices is very slim. The *Catechism* does not address them specifically; they are merely alluded to in a very general way at the very end of the section on the liturgy and the sacraments, titled "Popular Piety." The section on the liturgy and the sacraments spans nearly 150 pages; the three paragraphs on popular piety take up the last page (pars. 1674–1676). The tabernacle for the Eucharist (the receptacle for the consecrated host reserved for the sick and the dying), to take a specific example, is mentioned specifically in the *Catechism* only twice, and then very briefly: once to define it and once to discuss its placement (*Catechism,* pars. 1183 and 1379). Praying the rosary, too, is mentioned in passing only twice: once as a historical development associated

aged only in ways that did not interfere with or substitute for the corporate worship of the church.[58] Official sanction notwithstanding, the Catholic Church's desire to make a firm distinction between public liturgy and private devotion resulted in the disappearance of a variety of practices from public worship, along with the images and objects associated with them. In the words of one architect, many Catholic sanctuaries went from "baroque to beige" in very short order.[59]

This phenomenon converged with other changes in the Catholic Church and in society at large to create a sense of crisis. Some Catholics in the late 1960s and early 1970s pinned this crisis on the so-called "collapse of devotionalism" and a subsequent "piety void" that threatened Catholic identity and perhaps even the very future of the Catholic Church.[60] As an early critic put it, "[t]he casual discarding of traditional symbols, often with the implication that there was something ridiculous or unsavory about them, symbolized effectively a Church slowly dying, piece by piece."[61] With some historical distance from those turbulent days — turbulent not only for the

---

with the *Ave Maria* and once as an aid to contemplative prayer (*Catechism,* pars. 2678 and 2708). A variety of Catholic presses are the source for most discussions of the meaning and practice of these devotions.

58. "In keeping with the Church's very ancient tradition, it is lawful to set up in places of worship images of Christ, Mary, and the saints for veneration by the faithful. But there is need both to limit their number and to situate them in such a way that they do not distract the people's attention from the celebration. There is to be only one image of any one saint. In general, the devotion of the entire community is to be the criterion regarding images in the adornment and arrangement of a church" (General Instruction of the Roman Missal [GIRM], 4th ed., chapter 5, article 278).

59. Bob Czerew, personal conversation, January 12, 2007.

60. The phrase "piety void" was coined in 1965 by Dan Herr, a regular columnist for the *Critic* who was sympathetic to the reform of the liturgy ("Stop Pushing," *Critic* 24 [October-November 1965]: 4, 60). This is reiterated, with a slightly different focus, by Robert Ledogar in "The Question of Daily Mass," *Worship* 43, no. 5 (May 1969): 258–80. George Devine's analysis of the perceived piety void, written in 1974, describes it as a result of a "mistake" on the part of the church, which took away "a set of symbolic ways of relating to the Mass without installing another set that would be equally serviceable." His image for the impact of these abrupt changes is striking: "many Catholics found themselves in a situation not unlike that of one required to stare at the sun with the naked eye" (Devine, *American Catholicism,* p. 48).

61. James Hitchcock, *The Recovery of the Sacred* (New York: Seabury, 1974), p. 80. See the entire chapter on "folk religion" for Hitchcock's discussion of pre– and post–Vatican II popular devotion, pp. 97–128.

church, but also for the nation as a whole — it is easier to see the points of continuity underneath the seemingly radical discontinuities. In spite of the apparent piety void, there is evidence to support the claim that many Catholics, in fact, experienced a renewal of their personal prayer lives in the years following Vatican II.[62] Certainly, the Catholic Church has not collapsed; numerically, it is growing. As the theologian and historian Chester Gillis laconically observed, "Those who loudly proclaim that Catholicism is drawing its dying breath are most likely not very well acquainted with history."[63]

The response to devotional art, though, is directly related to the liturgical reforms described above. Not only did renewed attention to the liturgy channel the discussion about the role of the arts toward liturgical space, liturgical furnishings, and certain liturgical objects, it also diverted and subverted careful attention to the possible roles that existing objects and images could play. The laudable desire to increase "full, conscious, and active participation" among Catholic worshipers, it was assumed, required the removal or demotion of any works of art in the sanctuary that were not part of the public liturgy.

There are two challenges in making such a strong distinction between liturgy and devotion. First, the distinction relies on a problematic mental distinction between "private" and "public" that is more characteristic of European, post-Enlightenment habits of thought than of the habits of thought found in most other parts of the world.[64] Liturgy is envisioned as public and communal; devotion is envisioned as private and therefore individual. While it is true that liturgy is inherently communal, it does not follow that

62. Joseph P. Chinnici, "The Catholic Community at Prayer, 1926–1976," in *Habits of Devotion: Catholic Religious Practice in Twentieth-Century America*, ed. James M. O'Toole (Ithaca, NY: Cornell University Press, 2004), p. 20. The essay discusses continuities as well as discontinuities in Catholic practices over fifty years. It also contains an illuminating summary of studies on practices that continued throughout this period, but with changed emphases and intentions.

63. Chester Gillis, *Roman Catholicism in America* (New York: Columbia University Press, 1999), p. 274.

64. In 1960 already, Thomas Merton questioned the extent to which public and private worship had been oversimplified in discussions about the liturgy. "To judge by the statements made by enthusiasts on one side or the other one would almost imagine that there were thought to be two alternative ways to Christian fulfillment: the one exclusively public and corporate and the other exclusively private and individual. No wonder that the results are confusing!" ("Liturgy and Spiritual Personalism," *Worship* 34 [October 1960]: 250–51).

devotion is inherently individual. Note that almost any individual practice is still embedded in communal contexts and expectations. I pray a psalm in the morning as an individual, yes. But I do so because that is what Christians as a people do and what they have done for as long as there has been a church. Much of our imagined individuality and autonomy is more fiction than not, once we peel back the layers that conceal the communal norms that shape most behaviors.

Second, the distinction between liturgy and devotion tends to conflate objects and actions; that is, it seems to assume that the function of a work of sacred art is somehow embedded in the object itself rather than being located in the actions with which the worshiper engages it. If, in fact, this is the case, then it follows that works of sacred art must be *either* liturgical *or* devotional. They can't shift between the two. But is it necessarily the case that an image initially designed for devotion can't ever form part of the context for corporate worship? That a statue of a saint, for example, can't become part of the environment for worship — much like the presence of one's spouse or children deepens our joy in worship? James Empereur, SJ, makes this point in his chapter in the commentary on the Vatican's *Directory on Popular Piety and the Liturgy*. He uses the Advent wreath as an example, showing how such an object can easily be interpreted either as properly liturgical or as exemplary of one of a number of popular devotional practices, depending on the ways in which it is used, but in no way is it exclusively individual or private.[65]

Devotional Art and the Problem of Taste

One reason why it may have been difficult to imagine an overlap between the liturgical environment and devotional art was hinted at above — many works of devotional art were discarded "with the implication that there was something ridiculous or unsavory about them." This brings us to the challenge of taste — or, less charitably restated, the problem of kitsch.

On one level, Catholics celebrate kitsch and other Christians envy it. It is hard not to find some delight in the affectionate absurdities of "Pope-on-

---

65. See pp. 10–11 in Phan, *Directory on Popular Piety and the Liturgy: Principles and Guidelines — a Commentary*.

a-Rope" soap and the even more wonderful "Let Us Spray" lawn sprinkler that blesses your lawn with water sprayed from the top of John Paul II's mitre and upraised hands — just two of the many items that accompanied John Paul II's visits to the United States.[66] But these lighthearted ephemera aren't really the kind of "kitsch" that is at issue here. Rather, the disdain and condescension are aimed at mass-produced religious images that appear to certain contemporary eyes as unfortunate relics of conservative, nineteenth-century academic art (fig. 15). These are the statues and paintings that adorned many side chapels and high altars before Vatican II.

The stylistic problem consists of an airbrushed naturalism, a kind of "classicism lite" that emerged over the course of the nineteenth century, particularly in France, within academies and institutions that enjoyed, for different reasons, state support and church support. Artists like Eugene Delacroix, Gustave Courbet, Edouard Manet, and Claude Monet defined themselves *against* that style and against the institutions that supported it. These names are not inconsequential. They are conventionally taken to be the very founders of modern Western art: art that is internally self-sufficient; art that is not directed toward any use other than aesthetic contemplation; art that is independent of entanglements with church or state. In other words, "Art" with a capital *A*. Any religious art, much less religious art stylistically derived from French nineteenth-century academic painting, was for many twentieth-century artists, art historians, and critics genetically incompatible with Art.

Mass production is also part of the problem. Critics sometimes refer to mass-produced religious art as "l'art Saint-Sulpice" or "Barclay Street art" after the districts in Paris and New York that housed the religious image industry, thus showing that the distaste for such images is rooted as much in commerce and economics as in style. The Western idea of Art emphasizes singularity and independence. Any artistic product designed for mass production necessarily dilutes this. Though various artists and movements have sought to recuperate a more communitarian approach to art (the arts and crafts movement, for example, or even the Bauhaus), the artist is still imagined, by and large, as a singular genius, independent of social and economic

66. Pat Morrison, "Trademarking Holiness," *National Catholic Reporter* 92, no. 1 (August 15, 2003); Brett Webb-Mitchell, "True Kitsch Is Catholic Kitsch," *Regeneration Quarterly* 3, no. 3 (Summer 1997): 43–44.

Fig. 15. Devotional images in the Parish Hall of Saints Cyril and Methodius Catholic Church, Wayland, Michigan. This congregation dedicated a new sanctuary in 2003, turning their old sanctuary into a multipurpose gathering space. PHOTOGRAPH BY AUTHOR

entanglements that might compromise that singularity, and one who creates unique objects. No wonder we are deeply ambivalent about the status of any art that enjoys widespread popularity! We tend to assume that artists whose works are enjoyed by many have obviously sold out, have compromised their singularity. Popular religious imagery intended specifically for mass production can never possess any artistic integrity within this framework, even if it somehow manages to pass muster stylistically.

This inherited critical framework, however, has become more complicated in the last two decades. On the stylistic front, art historians are revisiting nineteenth-century religious painting and seeking to understand it on its own terms rather than merely as a foil for emerging modernism. They argue for more coherence within and continuity with the larger artistic debates of the day.[67] The growing role of dealers and galleries over the course of the nineteenth century and the emergence of museums of modern art in the early twentieth century have added a new set of "institutions" to the discussion of fine art's supposed autonomy. While avant-garde artists may have detached themselves from the academy, the state, and the church, they necessarily have embraced another set of institutions — galleries, dealers, and museums. This seriously compromises the extent to which an artist can be truly autonomous.[68]

Most importantly, though, historians with sociological and anthropological sympathies are helping us appreciate the work that mass-manufactured religious objects actually did and continue to do in the day-to-day lives of practicing Christians. Rather than anesthetizing a permanent underclass of aesthetically impoverished and politically compliant naifs, popular religious images are instead regularly pressed into service to express and embody genuine religious faith.[69] Though not primarily directed to art, Andrew Greeley's argument for a "Catholic imagination" has bearing here. In Greeley's opinion, the lively stories and vibrant images of popular Catholic culture represent a profound theological inclination to understand and experience God as immanent in the world around us. This sense of immanence lends the faith great resiliency in an otherwise hostile modern world.[70] Similarly,

67. See, for example, Bruno Foucart's *Le Renouveau de la peinture religieuse en France (1800–1860)* (Paris: Arthéna, 1987); Michael Driskel's *Representing Belief: Religion, Art, and Society in Nineteenth-Century France* (University Park: Pennsylvania State University Press, 1992); Nancy Davenport, "The Revival of Fra Angelico and Matthias Grünewald in Nineteenth-Century French Religious Art," *Nineteenth-Century French Studies* 27, no. 1–2 (Fall 1998/Winter 1999): 157–99.

68. For just two examples, see Oscar Bätschmann, *The Artist in the Modern World: The Conflict between Market and Self-Expression* (New Haven: Yale University Press, 1997), and Michael Fitzgerald, *Making Modernism: Picasso and the Creation of the Market for Twentieth-Century Art* (Berkeley: University of California Press, 1995).

69. For this argument, see the works of David Morgan listed in note 48 above. For a specifically Catholic appreciation of the complex roles the saints and their images have played in Catholic culture, see Joseph Varacalli et al., eds., *The Saints in the Lives of Italian-Americans: An Interdisciplinary Investigation* (Stony Brook, NY: Forum Italicum, 1999).

70. Andrew Greeley, *Catholic Imagination* (Berkeley: University of California Press,

in one of the earlier assessments of religious popular imagery, David Morgan and Sally Promey list the following roles for such images: they "[communicate] between human and divine realms in an economy of ritualized exchange . . . [consolidate and reinforce] a range of allegiances . . . help create and organize memory. . . . fuel constructive, synthetic acts of imagination in the kind of meaning making practices that form a basic aspect of religious experience."[71] If popular religious art truly aids prayer, creates identity, shapes memory, and makes meaning[72] — and there is no reason to doubt the growing consensus in the academic literature, or to doubt our own experiences — then it is no small wonder that the removal of so many popular images from Catholic churches created the sense of a "piety void" that could not entirely be made up by liturgical art.

Scholarship, experience, and charity all invite us to reexamine the easy dichotomy between good art and bad art, not to mention the tacit dichotomy in the Catholic discussion between liturgical art and everything else. This is not to say that bad taste is the new good taste. Hard conversations about which works of art are most fitting and why still need to happen.[73] But in having such conversations, we can't just assume that what we've taken to be "good art" will always be appropriate and what we've assumed to be "bad art" has no purpose. Rather, we will need to hold a bit more lightly our inherited ideas about what constitutes good and bad, appropriate and inappropriate, quality and kitsch. We also need to remember that our relationship to images and objects, whether "high" or "low," is as active as it is passive — and deeply embedded in our ways of being Christian.[74]

2000). Greeley gave an earlier formulation to this in *Religion as Poetry* (New Brunswick, NJ, and London: Transaction Publishers, 1995).

71. Morgan and Promey, *Visual Culture*, pp. 2–3.

72. Steven Schloeder is one of the few Catholic scholars to propose some guidelines for nonliturgical images in the church in chapter 7 (pp. 145–67) of *Architecture in Communion* (San Francisco: Ignatius, 1999). His argument for their legitimacy relies on themes laid out at the Council of Trent and subsequently reaffirmed. Art instructs, inspires, and aids memory.

73. For an argument that discussions of taste can become opportunities to practice virtue and strengthen the church, see Frank Burch Brown, *Good Taste, Bad Taste, and Christian Taste: Aesthetics in Religious Life* (Oxford: Oxford University Press, 2000), especially pp. 24–25 and 250–51. For some tools in discerning which works are fitting, see Nicholas Wolterstorff, *Art in Action: Toward a Christian Aesthetic* (Grand Rapids: Eerdmans, 1980), especially pp. 96–121.

74. Gender is also a very complicated part of the discussion of taste in art. Depending on who is casting the aspersion, both advocates of "good" liturgical art (members of mo-

The Artist in the Parish

If one set of challenges issuing from the liturgical reforms of Vatican II concerns the vexed relationship between art for worship and art for devotion that resulted from the otherwise laudable pastoral desire for the active participation of all assembled in public worship, a second challenge issues from the institutional structures and protocols that tacitly distanced the practicing artist in the pew from serving his or her parish. Hence the perplexing responses I received from Catholic artists to my question, "What do you think, as an artist, about the art in your church?" (I later learned to ask my question more precisely, using "parish" or "congregation" rather than "church." The initial confusion was nonetheless informative.)

As discussed above, the Catholic Church in the United States has worked hard to develop structures (diocesan liturgical commissions), protocols (mandated consultation with the diocesan liturgical commission), and resources (study guides and planning aids) to guide individual congregations in building or renovating their sanctuaries. Those structures, protocols, and resources themselves have encouraged the birth of a new profession — liturgical consulting. Liturgical consultants are often architects or artists, well networked to other architects and artists, whose natural inclination is to look to their own networks rather than to the local parish for talent. It becomes very easy to outsource most, or all, of the artwork in a sanctuary to outside experts. While local builders and craftsmen might be used for building or renovation, and while parishioners might volunteer their labor from time to time, major commissions will go to professionals. Furthermore, because Catholic congregations conceptualize "art and worship" as concerning worship space and a limited range of furnishings and objects, once the building project is over, the conversation about "art and the church" is done. This leads to a paradoxical situation. According to sociologist Mark Chaves,

---

nastic communities, priests, and artists) and the consumers of "religious kitsch" have been denigrated as "effeminate." Colleen McDannell implies that the drive for good art for the liturgy was in part an effort to masculinize the aesthetic of Catholicism. See McDannell, *Material Christianity*, p. 38. Devine points out that detractors of the liturgical movement sometimes sought to discredit it by stereotyping its proponents as effeminate (Devine, *Liturgical Renewal*, p. 40).

Catholic congregations are less likely than congregations in any other religious tradition to expose people to artistic activity inside the congregation. . . . If Catholic churches do offer more visual richness than other congregations, that visual richness does not sufficiently compensate for lower levels of other kinds of artistic practice to produce equivalent rates of subjectively experienced art among attenders. . . . Thus, data about both what congregations do and how individuals experience what they do support the conclusion that the only major religious difference in the quantity of exposure to art inside congregations is that Catholic congregations expose people to less art than do congregations in any other tradition.[75]

There are, of course, exceptions to the rule. Catholic religious orders consistently expect the artists in their midst to contribute directly to the life of their communities. The Marywood Center, the home of the Dominican Sisters in Grand Rapids, for example, has filled the hallways, the chapel, the dining hall, the common areas, and the sisters' rooms with works of art made by the artists within the religious community. The Franciscan Life Process Center in Lowell, just outside Grand Rapids, the home of the Franciscan Sisters of the Eucharist, offers a heavy rotation of art workshops and art classes as a crucial part of its ministry. Clearly, from-the-ground-up, grass-roots involvement with the arts is highly compatible with life in Catholic religious communities. But in these contexts, it emerges as an expression of mission (teaching, in particular), or ministry, or communal self-expression, and not primarily as liturgical expression. Perhaps there is something for Catholic parishes to learn from these communities.

I also discovered another especially lovely exception to the rule, and in a parish setting. In 2003, Saints Cyril and Methodius Church in Wayland, a small town south of Grand Rapids, dedicated a new sanctuary. Like Saint Sebastian in Byron Center, the congregation had received guidance and support for the design process from its diocese, and members worked with professional consultants and designers to envision their new space. But then, something unusual and wonderful happened. Due to site constraints, the sanctuary had to run along a north-south axis rather than the more typical

75. Mark Chaves, *Congregations in America* (Cambridge, MA: Harvard University Press, 2004), pp. 176–77.

Fig. 16. Working on a window at Saints Cyril and Methodius Catholic Church, Wayland, Michigan. PHOTOGRAPH BY AUTHOR

east-west axis. Built as designed, with plain glass windows in the clerestory, the sanctuary was flooded at certain times of year by blindingly bright and uncomfortably hot morning sunlight. One member of the congregation had some experience with stained glass and realized that she could do something about this problem. She approached the priest with a plan to train parishioners to make windows. Together, the priest and a small group of women devised a simple program of eucharistic symbols for the six windows on the east and west sides of the nave. They passed their ideas to a member of the congregation who was on the faculty at Kendall College of Art and Design. He drew up formal designs. As a substantial project destined for a worship space, the project required, and gained, the approval of the art and environment subcommittee of the congregation's Diocesan Worship Commission. For the next several years, this group of women met every Tuesday morning to work together (fig. 16). Window by window, the series took shape until the entire project was completed and all the windows installed. The women involved with this project expressed a deep sense of enjoyment in the work, in the fellowship, and in seeing the work of their hands in their own sanctuary. One spoke of it as a way of "doing God's work," others as "my contribution to the life of the church."[76]

Some elements of what happened at Saints Cyril and Methodius are absolutely typical for Catholic congregations: the origins of the project in a building program, the process of liturgical catechesis undertaken by the congregation, the role of the diocese in approving but also supporting the work. What is unusual here is the initiative of an individual parishioner/artist, and the close parish/artist relationship that was allowed to flourish, and which is now instantiated forever, in these simple, lovely windows.

76. Debra Nardin, along with Helen, Betty, and Claire, personal conversation, February 27, 2007, and June 10, 2013.

CHAPTER 3

Art as Activism:
The Visual Arts in Protestant Congregations

Art is not escapism but an invitation to activism.

— DANA GIOIA[1]

Six Vignettes

It's February 21, 2014, and First United Methodist Church (FUMC) in downtown Grand Rapids is celebrating the gala opening of its forty-second Celebration of the Arts exhibition. Since 1972, FUMC has hosted this two-week art festival, the centerpiece of which is a large, juried exhibition of religious and spiritually oriented work. According to its website, Celebration is now one of the largest juried sacred art shows in the United States.[2] Today, the show is supported by a committee of church members (some of whom joined the church because of Celebration) and receives upward of four hundred submissions from more than two hundred artists who generally live in the greater West Michigan area. Each year, the congregation purchases the "People's Choice" winner for its permanent collection. These works are displayed throughout the church, but not in the sanctuary, which is an early twentieth-century, neo-Gothic space, lit by spectacular stained-glass

1. Dana Gioia, preface to *The Arts and Civic Engagement: Involved in Arts, Involved in Life,* by National Endowment for the Arts (Washington, DC: National Endowment for the Arts, 2006).

2. www.thecelebrationofthearts.com, accessed July 4, 2013.

windows (seven of the windows are by Tiffany). While there may be a banner or a seasonal display on the communion table to mark a church season or to support a particular sermon series, the configuration of the space and the impact of the windows make it challenging to integrate other visual elements. In addition to Celebration, FUMC serves as a venue for ArtPrize, a city-wide art competition and a relative newcomer to the art scene in Grand Rapids. On their ArtPrize page, FUMC states, "The early Christian church was one of the greatest patrons of the arts, so we believe that it is natural that today both artists and observers find the church as home to the arts and a place to hear God's voice through artistic expression."[3]

A few blocks away, Fountain Street Church also serves as a venue for ArtPrize. Partnering with the American Civil Liberties Union, their shows have focused on themes relating to social justice, providing "opportunity for artists to be both creative and compelling across the social and political spectra, exploring issues such as capital punishment, prisoner's rights, racial justice, human rights, national security, HIV/AIDS, the rights of people with disabilities, free speech, voting rights, drug law reform, LGBT rights, gender rights, freedom of and from religion, technology and liberty, reproductive freedom, and much more."[4] Fountain Street Church, founded as a Baptist congregation in 1842, had already reidentified itself as a noncreedal, liberal congregation before the end of the nineteenth century. By the middle of the twentieth century, under the leadership of the Reverend Duncan Littlefair (himself a weaver of no mean talent), the church had developed a strong interest in the arts. Since the early 1960s, the church has had a standing art committee of more than twenty-five members. The committee enjoys strong connections to local colleges and universities and is funded by donations raised through the nonprofit Fountain Street Church Foundation. Over the years, the church has amassed a collection of museum-worthy art, developed an active gallery program, and trained docents to give tours of its neo-Romanesque facility and its permanent collection and Keeler Lounge gallery. Fountain Street's logo — a yellow triangle, a blue square, and a red circle — speaks to its universalist commitments: derived from a Bauhaus exercise, the three basic geometrical shapes wedded to the three primary

3. www.artprize.org/first-united-methodist-church, accessed July 4, 2013.
4. www.artprize.org/2011/fountain-street-church, accessed July 14, 2013.

colors are meant to represent a universal visual language that speaks to all human beings. Indeed, Duncan Littlefair's motto, "art is a window to the soul," lives on at Fountain Street.[5]

Across town, Church of the Servant began its days in the late 1960s as a loose fellowship of mostly Christian Reformed families interested in exploring new approaches to what it means to be a church. A number of these families were connected to Calvin College, an institution owned and operated by the Christian Reformed Church. For more than twenty years, Church of the Servant met in a series of temporary locations. Setting up and breaking down their worship space every Sunday created a keen sensitivity to the creative challenge of shaping space to support worship. Today, the congregation meets in a sanctuary designed by architect Gunnar Birkerts specifically to accommodate its patterns of worship and congregational life. Outside the building, processional banners flank the walkway to the entry. At the entry, a long, horizontal ceramic panel, designed by a member of the congregation, runs along the left wall, portraying the seasons of the church year. Inside the entry, the fellowship area and the adjacent hallways, known as the ARTery, play host to four art exhibitions every year that feature Christian artists, works by church members, or group shows on themes connected with Christian faith. The sanctuary itself is a light, bright rectangle lit by plain clerestory windows with a slight "apse" bowing out along one of the long sides. A large column with tree-like struts branches out to support a polygonal dome, also made of clear glass, that rises above the rest of the ceiling. The apse itself holds a low dais, on which sits an unusual, combined pulpit/communion table/baptismal font made of light, unstained birch. Bright streamers of cloth or strikingly vivid banners keyed to seasons of the church year hang above and behind the table. Almost all the liturgical art in the sanctuary is designed by members of the church, and themes from these visuals are reproduced on the weekly order of worship as well.

Northwest of downtown, Orchard Hill Reformed Church is preparing for its next summer arts camp, a program that began in 2000 under the leadership of its former director of art and worship. Enrollment in recent years has passed three hundred children between ages five and eleven,

5. Information provided by Tia Grass (interviews on July 13, 2007, and June 11, 2013), longtime chair of the art committee at Fountain Street Church.

most of whom are not from the congregation. Last year, the camp required the services of 130 volunteers, a number of whom are older teens who are themselves arts camp alumni. Orchard Hill is up front about the outreach-oriented purpose of the camp; after sharing the good news, however, the other purpose is to provide children with intense exposure to an art form of their choice. Children can choose from an impressive array of creative activities: interpretive dance, drama, puppetry, singing, acoustic guitar, photography, woodworking, moviemaking, paper crafts, and origami, as well as more unusual offerings like lure making, stage combat, creative duct tape, and creative invention, a course that would appeal to would-be mechanical engineers. In addition to arts camp, Orchard Hill hosts free classes in voice, guitar, and dance during the school year and coordinates private lessons for students who wish to pay for individual instruction. Until recently, the church was using the entire narthex for an ambitious program of rotating art exhibitions. Several factors converged, however, to render that less and less feasible. The narthex had always been a challenging space in which to display art — particularly 3-D pieces that interrupted the flow of foot traffic and became an attractive nuisance for the many children traversing the space. Then there was the burden of recruiting artists, hanging exhibitions, lighting them, and publicizing them — all of which takes a great deal of time and specialized expertise. With the arrival of new staff with different areas of expertise, the exhibition program was reenvisioned along more modest lines with the intent of underscoring the worship life of the church. Now Orchard Hill uses an area in the narthex to display posters and collections of objects that connect to current sermon series.[6]

Out in Grand Haven, a forty-five-minute drive west of Grand Rapids, Covenant Life Church gathers for worship in a repurposed space, the former Story & Clark piano factory. Entering the narthex/fellowship hall, worshipers typically find some sort of large installation keyed to the church season or to a particular sermon series. In past years, these have included a shower of multicolored origami birds, or hopscotch-like paths laid down on the floor, or large, clear Plexiglas panels "blocking" the way to the sanctuary. Inside the sanctuary, additional visuals — ranging from minimalist,

6. Interviews with Jim Fissel (July 7, 2007) and Wendy Huizinga (June 24, 2013, and July 15, 2013).

colored lighting, to dramatic swoops of fabric, to large-scale set-like environments — pick up and expand the visual themes found in the narthex.
The origami birds, for example, were used for a Pentecost sermon series
on the seven churches of Revelation. They were repeated in the sanctuary,
aligned with seven differently shaped paper lanterns, each associated with
a particular colored bird. The birds, the shapes of the lanterns, and the
intentional use of space and color created visual analogies to the character of each church, to the gifts of the Spirit, and to the call and challenge
of witness in response to the gift of the Spirit. From season to season, the
physical space of the church takes on very different characteristics, and the
congregational movements of gathering, worshiping, and being sent are
dramatically reinterpreted.[7]

Newcomers to Mars Hill Bible Church, an independent, suburban congregation southwest of downtown Grand Rapids, most likely had their first
encounter with the church through its extensive website. The Mars Hill
website is much, much more sophisticated than a typical church's website
and creates a substantial online presence for the congregation.[8] A small
number of well-designed, original images scroll across the home page, keyed
to the current sermon series and various ministries of the church. Each topic
area on the site has a visual theme created by Mars Hill's graphic designer.
The website does not rely on photographs or on stock images. Rather, the
designer works up imagery in collaboration with the pastoral staff. The
few photographs on the site all feature the same motif: close-ups of different people's ears, with or without earbuds. (If it's possible to imagine an
image that captures the word-driven culture of most Protestant churches,
this might be it!) In contrast to the savvy of its website, Mars Hill's physical
presence is markedly plain. Like Covenant Life Church, Mars Hill wor-
ships in a repurposed space: a former mall. Each Sunday, many hundreds
of people walk from the sprawling parking lots into the former corridors of
the mall. Classrooms and workrooms occupy the former retail spaces. Of
late, a handful of designs from the website have been scaled up and used as
murals in the hallways to better connect the church's virtual presence with

7. For descriptions and pictures of a sample of installations from the middle years of the
first decade of the twenty-first century, see http://issuu.com/cicw/docs/caton and http://
issuu.com/cicw/docs/caton-1.

8. This description reflects the state of the website in mid-July 2013 (www.marshill.org).

Fig. 17. Nicholas Napoletano, *Fraternal Co-dependence*. On view at ArtPrize 2011.
PHOTOGRAPH BY ARTIST

its physical campus. Walking down the wide corridors, worshipers make their way into the Shed, one of the former anchor stores. The Shed is a simple, flat-ceilinged, quasi-industrial space with a raised dais in the center. The congregation surrounds the platform, from which the musicians and the pastors lead worship. Above the platform, four screens create a giant square, each side of which projects images, songs, and Scripture passages that support worship. On occasion, they are used for a video that relates to the sermon. However, the screens never project images of the musicians or preachers. There is no Jumbotron-style spectacle here. On one of the Sundays I visited Mars Hill, a silent video showing an artist at work in his studio ran on the screens during the sermon, alternating with key terms and passages from the Scripture text of the day (1 John 3:2). Other than the images and texts projected on the screens, the Shed is unadorned, save for a recent addition — a very large figural painting, *Fraternal Co-dependence*, that was part of the 2011 ArtPrize competition (fig. 17). Mars Hill has displayed ArtPrize work at the church before, but only in the corridors. The arrival in the Shed of a conspicuously large painting, along with a spring event at the Grand Rapids Art Museum called "Art + Spirituality," sparked new conversations among Mars Hill worshipers about what might get to count as religiously relevant art. A new initiative, "Into the Noise," is meant to extend that conversation through an ambitious program of cultural plunges at major music and art festivals. According to the "Into the Noise" page on the

Mars Hill website, "In these dynamic, experiential learning environments attendees will learn to engage with the powerful forces of art that surround us. In each space attendees will be encouraged to have eyes to see God where he is at work through the art being presented while also better understanding the narratives that might be shaping our world in harmful ways."[9]

Six different congregations, at least six different approaches to connecting the visual arts to the life of the church: collaborating with ArtPrize, building permanent collections, hosting large regional competitions or more modestly scaled exhibitions closer to home, running a successful summer art camp, offering art instruction during the school year, using visuals more or less ambitiously to mark the church seasons or help interpret a sermon series, creating a visual identity for a congregation. Though these examples don't exhaust the ways in which art-committed Protestant churches integrate the visual arts into the life of a congregation, they do describe the range of common practice.[10] What they don't do is add up to any denominationally or theologically stable pattern for how the visual arts are contextualized in Protestant churches. First United Methodist's approach, for example, is highly compatible with traditional Methodist understandings of social witness, but one could also point to Methodist churches elsewhere in Grand Rapids and farther afield that operate like Mars Hill, or like Church of the Servant, or like Orchard Hill with respect to the arts. So, too, with Reformed congregations and independent Bible churches.[11] Though it's harder to imagine a nonsectarian, liberal congregation like Fountain Street choosing to use liturgical art like Church of the Servant does, it's not at all impossible to imagine Fountain Street running

9. http://marshill.org/pastors-teachers/into-the-noise, accessed July 17, 2013.

10. I'm aware of churches further afield that host artists-in-residence, and I've witnessed live "worship painting" — inviting an artist to create an image during worship — once, but not in West Michigan. The Mars Hill service described above might be thought to offer a virtual version of "worship painting," but it was clear that the artist shown was not understood to be responding in the moment to the message being preached.

11. Lester Ruth suggests that the Methodist and Reformed churches are among the most stylistically diverse because, as "centrist" traditions, they are pulled simultaneously in two directions: toward the high liturgy and ecclesiology of the Anglican and Lutheran traditions, on the one hand, and toward the decentralized activism of Anabaptist and Pentecostal churches on the other hand. Lester Ruth, "A Rose by Any Other Name: Attempts at Classifying North American Protestant Worship," in *The Conviction of Things Not Seen: Worship and Ministry in the 21st Century*, ed. Todd E. Johnson (Grand Rapids: Brazos, 2002), pp. 49–50.

a summer arts camp or building a savvy website to create a visual presence for its ministry.

Unlike Orthodox churches, where energy around the visual arts is channeled toward icons, which are then governed by a resilient covenant enacted and reinforced by liturgical practice, and unlike the Roman Catholic Church, where a vision for the arts is purposefully expressed by church documents and channeled through specific institutional procedures, it is not at all clear what, if any, covenants, documents, or institutional procedures — much less theological, confessional, or denominational distinctives — give shape to Protestant patterns of engaging the visual arts. Is there any underlying logic to the Protestant landscape? And if so, what do we gain by examining it? This chapter argues that there is in fact some underlying logic to the Protestant landscape and that we would do well to be more cognizant of its influence.

The Context: The Forces That Shape the Protestant Landscape

I'm not the first to claim that there is some general shape to how Protestant churches engage the arts. Within the last decade, a number of sociologists and historians have become intrigued by the relationship between congregations and the arts. Robert Wuthnow's 2003 book, *All in Sync: How Music and Art Are Revitalizing American Religion*, examines the implications of the deep sympathy between how Americans in general think of art and how Americans think of spirituality. Both art and spirituality, he argues, are connected by a particular idea of the imagination that, in the popular mind, functions as a counterweight to reason and science.[12] Wuthnow sees enormous implications in this convergence for institutional religion. On the one hand, taking the popular convergence between artistic and spiritual imagining at face value, "religious leaders need to understand the profound cultural shift that the current interest in the arts represents. It is a move away from cognition and thus from knowledge and belief, a move toward experience and toward a more complete integration of the senses into the

---

12. Robert Wuthnow, *All in Sync: How Music and Art Are Revitalizing American Religion* (Berkeley: University of California Press, 2003), pp. 190–91.

spiritual life. It is uncharted territory."[13] On the other hand, "religious leaders can engage in selective absorption of the arts with little to worry about and much to gain."[14] *Selective absorption* — it is a striking phrase, one that does indeed describe much of what we see in the Protestant world concerning the visual arts. Wuthnow's analysis argues that, in general, evangelical congregations tend to engage in less selective absorption than mainline congregations, but this result is shaped by what gets to count as "artistic engagement" in the study.[15]

Sociologist Mark Chaves, building on categories first introduced by Robert Putnam in his important book *Bowling Alone*, describes church-based arts activities as either "bridging" or "bonding." *Bridging* activities connect the congregation to social groups beyond the congregation. *Bonding* activities strengthen ties within the congregation. Within his analytical framework, Chaves notes that liberal Protestant congregations are more likely to engage in bridging activities, and more conservative Protestant congregations in bonding activities. New congregations are also more likely to favor bonding over bridging activities.[16] As a result, he concludes, "Religious differences in bridging artistic activities documented here may very well *increase* cultural stratification in American society. Liberal congregations and mainline congregations connect their people to secular art worlds, and thereby help to build conventional sorts of secular cultural capital. . . . Conservative congregations resist these connections partly because they wish to replace secular cultural capital — and the criteria for merit and achievement they imply — with explicitly religious cultural capital."[17] Historian Sally Promey comes to a similar conclusion: "a hierarchy of taste cultures continues to operate within American Protestantism. The split characterized by the alliance of evangelical Protestant Christianity with certain aspects of American mass culture on the one hand, and of liberal Protestant Christianity with certain aspects of American high culture on the other, informs religious

---

13. Ibid., p. 245.

14. Ibid., p. 237.

15. Ibid., p. 144.

16. Mark Chaves, *Congregations in America* (Cambridge MA: Harvard University Press, 2004), pp. 170–79.

17. Ibid., p. 179.

experience and shapes perceptions of these two expressions of American Protestantism."[18]

Chaves's and Promey's analyses fit, to some extent, the six churches introduced in this chapter. Fountain Street Church and First United Methodist's exhibition programs, their permanent collections, and their ArtPrize participation could be seen, as expected, as bridging activities; Covenant Life and Church of the Servant's worship-oriented arts programs could be described as the sort of bonding activities typical of more theologically conservative congregations. But what of the explicitly religious character of First United Methodist's Celebration of the Arts? Could that not act to "replace secular cultural capital . . . with explicitly religious cultural capital"? What of Mars Hill's website and Art + Spirituality program, or Orchard Hill's art education programs, which are definitely bridging activities, though hosted by theologically traditional congregations?

Is a high art/popular art divide, or a secular capital/religious capital divide, all that's going on here? What Wuthnow, Chaves, and Promey take for granted in their analyses is the character of the cultural capital that churches are either seeking to embrace, replicate, or replace. That is, they take for granted the shape of our art system. Liberal or conservative, bridging or bonding, secular or religious dyads do provide some helpful perspectives on intersections between the arts and Protestant churches. But what would we see if we focused our analytical lens on the nature of our art system? Gaining a better appreciation of the Protestant landscape involves venturing into territory far outside the church. You may begin to wonder, as you are reading the following sections of this chapter, where this is all headed. But please bear with me. To appreciate the complexity, the power, the obstacles, and the opportunities of the moment for Protestant churches working with the visual arts, we need to identify the forces at work. Those forces, three in particular, are often so naturalized, so reified, so taken for granted, that they've become virtually impossible to notice, much less question. These three forces are: our dominant notion of Art, inherited from the eighteenth-century Enlightenment and heavily inflected by the Romantic movement

18. Sally M. Promey, "Pictorial Ambivalence and American Protestantism," in *Crossroads: Art and Religion in American Life*, ed. Alberta Arthurs and Glenn Wallach (New York: New Press, 2001), pp. 220–21.

that followed close on its heels; our educational institutions and the professional communities they create; and the way we organize our arts economy.

"Art" with a Capital A

The most important, fundamental cultural commitment that most of us in North America share with respect to art, is to Art. That is, "Art" with a capital *A*. Historically speaking, the idea of Art is quite recent. Before the eighteenth-century Enlightenment, there was no clear, firm distinction drawn between well-crafted artifacts created for use and well-crafted artifacts created for aesthetic enjoyment.[19] From the Middle Ages through the Renaissance and well into the seventeenth century, people whom we now view as singular, uniquely gifted artists turned their talents to many activities beyond painting or sculpture. They illustrated books, fabricated theatrical sets, and even invented textile patterns or made furniture, in addition to making the sorts of things we now consider Art. Our modern notion of fine art, as opposed to craft, emerged in the mid-eighteenth century during the Enlightenment and is intimately connected to the rise of special cultural institutions for the advancement of Art. Galleries, museums, concert halls, art periodicals, art critics, and art schools began to flourish and multiply across Europe, all designed to separate Art from the hurly-burly of daily life so it could be properly appreciated. The academic disciplines of philosophical aesthetics and art history emerged to further define and refine the idea of Art. By singling out Art for special attention, by imagining it first and foremost as nonutilitarian, disinterested, and autonomous, these cultural developments helped create and continue to sustain our dominant idea of Art.[20]

To appreciate this vast sea change in pre- and post-Enlightenment thinking about Art, imagine the difference between encountering a painting of

19. For a brief discussion of this eighteenth-century development, see Paul Oskar Kristeller, "The Modern System of the Arts," *Journal of the History of Ideas* 12 (1951): 496–527, and 13 (1951): 17–46. For a discussion of the "uselessness" and uses of art, see Nicholas Wolterstorff, *Art in Action: Toward a Christian Aesthetic* (Grand Rapids: Eerdmans, 1980).

20. Larry Shiner, *The Invention of Art: A Cultural History* (Chicago: University of Chicago Press, 2001); Mary Anne Staniszewski, *Believing Is Seeing: Creating the Culture of Art* (New York: Penguin Books, 1994).

the crucifixion over an altar in a Catholic church and viewing the same painting in a museum accompanied by six other crucifixions. In the first case, especially if one is Catholic, our attention to the object is coupled with our participation in the Divine Liturgy. In the second case, our attention to the object is directed to the stylistic interpretation of the subject matter. Or imagine the traditional portrait gallery in an English country house. While one of those portraits hanging in the gallery might be a Gainsborough, it still functions as a family portrait while hung in the home. Transposed to a museum, it functions primarily as "a Gainsborough." This little thought experiment demonstrates how galleries and museums, along with the dealers, critics, and art historians who support them, have helped create the idea of Art we have today by directing our attention toward some elements of art (style, iconography, artist) and away from others (dramatizing the Eucharist, underscoring one's lineage). Try this imaginative exercise with icons, and our notions of Art become even more obvious. It's a testimony to the strength of the Orthodox covenant with icons that even when icons are exhibited in museums and galleries, Orthodox believers have been known to pray, prostrate themselves, and even try to kiss the icons. These are the gestures of worship, not of Art appreciation!

As strong as this idea of Art is — as something quite special, as set apart from daily life — it has nonetheless been constantly contested.[21] Ever since Art was institutionalized in museums, galleries, and academies, there have been regular attempts to reinvent a unity between art and the activities of daily life that was imagined to have been lost. The Nazarene movement in early nineteenth-century Germany and Italy, and during its first years, the Pre-Raphaelite Brotherhood in mid-nineteenth-century England, tried to recapture what they believed was the purer, more direct experience of art and faith embodied in the arts of the early Renaissance. After that, in their estimation, the corruptions of stylishness, affectation, and celebrity set in. The Nazarene and Pre-Raphaelite ideal of a natural, pure, spiritual role for art, though, was distinctly of its own day, deeply Romantic, highly individualistic, and — most tellingly — completely divorced from the rites, rituals, communities, and spaces that made the art they admired so meaningful in

---

21. One of Shiner's goals in *The Invention of Art* is to trace the history of resistance to Art within the art world.

its own day. Similarly, the founders of the arts and crafts movement in late nineteenth-century England and of the Bauhaus in early twentieth-century Germany were also skeptical of Art, seeking to recover a unity between art and life that was endangered by mass manufacture. But rather than focusing on a lost spirituality, they focused on a lost sense of community. By reinventing medieval apprentice-and-guild systems for a modern era, each of these movements hoped to overcome what it perceived to be an invidious and destructive separation between makers and users. Their goal was to create systems of production that sustained meaningful relationships between artisans and consumers, allowing talented craftspeople to enjoy their work while creating superior products for ordinary people.

Each of these movements has had some impact. The style of the Nazarenes and the Pre-Raphaelites, for instance, lives on, along with the airbrushed naturalism of nineteenth-century academic art, as the style of much popular religious art — the sort one finds in Christian gift shops and bookstores across the country. Some of the underlying economic concerns of the arts and crafts movement are shared today by "slow food" and "buy local" advocates, and a faint trace of the Bauhaus can be discerned in campaigns like Target Corporation's "Design for All" program, which some years ago successfully recruited the noted architect Michael Graves to design household implements for everyday use.[22] But as attempts to fundamentally realign the dominant relationship between fine art and daily life, all these restorationist impulses have failed. Neither the arts and crafts movement nor the Bauhaus significantly overturned the Enlightenment conviction that Art exists in a realm apart from daily life. And the afterlife of Nazarene and Pre-Raphaelite style remains firmly associated with popular, devotional, mass-produced kitsch, not real Art.

The concerns that motivated these resisters, however, are very much with us today and are a large part of our continuing challenge in integrating art into the life of the church. Though we may no longer believe in the inherent spirituality of a particular early Renaissance style or yearn for the days of the medieval craft guilds, we certainly do desire that Christians see

22. Graves acknowledges the debt to the Bauhaus in discussing his desire to design a chess set for Target. Linda Tischler, "Target Practice," *fastcompany.com* 85 (August 2004), fastcompany.com/magazine/85/graves_qa.html, accessed April 11, 2007.

the work of artists as spiritually meaningful, and we desire a more symbiotic relationship between artists and the church in hopes that ordinary worshipers will encounter beautiful and well-made artworks in our congregations that deepen our ability to worship and glorify God. All these desires and frustrations are rooted in a fundamental gap that has opened up over the last couple of hundred years between the ideas and related social structures that support our contemporary art system and the absence of structures (in the Protestant world, at least) that could reliably support the work of the artist in the worshiping church.[23]

Acknowledging these critiques of our dominant notion of Art, we must also acknowledge the miraculous and tremendous gifts that have flowed from the post-Enlightenment invention of Art. If Art hadn't been invented, we would never have seen the works of Delacroix, Monet, Matisse, or Rothko, much less been able to visit the museums and galleries and study in the classrooms in which we came to understand and love them. If Art hadn't been invented, we might also never have come to appreciate in quite the same way the wonder of objects made in the Middle Ages or made elsewhere around the globe.[24] Closer to home, if Art hadn't been invented, I would not enjoy the enriching and challenging work that I do as an art historian at a liberal arts college. Art makes all these things possible. While I know I am not alone in my frustration with particular elements of our art system as it now exists, I also know that it is bad faith on my part to fail to acknowledge the scale of my overall indebtedness to and investment in our cultural idea of Art.

The Socializing Role of Education

Schools are the second force at work shaping the Protestant conversation on the arts. To be "schooled" is to be trained, disciplined, formed. Being schooled is to be socialized in particular practices and understandings. It is to be inducted into and held accountable to a particular community. In the arts, one

23. For more on this, see James Elkins's short book, *On the Strange Place of Religion in Contemporary Art* (New York: Routledge, 2004).

24. For two interesting discussions of how Art made it possible to recover and appreciate medieval objects and works from elsewhere in world, see Wolterstorff, *Art in Action*, pp. 28–30, and Shiner, *The Invention of Art*, pp. 229–45.

can be schooled in a variety of ways: one can be schooled as a fine artist, as a designer, or as a K-12 art educator. One may be schooled in the arts in other ways, but for our purposes, these are the three dominant ways one is shaped as an artist. Each of them has a slightly different twist on what it means to be an artist, on why art matters, on the purpose of art, and on how art relates to an audience. These different understandings are at once the source and the product of the process of professionalization. A thumbnail history of art education in the United States will help us appreciate this dynamic.

Early advocates for teaching art in American schools were proponents of the industrial arts, particularly drawing. Drawing, so the argument went, "is necessary to the possession of taste and skill in industry, and is therefore the common element of education for creating an enjoyment of the beautiful, and for a profitable practical life." As such, "drawing should be regarded as a means for the study of other subjects, such as geography, history, mechanics, design. In general education it is to be considered as an implement, not an ornament."[25] Just as industrialists were lobbying the schools to train their future employees in draftsmanship, others were lobbying for the necessity of art on entirely different grounds: regardless of talent, so the alternative argument went, *seeing* and *making* are crucial components of learning in general. As such, drawing is a fundamentally democratic activity that fosters citizenship in a democratic nation. The roots of this view lie in the late eighteenth-century, Romantic pedagogy of Johann Heinrich Pestalozzi, whose student Friedrich Fröbel invented the notion of early childhood education that came to be known as *Kindergarten*. German immigrants brought *Kindergarten*, along with its philosophy of art education, to the United States in the 1860s. The effect of all this advocacy was the earliest educational mandate for art in the United States. In 1870, the State of Massachusetts legislated that any municipality with a population exceeding ten thousand (that is to say, any town that was a center of industry) was required to offer industrial drawing as part of a state-supported, common school curriculum.[26]

The two arguments, one offered by the industrialists and the other by the heirs of Pestalozzi, represent two different visions of art. The first represents

---

25. Arthur D. Efland, *A History of Art Education: Intellectual and Social Currents in Teaching the Visual Arts* (New York: Teachers College Press, 1990), p. 101.

26. Ibid., pp. 97–100.

"art-as-trade." The second represents "art-as-formative." The emphasis for the first is on skills, products, and commerce; for the second it's discovery, imagination, personhood, and democracy. Though the two are not mutually exclusive, there is tension between them, and each had, and continues to have, vigorous supporters.

We can see the social reification of this ideological divide in the concurrent foundation of two different professional associations: the College Art Association (CAA) and the American Institute of Graphic Arts (AIGA). Both organizations trace their roots to 1911. The CAA grew out of the Western Drawing and Manual Training Association and was founded to "promote art interests in all divisions of American Colleges and Universities" and to provide college and university educators with a venue to discuss their teaching and research. [27] The AIGA was founded not by educators, but by "the old guard of a new profession." According to the AIGA's self-described origins, "Its charter members were not the rebels typically associated with a cultural avant-garde but veteran professionals — craftsmen and artisans." Directed toward the needs of working printers and designers, its original mission was "[G]enerally to do all things which will raise the standard and aid the extension and development of the graphic arts in the United States."[28] Today, the AIGA remains focused on the concerns of professional designers, though changes in technology have necessarily broadened its interests beyond "graphic arts" as narrowly conceived. Its current mission is "to set the national agenda for the role of design."[29] Contrast that to the mission of the CAA, which works to "cultivate the ongoing understanding of art as a fundamental form of human expression."[30]

---

27. In 1911 the College Art Section of the larger Western Drawing and Manual Training Association first met as an independent group due to its unique interests and concerns. Holmes Smith, "Problems of the College Art Association," *Bulletin of the College Art Association* 1 (1913): 6–10. This publication later became the *Art Bulletin*.

28. AIGA was officially organized in 1914, but it originated in a core group of designers and printers who had been meeting together from 1911 onward. From Steven Heller and Nathan Gluck, "Seventy-Five Years of AIGA," 1989, www.aiga.org/content.cfm/about-history-75thanniversary, accessed April 26, 2007.

29. AIGA, constitution and bylaws, http://www.aiga.org/resources/content/1/0/0/3/documents/Bylaws.pdf, accessed April 26, 2007.

30. CAA website, http://www.collegeart.org/aboutus/mission.html, accessed April 24, 2007.

The tug-of-war between those who endorsed the business-oriented, art-as-trade view and those who endorsed the art-as-formative view in American schools was not settled until the mid-twentieth century. The founding of the National Art Education Association (NAEA) in 1947 is one marker of the growing professional structures that supported arts education along art-as-formative lines.[31] Another, some fifteen years later, was the success of the NAEA in working with the administrations of John F. Kennedy and Lyndon B. Johnson to get the arts more firmly integrated into school curricula via the Arts and Humanities Program of the US Office of Education. As a result, the arts were recognized as a content area. The founding of the National Endowment for the Arts (NEA) and the National Endowment for the Humanities (NEH), both in 1965, with their educational mandates, provided further resources, not to mention cultural cachet, for arts education.[32] These initiatives, along with the subsequent efforts of Kathryn Bloom in the Arts and Humanities Program, inspired many states to create mandates for art in their elementary and secondary school curricula and to require some art instruction in teacher training. Though state mandates rarely went far enough to satisfy arts advocates (and continue to fall short), they nonetheless made substantial progress, and most certainly made debates about the importance of art education a regular part of national and state conversations about education as a whole. The emergence of the NAEA and the federal endorsement of art represented by the creation of the NEA sealed the triumph of the art-as-formative view in our primary and secondary schools over the industrialists' ideal of a curriculum that trains draftsmen for industry.

Art-as-formative is now the root commitment of our art system. Even design now draws its authority from the expressive power of the visual realm — art-as-formative reframed as visual communication. College-level programs in graphic design, illustration, animation, interior design, and the like may come closest to the art-as-trade vision of the late nineteenth

31. The NAEA itself was a merger of several arts education organizations that went back to the 1870s. Efland, *History of Art Education,* p. 185; see also Frederick M. Logan, *Growth of Art in American Schools* (New York: Harper and Brothers, 1955), pp. 142–44.

32. See also Charles Dorn, *Art Education: The Development of Public Policy* (Miami: Barnhardt and Ashe, 2005), especially pp. 127–52, "The Federalization of American Art Education Policy 1960–1997."

century, yet they understand themselves to be a form of "applied formation," if you will.

Finally, art-as-formative also sustains a third domain of our art system: "art-as-identity." Though hardly new to human experience — and certainly not new to post-Enlightenment societies — the notion of art-as-identity has only recently become professionalized. Graduate art programs play the key role in forming those who adopt the identity of artist as opposed to designer or educator. A student might be good at art in high school, but college and especially postbaccalaureate programs determine whether that student will begin to identify as an artist. This distinction is created, represented, and maintained by the fairly recently invented master of fine arts degree (MFA). As Howard Singerman neatly summed it up: "In grammar school, teachers teach art; in my undergraduate college, artists taught art. In graduate school . . . artists teach artists."[33]

The MFA arose in response to the need to determine who was certified to teach art at the college and university level in the wake of the explosive growth of higher education after World War II. The population boom that had created a great need for elementary and secondary art teachers was also creating a demand for college teachers to staff the classrooms filled by returning GIs.[34] The consolidation of opinion around which degree was the appropriate terminal degree for artists required hashing out whether advanced work in art was about making art or studying it. The PhD was associated with a notion of pure research that excluded physical making. Yet the bachelor of arts (BA) in art was clearly not enough preparation for advanced work or teaching. The eventual solution was the MFA, based on the conviction that by making art at an advanced level, one was therefore studying it at an advanced level. This accommodated the need both for hands-on work and for a properly academic approach to that work. Just as advanced work in biology trains and certifies biologists and advanced work in history trains and certifies historians, advanced work in the visual arts trains and certifies

33. Howard Singerman, *Art Subjects: Making Artists in the American University* (Berkeley: University of California Press, 1999), p. 3.

34. Efland, *History of Art Education,* especially chapter 4, "Art Education from World War II to the Present." James Ackerman provides his assessment of the midcentury boom and its ramifications in his 1973 essay, "The Arts in Higher Education," in *Content and Context: Essays on College Education*, ed. Carl Kaysen (New York: McGraw-Hill, 1973), pp. 219–66.

artists. The MFA creates artists through a process of socialization that instructs them in the questions of art as well as in the methods and practices of art and inducts them into the larger community of artists. In doing so, it fulfills one of its primary roles: "to separate its artists and the art world in which they will operate from 'amateurs' or 'Sunday painters.'"[35] Even more than that, this degree symbolizes an art world distinct from the worlds of the K-12 art educator and the career designer. This is the world of *Flash Art*, *Art in America*, and *Artforum*, of certain A-list galleries in major cities, and of one-person retrospectives at the Whitney. Insofar as the MFA is the required degree for teaching and an asset in gaining access to elite galleries, dealers, and publications, it has been described (somewhat cynically) as "an academic certification pyramid that only promises to certify the certified to be qualified to gain employment as certifiers."[36] Of course, the same could be said of just about every branch of academic study.

First awarded with great rarity in the 1920s, the MFA became increasingly common in the 1960s and 1970s. In 1950–1951, there were thirty-two MFA programs enrolling 320 students. By 1960, when the College Art Association first recommended the MFA as the appropriate terminal degree for college and university teachers, those numbers had grown to seventy-two programs enrolling 1,365 students. In 1977, CAA formally specified the MFA as the requisite degree for teaching art at the college level; since then, the number of programs and students has grown exponentially. In 1995, more than seven thousand MFA degrees were awarded by American universities. By 2005, Robert Storr estimated that number had risen to thirty thousand MFAs a year.[37]

So what do we glean from this history? By paying attention to the history of art education in the United States, we can see the roots of three ways of inflecting the meaning of art and three different notions of the artist, each located in related but distinct parts of our culture. Designers are the legacy

35. Singerman, *Art Subjects*, p. 6.

36. Mark van Proyen, "The Educators Educated," *New Art Examiner* 27 (Fall 2000): 24–27. Proyen's essay responds to a prior, critical examination of the MFA by Karen Kitchel, "The M.F.A.: Academia's Pyramid Scheme," *New Art Examiner* 26 (Fall 1999): 33–37.

37. Singerman, *Art Subjects*, pp. 187–213; Robert Storr, "View from the Bridge," *Frieze* 92 (June-August 2005); www.frieze.com/issue/article/view_from_the_bridge4, accessed July 10, 2013.

of the art-as-trade tradition. They emphasize skills and products and are accustomed to bending their talents toward the goals of others. The American Institute of Graphic Arts (and a handful of other associations) establishes professional criteria and represents designers' interests in the marketplace. K-12 art teachers are the legacy of the art-as-formation tradition. They emphasize the creativity of every person and understand the power of art as aiding discovery, cultivating inventiveness, and encouraging individual expression. By definition, K-12 educators work for our school systems, though as we'll see, many work in our churches as well. The National Art Education Association establishes professional standards for the teaching of art at the primary and secondary level and advocates for art education and for art educators. The MFA is the invention of art-as-identity. Art-as-identity focuses the formative power of art on the person of the artist, intensifying the qualities of creativity and expressiveness and sharpening them with critical and analytical tools from the academy at large. Essentially, those holding MFAs work for themselves. Even those who teach at the college or university level will have a personal practice that is self-determined. The College Art Association represents the holders of this degree who teach at the university level and establishes the professional norms that define the degree. Designers, educators, and those with MFAs are all part of our art system. But they inhabit different subcultures within it, each with its own assumptions, practices, professional identities, and operational norms.

This is a lively, powerful, and rather extraordinary history. In the long view, it is also amazingly recent. If our definition of Art has roots in the eighteenth century, the influence of these three educational streams is basically a post–World War II story, a legacy of the last sixty years. In 1955, Frederick Logan, a historian of American education, gave us the view from midcentury in his book *Growth of Art in American Schools*. Ending with a chapter titled "The Shape of Things to Come," Logan predicted with great accuracy the trends that would significantly shape the American art scene in the years ahead. He forecast the growing importance of art-education associations like the NAEA and the CAA for the study of and advocacy for art, the continued formalization of the place of art in school curricula, and, most tellingly, the enormous impact college-based art programs would eventually have. "It would seem impossible," he wrote, "for these schools not to produce in the next quarter century a flood of students who will radically alter the practice and public acceptance of the arts. . . . The increase in the proportion of art-trained persons to the rest of the population is bound to make itself felt."[38] Indeed, it has been felt.

Artists as Activists

The third force shaping Protestant engagement with the arts in their worshiping communities — and the hardest to notice — is the way in which our decentralized American economy funds artistic activity. While public attention is often fixed on federal funding, fanned by the flames of some *scandale du jour*, the truth is that direct federal funding for all the arts is a minuscule portion of our overall federal budget (0.028 percent, or less than three cents for every hundred dollars, of spending).[39] As for how much of the total funding for the arts comes from the federal government, that's also much lower than many people would think — less than 9 percent (and this figure includes support for symphony orchestras, opera and dance companies, and major museums).[40] Given the paltry amount of federal support, how *are* the arts funded in the United States? As Dana Gioia, the former chairperson of the NEA, explains,

> In countries like France, Germany, Mexico, or China, most arts funding comes from the government — either at a federal or local level. For the most part, these systems tend to be centralized, often located in a large ministry of culture. These organizations are also typically political, as arts personnel are usually either members of civil service or political appointees from the ruling party. These systems provide smooth and stable planning for arts organizations, but they run the risk of dividing the cultural world into insiders

38. Logan, *Growth of Art*, p. 271.

39. The advocacy group Americans for the Arts points out that as a proportion of the federal budget, the National Endowment for the Arts (NEA) has been losing ground for thirty years. If appropriations for the NEA had remained proportionally the same as 1982, the 2012 appropriation would have been $633 million, rather than $155 million. See http://aftadc.brinkster.net/handbook/2012/issue_briefs/NEA_Final.pdf as well as the AFA information sheet posted at www.providenceri.com/efile/3402 (accessed July 12, 2013).

40. That figure comes from Dana Gioia, "How the United States Funds the Arts" (Washington, DC: National Endowment for the Arts, 2007), p. v. Since the recession of 2008, those numbers have gotten even smaller.

and outsiders. . . . In contrast to the European models, the U.S. system of arts support is complex, decentralized, diverse, and dynamic. It combines federal, state, and local government support with private subvention from individuals, corporations, and foundations, as well as box office receipts.[41]

Federal dollars, even if few in number, are worth our attention because of the way they work: the creation of the NEA in 1965 necessitated the establishment of state arts agencies through which the NEA was mandated to disburse a set proportion of its funds; this, in turn, over the next decades, generated the founding of more than four thousand civic and regional arts councils. These local organizations combine federal dollars with state and local monies, greatly multiplying the impact of federal support.[42] Just a few federal dollars can give an organization tremendous legitimacy, but the organization must raise the rest of its support on its own. In West Michigan, for example, the Arts Council of Greater Grand Rapids grew out of a local campaign to commission a large public sculpture for Federal Plaza in the downtown area.[43] The group began work in 1967 and was formally organized as an arts council by 1969 when Alexander Calder's *La Grande Vitesse* was dedicated (fig. 18) and feted with a three-day arts festival that became an annual June tradition.[44] "The Calder," as it's locally known, was the first public work of art in the country to be partially funded with federal dollars through the NEA's newly minted Art for Public Places program. Its arrival

41. Ibid., p. v.

42. Ibid., p. 8.

43. In 2012, the Arts Council of Greater Grand Rapids disbursed all its remaining assets and ceased operations. Some presented this as the result of the council having fulfilled its mandate to foster arts organizations in Grand Rapids, which are now seen to be self-sufficient. Others point to plummeting state support for the arts (from $25 million around 2001 to $2 million in 2011). Still others wonder if ArtPrize has begun to divert funds, attention, and volunteer hours away from a wide range of art activities toward its own business-oriented agenda.

44. www.nea.gov/about/40th/grandrapids.html, accessed July 4, 2013. For more on Calder's *La Grande Vitesse* and its role in the art life of Grand Rapids, see Jennifer Geigel Mikulay, "Producing *La Grande Vitesse*: Civic Symbolism, Vernacular Archives and Public Sculpture in Grand Rapids, Michigan," in "Focus: Public Art," special issue, *Collections: A Journal for Museum and Archives Professionals* 4, no. 3 (Summer 2008): 211–24, and Jennifer Geigel Mikulay, "Another Look at *La Grande Vitesse*," *Public Art Dialogue* 1, no. 1 (March 2011): 5–23.

Fig. 18. Alexander Calder, *La Grande Vitesse,* 1969. © 2015 CALDER FOUNDATION, NEW
YORK/ARTISTS RIGHTS SOCIETY (ARS), NEW YORK

inspired an arts boom in Grand Rapids. Forty years on, Calder's *La Grande
Vitesse* is now a beloved symbol of the city, reproduced on everything from
city letterhead to street signs to garbage trucks.

The most significant form of art support in the United States, however,
is as inconspicuous as our contentious debates about federal spending for
art are conspicuous. It's our tax system. Tax exemptions for nonprofit organizations and tax deductions for charitable donations are the main source
of financial support for the arts.[45] Exemptions and deductions are also extended to explicitly religious or church-based arts groups (like the Fountain
Street Church Foundation, mentioned earlier), whereas direct federal and
state funds can be less accessible for these groups. This ground-up, decentralized arrangement, so the argument goes, creates a dynamic environment

45. Volunteerism is another invisible economic component of our arts landscape. The
NEA estimated the worth of Americans' art-oriented volunteer time in the 1990s (the most
recent decade for which such statistics were calculated) to be between $20 and $25 billion,
the equivalent of 390,000 full-time employees (Gioia, "How the United States Funds the
Arts," pp. 18–19).

that directs arts funding to those organizations and activities that enjoy the most public support. The need to garner support, in turn, results in an entrepreneurial system that relies on local fund-raising efforts and local volunteer support.[46]

And therein lies the challenge. Federal grants, state agencies, regional arts councils, and local nonprofits, all dependent on generous donors and energetic volunteers, not to mention the commercial realm of for-profit galleries and design studios, taken together create a hugely decentralized, free-form system of support and funding. Whether or not you agree with our American economic arrangement for supporting the arts, the economy is a major structural force that shapes the way we organize and value artistic activity in our society. Surviving in this alternative economic landscape requires constant awareness of opportunities, an entrepreneurial attitude, a willingness to cultivate patrons, and unceasing advocacy for art in general and for one's own (or one's students') art in particular. Surviving as an artist or as an art educator is training for activism and advocacy.

The epigraph at the opening of this chapter comes from an NEA study touting the link between engagement with the arts and broader civic engagement as though the second were a happy consequence of the first. I think, however, the connection is the other way around. To be an artist or art lover *is* to be a civic activist. If Robert Wuthnow is right and contem-

---

46. The enthusiasm on the ground for local arts activities, endorsed and supported by local communities, and seeded with federal dollars — as demonstrated by the experience of Grand Rapids in the 1960s and 1970s — should temper the fears of alarmists who focus only on a small number of nationally known controversial cases. Research bears this out. A group of sociologists studying the frequency of controversies over the arts in Philadelphia discovered "no upsurge of conflict between religion and the arts during the 'culture war' years" of the late 1980s and early 1990s. Rather, the previous decade (mid-1970s to mid-1980s) saw more conflicts between art and religious communities — though even then, religiously motivated conflicts were few. They conclude, "By the late 1990s, Philadelphia boasted more than 3,000 churches and about 1,200 nonprofit arts and cultural organizations. Given the potential of many of the latter to offend many of the former, the degree of controversy we discovered seems low indeed." Paul DiMaggio et al., "The Role of Religion in Public Conflicts over the Arts in the Philadelphia Area, 1965–1997," in Arthurs and Wallach, *Crossroads: Art and Religion in American Life*, p. 130. See also Paul DiMaggio and Becky Pettit, "Public Opinion and Political Vulnerability: Why Has the National Endowment for the Arts Been Such an Attractive Target?" Working Paper #7 (Princeton: Center for Arts and Cultural Policy Studies, Princeton University, 1999); www.princeton.edu/~artspol/workpap7.html, accessed July 12, 2013. See also Chaves, *Congregations in America*, p. 167.

porary Americans see both art and religion as exercises of the imagination, we should not be in the least surprised that activist artists and art lovers are showing up in our churches in increasing numbers.[47] We should be even less surprised when they show up in artistically barren Protestant churches, and not only see work to be done but are prepared and willing to do it!

The Discussion: Protestant Churches and Our Art System

My claim in this chapter is that the dominant forces shaping the Protestant conversation on the arts are drawn more often from our larger North American art system than from any stable, communal covenant or confessionally oriented, denominationally supported structure arising from within our churches. We are all too familiar with the absence of enthusiasm for the visual arts in many Protestant churches, and we understand the historical and theological roots of the problem. We tend to rehearse this history and lament our predicament at every opportunity. But it has not often occurred to us to question whether the assumptions, practices, and values of our surrounding American art system are the most appropriate way to fill the vacuum. More often than not, we've simply taken the varied assumptions about art in circulation in our culture and imported them into church without much self-awareness or discernment. Understanding the Protestant situation, then, entails a more clear-eyed understanding of our surrounding cultural art system. Our dominant ideas about Art, the ways in which we are socialized as various kinds of artists in our schools, and the ways in which our economy teaches artists and art lovers to mobilize on behalf of art, all give shape to a powerful, coherent, if often invisible set of assumed norms. Recall Larry Shiner's definition of an art system:

> [A]n art system has a larger scope that includes the various art worlds and
> sub-worlds. . . . Art worlds are networks of artists, critics, audiences and

47. James K. A. Smith's "cultural liturgies" project aims to nuance our grasp of how the imagination works. See James K. A. Smith, *Desiring the Kingdom: Worship, Worldview, and Cultural Formation* (Grand Rapids: Baker Academic, 2009) and *Imagining the Kingdom: How Worship Works* (Grand Rapids: Baker Academic, 2013).

others who share a common field of interest along with a commitment to certain values, practices, and institutions. An art system embraces the underlying concepts and ideals shared by various art worlds and by the culture at large, including those who only participate marginally in one of the art worlds.[48]

If we parse Shiner's definition, we see various art worlds (holders of MFA degrees, designers, and art educators, for example) that each has its own network of members, supporters, critics, audiences, and professional associations. These, in turn, are organized and energized by our entrepreneurial arts economy. Yet, all are united in a larger art system that represents shared underlying concepts and ideals. The underlying concept of our art system is the core belief, shared across the spectrum of art worlds from the A-list gallery director to the avid craft aficionado, that art is profoundly valuable — a manifestation of something deeply, intrinsically human that at once expresses and sustains individuality, originality, creativity, and freedom. For participants in our art system, it follows almost without thinking that a failure to appreciate art is a defect; that depriving people of art, especially children, is a violation of their humanity; and that using art to persuade or communicate is possible, powerful, and perhaps even potentially dangerous. Art is a good. Art is a gift to be received and enjoyed, not crassly exploited. To commit to Art is to commit to proselytize on its behalf. To the extent that Art in our current art system is believed by many to both represent and call forth true humanity, it parallels the Catholic and Orthodox understandings of the Divine Liturgy.

While I don't want to discount the sad state of public funding for the arts, especially in this postrecession era, or to downplay the serious consequences of our shrinking investment in art education, I do want to emphasize the remarkable arts landscape that has been built in the United States since the middle of the twentieth century.[49] Our culture is training more artists than

48. Shiner, *The Invention of Art*, p. 11.

49. The NEA began surveying public participation in the arts in 1982. Participation rose steadily between 1982 and 2002 and declined markedly in 2008. Some of the decline, it's surmised, is the result of the economic crash of 2008. Some of it is likely due to shifting modes of participation, with more people participating via new media. Questions about new media use were only added in 2008, so there is no longitudinal data with which to estimate their

ever before. More people know a self-identified designer, art educator, or artist than ever before. Our very agitation on behalf of the arts is due to the efficacy of this system. With this context in mind, let's return to our opening vignettes. Perhaps now we'll be able to see more clearly the ways in which the Protestant conversation is largely shaped and guided by the governing assumptions and structures of our larger American art system.

The Visionary

The character of an art program or arts ministry in a Protestant setting is very likely to be determined by one energetic, inspiring, entrepreneurial artist or art lover who has the ability to rally others around the cause. This may seem patently obvious. John Dillenberger, a doyen of Protestant scholarship on the visual arts, takes it for granted that "[n]othing happens, of course, without the initiating decision of individuals."[50] Most Protestant churches, after all, are starting from scratch with the visual arts. *Someone* has to get the ball rolling. And God bless those who do! That person might be an art-loving pastor, as was the case with Duncan Littlefair at Fountain Street Church. Or it might be a music minister, whose socialization as a musician parallels that of visual artists. A music minister with a deep sympathy for the visual arts was the instigator of Celebration of the Arts at First United Methodist. It might be a staff member who began life as a K-12 educator, as was the case at Orchard Hill and Covenant Life, or a graphic designer brought on to communicate the vision of a charismatic pastor, as at Mars Hill. A philosopher from a local Christian college with an interest in the relationship between liturgy and aesthetics helped establish the vision for the arts at Church of the Servant. In each case, it's very easy to imagine a very different art program, or no program at all, but for those specific individuals. Church-based art programs in the Protestant realm bear the stamp of their founder.

---

impact on arts participation over the long term. National Endowment for the Arts, *Public Participation in the Arts* (Washington, DC: National Endowment for the Arts, 2008). See also the 2011 NEA study, *Arts Education in America: What the Declines Mean for Arts Participation.*

50. John Dillenberger, "Artists and Church Commissions: Rubin's *The Church at Assy* Revisited," in *Art, Creativity, and the Sacred*, ed. Diane Apostolos-Cappadona (New York: Crossroad, 1988), p. 194.

The larger issue at stake here is that for the most part, each of these art-loving movers and shakers has been shaped by the orienting assumptions of a particular sector of our art system as much as (if not more than) by the internal resources of his or her denomination or confessional tradition. A visionary may have the impulses of the designer (art-as-trade), the educator (art-as-formative), or the fine artist (art-as-identity). Design-minded arts ministers care deeply about quality and consistency, about content and message. They don't mind being given a set task. It doesn't bother them that their work is expected to communicate a message. In fact, for them, that's the point. Contrast that to the fine-art point of view, where the desire for message-driven art is deeply frustrating and felt to be a profound misunderstanding of how art works. Like design-minded art leaders, fine-art-minded art leaders are concerned about quality: it's not appropriate to offer God sincere but ham-fisted efforts. Rather, we offer God and one another only our best, most sensitive, most sophisticated efforts. Education-minded art leaders are most concerned about broad-based engagement and about learning through the arts. It's not that quality doesn't matter, but it's not as important as participation and growth. Inviting people to engage, to learn, to express, and to imagine is the primary goal, no matter how amateurish the results.

This description is schematic and oversimplified, to be sure. Life on the ground is always complicated, and obviously the sensibilities of the designer, the educator, and the fine artist can overlap and support one another. But they can also, on occasion, work at cross-purposes. Any given congregation probably has all three sensibilities in circulation. Not all will be represented by the actual art program. The lead pastor might not share the art-world sensibilities of the lead visionary. The congregation might be very deaf to an educator's call for participation or frustrated by a fine artist's preference for ambiguity and open-endedness over a clear-cut message. Differing expectations rooted in different art-world assumptions can easily lead to contention, hurt feelings, and wasted resources.

Stability/Fragility

If success has anything to do with sustainability, the six churches I described in the opening can be viewed as success stories. Their arts ministries and arts programs have survived leadership changes in their congregations and have remained in place, in some cases for fifty years. This is the exception rather than the rule. I began this project by initiating conversations with denominational agencies and church-based art workers from all over the United States, across the Protestant denominational spectrum. Over the course of three years, I built up a list of a couple hundred contacts in more than twenty-five denominations and church associations. My intent was to use these informal phone and e-mail exchanges to create a survey that would help me inventory church-based arts programs, get details on how they were staffed and supported, and eventually discern if there were any patterns to be found.

My first discovery — not entirely surprising — was that in the visual arts, denominations often have no idea what's happening on the ground in their member congregations. In most cases, the connection between denominational structures and art workers in churches was entirely informal — person *x* in agency *y* knew of so-and-so in such-and-such church who was doing a lot with the visual arts. Sometimes I found my way to the right people by asking other art workers who they talked to, who they looked to for ideas and encouragement. These connections were more likely to be crosstown and cross-denominational than not. In the absence of denominational conversation partners, art workers talk to their counterparts in other denominations. This alerted me to the local character of Protestant church-based arts programs and led me to reframe my approach.

My second discovery was more sobering. When I returned to my contacts a year or two later, all too often I learned that the program had folded. The most common reason? The visionary had moved. Without that one entrepreneurial person, the program could not sustain itself. Some of my contacts had started programs in three or four congregations, only to see each initiative die on the vine once they moved away. The activism of these individuals is admirable. But I can only imagine their cumulative hurt and frustration at seeing their work so easily set aside. As so often happens in the research process, I was learning, but not what I'd expected to learn. Clearly, the instability of my survey pool made any purely data-driven approach less than tenable. But more importantly, I was seeing a key characteristic of arts programs in all too many Protestant settings. They are fragile. Visionaries are indispensable. As in our art culture at large, individual initiative counts enormously. But one visionary — no matter how committed and energetic — isn't enough to sustain a program.

Returning to our six success stories, we ask, what makes them work? On one level, the answer is simple: successful programs are woven into the finances and governance structures of their congregations. Already in 1954, Duncan Littlefair established a memorial trust for Fountain Street Church that to this day provides funds for art acquisition and supports the work of the art committee. In addition to stewarding the permanent collection and supervising the exhibition schedule for the Keeler Lounge gallery, the art committee works with several other arms of the church: it helps design the church's monthly newsletter, supervises memorial gifts, arranges occasional art workshops, and assists the character school's (Fountain Street's equivalent of Sunday school) staff with its curriculum. At First United Methodist, the art committee's main task is organizing Celebration of the Arts, which is largely self-funded through entry fees. Though the art committee is not considered a regular committee of the church, making sure that Celebration happens every year is an official responsibility of the church's Director of Music and the Arts. At Church of the Servant, the integration of visual elements into worship means that the visual arts committee is a subcommittee of the worship committee, under which music, liturgy, and dance subcommittees also serve. The art committee can range from five to ten members and has a modest line item in the church budget to support the gallery program and pay for the occasional design and fabrication of new seasonal paraments and other visuals for the sanctuary. On occasion, individual donors supplement the art committee budget for special projects. Orchard Hill's Art Camp on the Hill is now firmly part of the church's identity. Specific staff members are responsible for making it happen; the church budget funds it as part of the education and mission outreach of the congregation; church members embrace it, volunteering in great numbers to serve as leaders, teachers, assistants, and aides. As at Church of the Servant, the arts team at Covenant Life Church is intimately connected with the worship life of the church, but because their approach encourages major reenvisionings of the church facility, the arts team must plan systematically, months in advance, in consultation with the pastoral staff. They also enjoy a fairly generous budget, though it, too, is sometimes supplemented by individual donors. (Furthermore, though it may seem trivial, storage is a major challenge for arts-committed churches. One of the advantages of moving into an old factory or a former mall is the physical advantage of abundant storage.) Mars Hill doesn't have an art team or arts budget per se. Rather, its financial and organizational commitment to visual art is embedded in its sense of what it means to engage in ministry, what it means to have a presence in and be present to contemporary culture. Mars Hill contracts with a professional designer for the original work on its website — work that is now also used for the murals inside the church. The church's "Art + Spirituality" and "Into the Noise" initiatives are considered part and parcel of its call to bear witness in the world today.

A sustainable visual arts program requires the nuts and bolts of financial support and stable governance. But in Protestant settings, even money and committee members might not be enough to sustain a ministry. In each of the six cases above, there's an additional component that's essential for sustainability: each congregation has found a vital, motivating link between one of the dominant norms circulating in our art system and the mission, values, and identity of the congregation.

Cultural Convergence

The activities of art-committed Protestant churches tend to track with the way the arts work in our culture at large. The arts thrive in large, urban settings, especially urban settings with a few colleges or universities (testifying again to the centrality of education in our art system). Protestant churches engaged with the visual arts are overwhelmingly urban, and their members college educated. Some enjoy a number of college and university faculty among their membership. Whereas every Orthodox congregation, no matter how remote, will have its icons, and every Catholic church, no matter how rural, will have a few basic images and the necessary liturgical objects, the more rural and less educated a Protestant church, the less likely the visual arts will be seen as relevant to the life of the church. This is a sobering fact for those of us committed to the belief that art really does matter in the life of the church — for all churches.

Beyond demography, the art life of Protestant churches tracks with the cultural trends of American society in general. It's no coincidence that Fountain Street Church and First United Methodist branched out into the visual arts when they did — just after the middle of the twentieth century. In our discussion of Art above, we maintained that it made perfect sense to align Art with the experience of faith. With its allusive, expressive, transcendent qualities and apparently universal language of color and form, Art seems deeply compatible with transcendent, religious experience. The one is easily mapped onto the other.[51] As the founder of the program at First United Methodist put it, "Quality art has a spiritual character regardless of the subject. Every subject is spiritual. The church's role is to touch the spiritual, to engage the spiritual, and the spiritual is in the arts. We are not just appending a program to the church. This is the church's business."[52] That resonance, combined with the powerful jolt to the American arts scene provided by our postwar educational system, the founding of the NEA, and the cascade effect of public recognition for the arts, resulted in real traction for art lovers in congregations where there was already a modernist sensibility toward both art and gospel. It also makes sense that the congregation's Celebration of the Arts began in 1972. The church already had a handful of members who were notable art boosters in Grand Rapids and supported the symphony and the art museum. With the advent of Alexander Calder's *La Grande Vitesse* just a few blocks away, along with the founding of the annual downtown Festival of the Arts, it made all the sense in the world to launch a parallel, church-based, spiritually oriented Celebration of the Arts.

If liberal and mainline churches align themselves easily with Art, evangelical churches often align themselves easily with media. Historians have long recognized the willingness of evangelicals to leverage the cadences of popular culture, using the latest technology, to communicate the gospel. Radio, then television, and now the Internet have all been pressed into service. The goal is communication, and, as such, designers make the best allies. The restrained but sophisticated visual language at Mars Hill speaks to our broader visual culture, even as it inflects that culture with the message of the gospel.

Communication, however, goes both ways. If art can be used to communicate from the church to society at large, then it's also true that the arts

51. The elision of art and spirituality began already with the Romantics. For an early examination of this phenomenon from an art historical perspective, see Joseph Koerner's *Caspar David Friedrich and the Subject of Landscape* (New Haven: Yale University Press, 1990). For a contemporary version of this argument, see Gordon Kauffman's *Jesus and Creativity* (Minneapolis: Fortress, 2009).

52. Interview with Dick and Marion DeVinney, May 27, 2007. Dick DeVinney served as Director of Worship and Art during the early years of Celebration.

of the world around us might have something to say to the church. If we envision art as a medium that can speak both from and to the church, then it's also not a surprise that ArtPrize is having an effect on Mars Hill. One of the goals of ArtPrize is to foster grassroots engagement with art such that "anyone can find a voice in the conversation about what is art and why it matters."[53] Given the momentum in Grand Rapids around ArtPrize, it only makes sense for a culturally attuned church like Mars Hill to join in. "Art + Spirituality" and, even more so, "Into the Noise" are based on the assumption that the arts communicate, and the church would do well to pay attention.

The art camp and art lessons offered by Orchard Hill and the ambitious program of seasonal installations at Covenant Life owe their origins to church leaders who began their working lives as K-12 educators before moving into church work. These founding visionaries were already convinced of the formative power of the arts. Though each program acts that commitment out differently, the two programs share an underlying belief that art is central to learning and to growth. Orchard Hill focuses on helping children learn and grow through engagement with the arts; Covenant Life focuses on the learning and growth of the worshiping congregation. At Covenant Life, the rationale for the visual arts was originally explained to me as an appreciation of the varied learning styles present in any congregation — a rationale drawn straight from debates in our schools about how best to teach students.[54] A subsequent Director of Worship and Art reframed the rationale as encouraging full-bodied, multisensory worship, explaining it to me as a way of helping all members of Covenant Life expand their capacity to receive and respond to God.[55] Regardless of differences in articulation, the underlying commitment to the educator's vision of art-as-formative remains clear.

53. www.artprize.org/about, accessed July 15, 2013. ArtPrize has other goals, too, chief among which is generating tens of millions of dollars for downtown businesses.

54. Conversation with Steve Caton, Director of Worship and Arts at Covenant Life Church in Grand Haven, Michigan, March 27, 2007.

55. Conversation with Chris Walker, Director of Worship and Art, Covenant Life Church, Grand Haven, Michigan, January 30, 2012. See also Craig Douglas Erickson, *Participating in Worship: History, Theory, and Practice* (Louisville: Westminster John Knox, 1989). See especially chapter 8, "With Heart and Hands and Voices (Multi-Sensate Worship)," for a more theoretical statement of this rationale.

The cultural convergence at Church of the Servant (COS), however, comes from a slightly different angle — it derives from the liturgical renewal movement. In a very real sense, the vision for the arts at COS does come from within the church, but not from within its denomination, the Christian Reformed Church. Rather, it comes from "the church" writ large. The Reformed tradition in general has been a latecomer to the ecumenical conversation on worship and liturgy that emerged over the last half-century.[56] When COS took shape in the late 1960s and early 1970s, it was definitely the exception rather than the rule within the Christian Reformed Church. No other church in the denomination held weekly communion, used set liturgies, employed simple liturgical vestments, or observed the entire church year. At that point, few Christian Reformed churches even observed Advent or Lent! With the advantages of an urban setting and more than a few college faculty among its ranks, though, it was possible for COS to imagine that Reformed worship could look different than it did in the typical midcentury Christian Reformed congregation. Over the years, the ethos of Church of the Servant, via its leaders and members, has had considerable influence in the denomination as a whole, helping foster and support more intentional and more ecumenical approaches to worship in the Reformed tradition.

What is remarkable in these snapshots of cultural convergence is the ways in which our contemporary art system, in all its force, in all its variety, and in all its complexity, shows up in our Protestant churches. We should not take this for granted. Compared to Orthodox and Roman Catholic congregations, Protestants do indeed face particular challenges in embracing the visual arts. David Taylor's description of these challenges is a nice summary of this chapter: "Protestantism — in my case evangelical Protestantism — handed me neither a big picture (a theology) nor a sense of how art and the church could hold together (a tradition). What I was left with were

---

56. In the late 1960s, Michael J. Taylor gave a fairly pessimistic assessment of Presbyterian churches' engagement with liturgical renewal (*Liturgical Renewal in the Christian Churches* [Baltimore and Dublin: Helicon, 1967]). For a recent, more optimistic account, see Alan D. Falconer, "Word, Sacrament, and Communion: New Emphases in Reformed Worship in the Twentieth Century," in *Christian Worship in Reformed Churches Past and Present,* ed. Lukas Vischer (Grand Rapids: Eerdmans, 2003), pp. 142–58. See also the history of the Association for Reformed and Liturgical Worship at http://www.arlw.org/docs/beginning.html, accessed July 15, 2013.

strategies and programs."[57] Viewed from a different angle, however, these very challenges are a kind of strange gift. As William Dyrness notes, "We are in a period of what one might call ad hoc experimentation with the arts in Protestant worship. Thanks to a growing number of artists in Protestant churches, their presence and gifts are increasingly being embraced."[58] And Lauren Winner notes that in spite of supposed Protestant indifference to the visual realm, "[i]ronically, the number of symposia, journal articles, and informal conversations devoted to the 'problem' of faith and the arts demonstrates just how much energy there is around the arts in Christian communities."[59] Perhaps it's not ironic at all. Perhaps it's just what happens when the force of our art system collides with the undifferentiated, open, yet-to-be-defined Protestant arts landscape. The very lack of shared traditions, the very absence of clear denominational expectations, the vast blank slate from which most churches begin their work with the visual arts actually create space for experimentation, for creativity, and for initiative. This lack encourages the advocacy-minded designers, art educators, and artists in our midst to dream of using their gifts for the good of their congregations.

Art, Inculturation, and Enculturation

Interestingly, Protestant conversations about art in the church bear some resemblance to the conversations that were occurring in the Catholic Church before promulgation of the *Constitution on the Sacred Liturgy* and before documents like *Environment and Art in Catholic Worship* and *Built of Living Stones* were drafted. Prior to 1963, there were only tangential connections between what the church officially believed about art as articulated in canon law, and what was said for and against art's place in the church by those who cared about art. The real sources of interest in the arts originated outside the Catholic Church and were "based less on canon law than

57. W. David O. Taylor, introduction to *For the Beauty of the Church: Casting a Vision for the Arts,* ed. W. David O. Taylor (Grand Rapids: Baker, 2010), p. 21.

58. William Dyrness, "Hope That Is Seen Is Not Hope: Visual Explorations of Advent," *Interpretation* 62, no. 4 (October 2008): 395.

59. Lauren Winner, "Someone Who Can't Draw a Straight Line Tries to Defend Her Art-Buying Habit," in Taylor, *For the Beauty of the Church,* p. 77.

on the philosophies, tastes, and biases" of those involved in the arts in any given parish.[60] This is very much the case in most art-interested Protestant congregations today.

At issue here is the difference between the normative claims we may make about what we are doing and the actual tools, training, and ideas we take to the job. Scripture, theology, and confessional identity, while influential, do not ultimately determine how the visual arts are integrated into the life of any given Protestant church. Rather, particular people in a congregation shape what is happening on the ground. Their commitments, in turn, may be couched in whatever scriptural, theological, confessional, or stylistic language is native to a particular congregation, but the starting point is the visionary, whose ideas about art are a product of the varied sectors of our art system. If there is enough resonance between the visionary's ideals and the mission and identity of the church, the program has a chance at embedding itself into the finances and governance of the congregation. If not, not.

With respect to the visual arts, art-committed Protestant churches are basically arenas of intense, mostly unexamined cultural exchange. In some cases, we might call the exchange one of inculturation — the embedding of the gospel in a specific cultural context. In other cases, we might call the exchange one of enculturation — the dominant cultural norms domesticating the gospel. I suspect that for many of us, our vision for the arts in our churches is first and foremost shaped by our North American art system, not by the internal resources of our churches. For some of us, this may be an uncomfortable argument. I know that, personally, I would prefer to believe that my thoughts and habits as a Christian are shaped first and foremost by my faith in Christ. Yet I also know that my thoughts and habits as a Christian are deeply inflected by my North American, white, Protestant, economically privileged socialization. It would be disingenuous as well as dangerous not to admit this. It is no surprise, then, that because my particular denomination does not have a rich tradition of theological reflection on visual art, my thinking about art is more indebted to ideas drawn from my Western educational context than from any guidance I received from the church. This, even though eighteen of my twenty-six years of formal

60. William Rubin, *Modern Sacred Art and the Church of Assy* (New York: Columbia University Press, 1961), p. 64.

education took place in church-related institutions! Though I can justify basic convictions about art with biblical and theological rationales, the fact remains that most of my operational assumptions are more firmly rooted in my particular slice of North American culture than in any transcultural, normative, Christian rationale I might try to claim for them.

It is easier for most of us to recognize inculturation when we see it at work elsewhere. We're able to recognize something as new or different in contrast to what's "normal," or enculturated for us. The challenge, however, is to see what's normal for us as being equally culture bound. Then we're left with the task of discernment. At its best, inculturation is culture in service to the gospel, a rich and rewarding dialectic between local lifeways and theological reflection that deepens the worship and witness of the church as a whole. At worst, it is probably closer to enculturation — the gospel in servitude to the dominant culture, an accommodation to local norms and assumptions that distorts the worship and witness of the church. Either way, understanding the cultural categories that have shaped our discussion of art in North America allows us to see our work as Christians, artists, art lovers, and members of our churches in a broader context and in a clearer light. It is my hope that this realization will temper our human tendency to globalize our own experience and encourage us to listen more carefully to brothers and sisters whose artistic cultural contexts, and faith contexts, are very different. We are invited to practice the spiritual discipline of humility, even as we continue to advocate for the arts in our own churches.

Part Two

DISCERNMENT

INTRODUCTION

In providing the categories on which accounts rest,
the comparative method is indispensable.

— ROBERT SEGAL[1]

I began this book with a story, the story of my students' experience in discovering the unanswered questions that lay beyond their commitment to connect their gifts as artists to the life of a worshiping community. They enthusiastically entered our grant project with biblical grounds to justify the validity of artistic activity. They could use doctrinal concepts to locate the arts in an overarching, theologically informed, Christian world-and-life view. But Scripture and doctrine, the focus of much of the Protestant literature on the arts and the church, it turns out, are only starting points and can't give direction to the "OK, now what?" questions that inevitably come next. My students' dilemma was the genesis of this project.

Over the many years I've spent framing and reframing their questions to discern how to respond, I became convinced that the answers to those "now what?" questions do not lie primarily in Scripture and doctrine. While Scripture and doctrine *are* important — foundational, in fact — they are not

---

1. Robert A. Segal, "In Defense of the Comparative Method," *Numen* 48 (2001): 373. Segal's essay analyzes the general suspicion that comparative methods have engendered, especially in the social sciences, but argues that most objections are not to the method per se, but to poor use of the method.

enough. There are any number of edifices one could build on that foundation, and the shape of those edifices, it turns out, is more concretely cultural than abstractly theological. In fact, even our *use* of doctrinal concepts varies from confessional community to confessional community.

The grounding of visual arts in Christian life and worship has tended to start with one of three doctrinal concepts: creation, incarnation, or sacrament.[2] Each has opened useful and fruitful perspectives on the arts. But none is as straightforward as we may at first assume because different Christian communities sometimes use the same term but mean quite different things by it.

The doctrine of creation, for example, can be used to quite different ends. My students will often justify their artistic interests by aligning their creativity with the *imago Dei* placed in us at creation. As God is creator, so human creativity mirrors the character of God. Nurturing our artistic creativity is a way of honoring God's intention for humanity. Interestingly, fewer students turn to the doctrine of creation to justify their immersion, as visual artists, in the physical, material stuff of this world — an equally valid, but much less romantic, use of creation as a legitimation for the arts.[3]

"Sacramentality" is another term that takes on different resonances in different settings. When Orthodox and Catholic Christians invoke sacramentality, it is generally as an affirmation of God's work through the material world toward our salvation. When Protestants with a more commemorative understanding of the sacraments invoke the term, it sometimes names a spurious, insidious spiritualizing of the world that, to some sensibilities, actually denigrates the value of the material world. In that case, "sacramen-

---

2. Wilson Yates, in *The Arts in Theological Education: New Possibilities for Integration* (Atlanta: Scholars Press, 1987), argues for a larger range of theological concepts to help make the case for the value of the arts. His emphasis, however, is less on making and using the arts in a religious context than on understanding the value of the arts for theological education.

3. For a juxtaposition of these two uses of the doctrine of creation, see Nicholas Wolterstorff's discussion of Dorothy Sayers's *Mind of the Maker* in "The Artist as a Responsible Servant," in *Art in Action: Toward a Christian Aesthetic* (Grand Rapids: Eerdmans, 1980). Steve Guthrie presents a socially oriented, nuanced discussion of the resonance between divine and human creativity in *Creator Spirit: The Holy Spirit and the Art of Becoming Human* (Grand Rapids: Baker Academic, 2011).

talizing" something is to indulge in category confusion, attempting to assign something a spiritual value it already has.[4]

"Incarnation," too, shows up in apologias for art in at least two different ways: as an extension of the doctrine of creation ("incarnation" is the definitive word on the goodness of God's creation and its full redemption in Christ) and as an extension of the doctrine of God ("incarnation" is the fullest revelation of the mystery of God's character and nature). Catholic uses of "incarnation" in discussions of art tend toward the latter; Protestant uses toward the former.[5] While these understandings of incarnation are not mutually exclusive, the emphasis falls for the one on the goodness of the material world, for the other on the mystery of the Godhead. Such varied emphases in using the same doctrinal concept underscore not just the range and power of doctrinal foundations, but also the particularity with which specific communities develop and employ them — and the attendant potential for inadvertently talking past one another.

All of which means that answering the "now what?" questions that my students were asking requires as much conscious attention to the social and cultural embeddedness of theological reflection as it does to the social and cultural embeddedness of artistic activity. The three previous chapters, sketching out the ecclesial and aesthetic assumptions that organize artistic activities in Orthodox, Catholic, and Protestant churches, are meant to help demonstrate that point. But we can go deeper. Setting these traditions alongside one another invites us to notice things that we probably would never have noticed otherwise. The following chapters undertake a more

---

4. Interestingly, within the last ten years, the phrase "sacramentalized but not evangelized" has become a rallying cry in both Orthodox and Catholic circles, describing the need for continued education in the gospel message among cradle Catholic and Orthodox members.

5. Compare, for example, the understanding of incarnation at work in Pope John Paul II's 1999 *Letter to Artists*: "This prime epiphany of 'God who is Mystery' is both an encouragement and a challenge to Christians, also at the level of artistic creativity. From it has come a flowering of beauty which has drawn its sap precisely from the mystery of the Incarnation" (n.p.), the way the doctrine is invoked in the Lausanne Occasional Paper #46: "Incarnation is central to the gospel and poses a clear challenge to all negative claims about the created order" (Colin Harbinson et al., "Redeeming the Arts: The Restoration of the Arts to God's Creational Intention," Lausanne Movement [2005], http://www.lausanne.org/wp-content/uploads/2007/06/LOP46_IG17.pdf, p. 14, accessed January 15, 2007).

systematic investigation of what issues, questions, and perspectives emerge when we examine our three traditions side by side.

Compare and Contrast

Essentially, part 2 is an extended "compare and contrast" exercise. Perhaps because I teach art history, a discipline that originated in a fundamentally comparative method, I find the approach both liberating and illuminating. Comparisons can be liberating because sometimes it is only in comparison that particular facets, characteristics, or grounding assumptions for any given phenomenon become noticeable. Comparison invites us to see things we might not otherwise be able to see. Comparison can be illuminating because once we've noticed these previously hard-to-see properties, we can ask more interesting, more precise questions that better honor the particularity of the object of our study.

A word of caution is in order, however. The comparative method can also be destructive, especially when the terms of the comparison are unexamined and norms from one culture are inappropriately imposed on another. The earliest art historical comparisons, for example, were driven by an assumed, unexamined set of classicizing norms that inevitably judged all nonclassicizing art (Gothic, rococo, baroque, Romantic, realist, and most non-Western art) as deviant and defective. Over time, thankfully, attempts to understand nonclassical and non-Western art in its own terms exposed the classical bias that had been built into the traditional practices of the discipline.[6] Fair-minded comparisons, then, do have to be as self-aware as possible regarding the very terms of the comparison. Avery Dulles makes a similar point with respect to comparative ecclesiology: "[A]rguments in favor of one's own preferred model are generally circular: They presuppose the very point at issue. . . . In any effort at evaluation we must be aware of

---

6. For one statement of what art history's traditional norms might be and how they've worked themselves out in the discipline, see Ernst Gombrich's classic essay "Norm and Form: The Stylistic Categories of Art History and Their Origins in Renaissance Ideals," in his *Norm and Form: Studies in the Art of the Renaissance* (London and New York: Phaidon, 1971), pp. 81–98. For a radical reconsideration of those norms, see David Summers's *Real Spaces: World Art History and the Rise of Western Modernism* (New York: Phaidon, 2003).

the tendency of each contestant to polemicize from a standpoint within his own preferred position. To make any real progress we must seek criteria that are acceptable to adherents of a number of different models."[7] In other words, when using comparisons to draw conclusions, all parties involved in the comparison should see themselves fairly represented and agree to the terms of the comparison.[8]

Now that we have read chapters 1 through 3, what possible terms of comparison might we notice more readily after having examined the social and cultural dynamics of the visual arts in these particular Orthodox, Catholic, and Protestant settings? What points of contact and contrast emerge? What new questions might we ask, given what we now notice a bit more clearly? Two sets of questions emerge. The first set of questions has its origins "in church," so to speak; the second set in our larger, North American art system.

Ecclesial Questions

The questions that emerge "in church" circulate around ecclesiology. How do the arts help express a congregation's theology of itself as a church? Is a congregation's engagement with the arts meant to express the universal character of the church or the local character of the congregation? How do the arts help express a congregation's ideas of the purpose of their church by enacting the story of our faith or by helping us encounter God's presence in worship? How do the arts, used in worship and devotion, help us notice the ways in which the church constitutes us both as a people and as individual persons? These questions help expose what John Witvliet calls the "lived theology" of a congregation.

In the introduction to *Worship Seeking Understanding*, Witvliet writes, "Common worship is the locus where the church's distinctive vocabulary, narratives, and rituals are developed and enacted." Common worship, he continues, "as much as any other dimension of the church's life, writes the

---

7. Avery Dulles, *Models of the Church* (Garden City, NY: Image Books, 1987), p. 182.

8. I've striven to be as fair-minded as possible, asking Orthodox, Catholic, and various Protestant readers to comment on drafts of every chapter. It is, of course, for others to determine whether the analysis is, in the end, sufficiently self-aware and fair-minded!

'lived theology' of the Christian community — that is, the theological vision that most believers live by, whether or not that vision matches that of official creeds, confessions, and classic texts."[9] One element of a church's lived theology includes its theology of itself as a church. How does a congregation, through its worship, its ministry, its organization, and its patterns of life together, live out its self-understanding as church? This is where official theology and lived experience may part ways. No matter how theologically elevated our beliefs about "church" are, it's equally true that the church is also a human, social organization. It is, as Craig Van Gelder puts it, "spiritual territory that occupies earthly terrain."[10] He continues: "There is a duality within the church's nature which we must understand if we are to address properly the ministry and organization of the church. The church is God's personal presence in the world through the Spirit. This makes the church, as a spiritual community, unique. The church also exists as a social reality with human behaviors organized within human structures."[11]

It is precisely this duality — that the church is at once a holy, transcendent creation of God and a wholly human, temporal community — that makes ecclesiology so central for understanding the relationship of the visual arts to the worshiping church. As illuminating as "creation," "incarnation," or "sacrament" may be, none gives access to the communal, social aspects of our life together, either as Christians or as artists. Ecclesiology as a theological framework, however, does. The church, as "God's personal presence in the world through the Spirit," but also as "a social reality with human behaviors organized within human structures," encourages us to recognize the force of social and cultural practices in our analysis that are not so easily recognized when using the theological lenses of creation, incarnation, or sacrament.[12] Three ecclesial themes emerge in cross-confessional comparison of how the arts function in our congregations: the relationship between the universal and the local, the relationship between "story" and "presence" in worship, and the relationship between corporate and individual identity.

9. John D. Witvliet, *Worship Seeking Understanding: Windows into Christian Practice* (Grand Rapids: Baker Academic, 2003), p. 17.

10. Craig Van Gelder, *The Essence of the Church: A Community Created by the Spirit* (Grand Rapids: Baker, 2000), p. 15.

11. Ibid., p. 25.

12. Ibid., p. 25.

Exploring these ecclesial themes leads to a second set of questions about how our lived ecclesiologies inflect our interaction with our larger art system. These questions originate outside the church and are then invited, with varying degrees of modification, into our congregations. Pausing to note them helps us appreciate the dynamics of cultural exchange between churches and our broader North American art system: How do congregations train their artists in ways distinct from or compatible with our larger art system? How do our patterns of artistic activity in our congregations yield to, or resist, the activism and agency fostered in our art system at large? How do stylistic choices take on cultural meaning, especially with respect to the fascinating and complicated role of Western naturalism in the visual arts of our churches? How can attention to the visual arts sharpen our appreciation of the challenges of inculturation; or, when are we speaking the gospel message in our own local idiom and when are we merely advancing our own culture in the guise of the gospel? The art-system questions that emerge in cross-confessional comparison concern questions of artistic socialization (institutionalization and professionalization), questions of the meaning of style (naturalism and abstraction), and finally, the visual arts as a site of cultural exchange (inculturation and enculturation).

Stepping back from these six themes — three originating in ecclesiology and three originating in our art system — we notice that two, the first and the last, are profoundly linked. The universal and local identities played out in our operative ecclesiologies take shape in part through the ways in which the visual arts serve as agents of inculturation or enculturation. All our other themes flow from this fundamental dynamic.

CHAPTER 4

Universal & Local

When we encounter the church, we move into spiritual territory that occupies earthly terrain.

— CRAIG VAN GELDER[1]

All Christians acknowledge the *universal* character of God's church. Though we may parse it in different ways — as visible and invisible, as institute and organism, as eschatologically "already" and simultaneously "not yet" — Christianity's focus on the vast scope of the kingdom of God makes clear that no single congregation represents the totality of the church universal.[2] Yet congregations vary on how they imagine themselves as part of the church universal. On one end of the spectrum, for example, a congregation might understand its relationship to the church universal as a function of belonging to a transhistorical, confessing community joined in worship of the one, true, triune God. The accent falls on the mystery of the congregation as a communal, corporate entity that constitutes part of the kingdom of God. Other congregations, by contrast, might understand their relationship to the church universal as less corporate and more collective. Such a congregation contributes to the church by bringing people to a saving knowledge

---

1. Craig Van Gelder, *The Essence of the Church: A Community Created by the Spirit* (Grand Rapids: Baker, 2000), p. 14.
2. See especially Brad Harper and Paul Louis Metzger, *Exploring Ecclesiology: An Evangelical and Ecumenical Introduction* (Grand Rapids: Brazos, 2009), pp. 47–77.

of Christ and by encouraging those people to bear witness to Christ's power in their lives. The emphasis there is less on the congregation as a whole as an expression of God's kingdom and more on the life and witness of its members as an expression of that kingdom.

Avery Dulles describes these two views as "body of Christ" and "people of God." Both images are biblically and theologically grounded, but the image of the people of God, as Dulles describes it, "differs from that of the Body of Christ in that it allows for a greater distance between the Church and its divine head. The Church is seen as a community of persons each of whom is individually free."[3] However, with the exception of some extremely sectarian congregations, no matter how the church universal is imagined — as mystical communion or as a community of persons — it remains, in this life, beyond our full comprehension. The full scope of the body of Christ and the numerous individuals who make up the people of God stretches across space and time, beyond our present experience. The reality of the church universal is taken on faith.

Our local congregations, by way of contrast, are much less an item of faith than part of our concrete, lived, day-to-day experience. Just as all Christians acknowledge in faith the church universal, all Christians encounter that through the *local* character of a particular congregation. Tellingly, this aspect of our life in God's church is often harder for us to recognize because it requires that we understand our own experience *as* local. Just as a fish in water can see the other fish around it, the plant life, the stones and pebbles in the river, but not the very water it is swimming in, we are often unable to recognize our native context as the water we swim in. As the famously outspoken Anglican bishop Hugh Montefiore noted, it's "comparatively easy to ask awkward questions about the suitability of another culture as the vehicle for communicating the Gospel; but it is very difficult to ask them about one's own."[4] Bryan Spinks points to the flip side of this dynamic: "[O]ften it is only someone from another culture who can spot the cultural

---

3. Avery Dulles, *Models of the Church* (Garden City, NY: Image Books, 1987), pp. 45–46

4. Hugh Montefiore, *The Gospel and Contemporary Culture* (London: Mowbray, 1992), p. 1, as quoted in John D. Witvliet, *Worship Seeking Understanding: Windows into Christian Practice* (Grand Rapids: Baker Academic, 2003), p. 116. Lesslie Newbigin's *Foolishness to the Greeks: The Gospel and Western Culture* (Grand Rapids: Eerdmans, 1986) is an impressive argument for the barriers to a full understanding of the gospel within Western culture.

elements in another's liturgy, and who may perhaps alone be the best judge of the balance between the human and the divine."[5]

Christ's incarnation in flesh and bone, two millennia ago in the ancient Near East, makes it clear that God's Word enters our world in all our world's specificity and particularity. But to confess that God entered our human particularity in Christ is not to imply that the reverse is also true. We do not take on God-in-Christ's omniscience and omnipotence as a consequence of the incarnation. We remain particular, finite, and decidedly local — not to mention fallen — creatures even as we belong, redeemed, to God's glorious kingdom. It is a constant challenge to humbly and appropriately discern the particular from the universal or to see the universal within the particular. One of the great joys of traveling outside the United States with young Christian college students is to see them encounter God's church in other parts of the world and notice for the first time that taken-for-granted elements of their experience of Christianity are actually more locally American (or even southern Californian) than universally Christian, and also experience for the first time the ways in which other elements of worship bind all cultures together in Christ. Most of us — even those of us whose ecclesiology emphasizes the church universal — probably underestimate the *localness* of our sense of "the church." The problem here is not that our churches *are* local in character. They cannot be anything less. Rather, the problem is in our tendency to unwittingly universalize our local experience without recognizing the possible repercussions.

This is the challenge of inculturation, the challenge at the heart of all the debates about "Christ and culture," as H. Richard Niebuhr famously put it, the challenge that has confronted the church ever since the council of Jerusalem had to decide whether circumcision would be required of all those entering the church. How do we adequately honor the transcultural, universal truth of the gospel while fully honoring the rich diversity that arises from our divinely ordained, creaturely, embedded condition? We profess "one, holy, catholic church" as an item of faith; we inhabit local instantiations of that church. Holding fast to the unseen mystery of the church universal in

5. Bryan D. Spinks, "Liturgical Theology and Criticism — Things of Heaven and Things of Earth: Some Reflections on Worship, World Christianity and Culture," in *Christian Worship Worldwide: Expanding Horizons, Deepening Practices*, ed. Charles E. Farhadian (Grand Rapids: Eerdmans, 2007), p. 245.

the midst of our seen, known, and loved local congregation is at once an exercise of faith and an invitation to discernment and humility.

The arts have their own version of the universal/local dynamic. Claims for the importance of the visual arts often rest on assumptions about their supposed universality. One of the governing assumptions of much modernist art and art criticism was that color, line, form, texture, and the like constitute a universal formal language that transcends the barriers of spoken language.[6] Other Christian apologists for the arts have begun with beauty, which, rooted in the beauty of God, renders the arts at once universal and transcendent.[7] Still others, like the many artists and art lovers interviewed by Robert Wuthnow in his two studies of religion and art (and like the apologists for the arts at Fountain Street Church and at First United Methodist), see the arts as universal due to an inherent spirituality.[8] But as is the case with our assent to the belief in the universality of God's church, our *experience* of art is irreducibly local. No matter our convictions about the universality of art (not to mention the problems and challenges one must sort through to hold any of these universalizing positions), our encounter with any given art form is always necessarily specific, particular, and culturally located in space and time. Once again, we often tend to mistake the particular for the universal, assuming that *this* formal vocabulary, *this* style, *this* beauty resonates universally across time and space. Holding to the conviction of the unseen in the presence of the seen, while remaining sensitive to the difficulty of discerning the one in the other, is an ongoing challenge.

In our extended "compare and contrast" exercise, our three brief sketches

6. One classic and influential statement of this view is Clive Bell's *Art* (London: Chatto and Windus, 1914). For a more nuanced variant, see Nicholas Wolterstorff's *Art in Action: Toward a Christian Aesthetic* (Grand Rapids: Eerdmans, 1980), pp. 90–113. Wolterstorff grounds art's potential universality in the expressive power of what he calls "cross-modal similarity." But he also qualifies that potential universality by relating expressiveness to intended purpose: "In its expressiveness, unlike its intended uses, a work of art transcends the boundaries of culture and makes itself available to all" (pp. 112–13).

7. For an introduction to the theological discussion of beauty, see Patrick Sherry, *Spirit and Beauty: An Introduction to Theological Aesthetics* (Oxford: Clarendon, 1992). Gesa Elsbeth Thiessen provides a substantial set of primary source texts on the question in *Theological Aesthetics: A Reader* (Grand Rapids: Eerdmans, 2004).

8. See Robert Wuthnow's *Creative Spirituality: The Artist's Way* (Berkeley: University of California Press, 2001) and *All in Sync: How Music and Art Are Revitalizing American Religion* (Berkeley: University of California Press, 2003).

of how the ways in which Orthodox, Catholic, and Protestant Christians engage the visual arts demonstrate the ways in which the universal/local dynamic plays out in real communities. One of the dominant factors in determining what will happen with the visual arts in any given congregation is the congregation's orientation toward the universal or local elements of "church."

Orthodox

For Orthodox Christians, the universal/local dialectic swings decidedly toward the universal. Because the liturgy is the central articulation of Orthodox theology, it is there that we see most clearly the universal, eschatological character of its lived ecclesiology. In worship, Orthodox Christians understand themselves to be entering the "already" part of the "already/ not yet" experience of Christian faith. The already is so strong, in fact, that the eucharistic prayers in the Liturgy of Saint John Chrysostom (the standard weekly liturgy for most Orthodox churches) thank God, who "left nothing done until you brought us to heaven and gave us your kingdom to come." Later in the liturgy, the congregation "remembers" the second coming of Christ, thanking God for "all that came to pass for our sake, the cross, the tomb, the resurrection on the third day, the ascension into heaven, the enthronement at the right hand of the Father, and the second, glorious coming."[9]

In Orthodox worship, Christians mystically join the heavenly throng of saints and angels worshiping around the throne of God. For Alexander Schmemann, the essence of the liturgy is that the kingdom of God "is already now *among us, within us.* Christianity is a unique historical event, and Christianity is the presence of that event as the completion of all events and of history itself."[10] Stanley Harakas explains that liturgy is "that action which most of all characterizes us as the Church, empha-

9. See the liturgy available at www.goarch.org/chapel/liturgical_texts/liturgy_hchc, and as commented on by David Petras, "Eschatology and the Byzantine Liturgy," *Liturgical Ministry* 19 (Winter 2010): 29–35.

10. *The Journals of Father Alexander Schmemann* (Crestwood, NY: St. Vladimir's Seminary Press, 2000), p. 234.

sizing our real existence as members of God's Kingdom, beginning in this life and extending into eternity. It is *the* location where time past, time present, and time future are gathered up for us in ultimate meaning and significance."[11] John McGuckin writes, "[t]he church, as the apostle clearly taught, is the mystical Body of Christ. . . . Orthodoxy sees the church as the living icon of Christ."[12] If the worshiping church is a living icon of Christ, and the icons of Christ and the saints help make present the eschatological reality of the church, then, it follows, as Ouspensky explains, that "[t]he icon completes the Liturgy and explains it, adding its influence on the souls of the faithful. The contents and the meaning of the icon and the Liturgy are the same, and this is why their form, their language, is also the same."[13]

The worshiping church is the church universal. The Divine Liturgy is eternal. And icons, with their "eschatological realism," as Mahmoud Zibawi puts it, help make present that mystical reality.[14] This identification of the local church with the church universal means that changing the liturgy or even changing the look of icons is very difficult to imagine. To use Peter Galadza's phrase, it would constitute a "remodel of the heavenly city."[15] The dialectic, in fact, goes in the other direction. It is human presumption to tamper with the mysteries of God. "To the degree that [Orthodox Christians] sense the church's unfailing Christ-energy in the world, the Orthodox faithful expect themselves to be reformed by the church, rather than to see how they can constantly reform it."[16] We are not to change the liturgy. Rather, the liturgy is to change us.

---

11. Stanley Harakas, *Living the Liturgy: A Practical Guide for Participating in the Divine Liturgy of the Eastern Orthodox Church* (Minneapolis: Light and Life Publishing, 1974), p. 27.

12. John McGuckin, *The Orthodox Church: An Introduction to Its History, Doctrine, and Spiritual Culture* (Oxford: Blackwell, 2008), p. 240.

13. Leonid Ouspensky, *Theology of the Icon*, trans. Anthony Gythiel with selections translated by Elizabeth Meyendorff, 2 vols. (Crestwood, NY: St. Vladimir's Seminary Press, 1992), p. 9.

14. Mahmoud Zibawi, *The Icon: Its Meaning and History* (Collegeville, MN: Liturgical Press, 1993), p. 33.

15. Peter Galadza, "Restoring the Icon: Reflections on the Reform of Byzantine Worship," *Worship* 65, no. 3 (May 1991): 242.

16. McGuckin, *The Orthodox Church*, p. 245.

Roman Catholic

Until Vatican II, the operational ecclesiology of the Roman Catholic Church was often, as Avery Dulles has described it, "institutional" in character. The church was understood and described "primarily in terms of its visible structures, especially the rights and powers of its officers."[17] This institutional ecclesiology emerged as a mirror image of the Reformation, with dogmatic defenses of exactly those elements the reformers had brought into question (the papacy and the priesthood in particular). Just as the Orthodox Church's "mystical communion" ecclesiology placed a great emphasis on the universal identity of the local congregation, so too did the institutional ecclesiology of the pre–Vatican II Catholic Church, which identified the church universal with the history, centralized structures, and magisterial teaching of the Roman Catholic Church. All of which renders the ecclesiology that emerged from Vatican II even more remarkable.

Pope Paul VI signaled this sea change in his opening address to the council, which began, "The Church is a mystery. It is a reality imbued with the hidden presence of God. It lies, therefore, within the very nature of the Church to be always open to new and ever greater exploration."[18] The council's core document on the nature of the church, *Lumen Gentium* (known in English as the *Dogmatic Constitution on the Church*), contains in its opening chapter a range of biblical images to describe the mystery of the church. Some of these images underscore its mystical, eschatological reality: bride of Christ, body of Christ, dwelling place of God among men, our holy mother who gives us birth. Other images are more earthbound and temporal: the church is a field to be tilled, the branches on a vine, or a vineyard to be tended; the church is a flock, or the sheepfold that shelters the flock; the church is a building whose cornerstone is Christ, the stone the builders rejected.[19] Dwelling on all these images and

17. Dulles, *Models of the Church*, p. 27.

18. Hans Küng, Yves Congar, and Daniel O'Hanlon, eds., *Council Speeches of Vatican II* (Glen Rock, NJ: Paulist, 1964), p. 26, as quoted in Dulles, *Models of the Church*, p. 10.

19. *Lumen Gentium (Dogmatic Constitution on the Church)*, par. 6. *Lumen Gentium* and all other official documents of the Roman Catholic Church can be easily accessed in English at the Vatican's website: www.vatican.va. For an extensive discussion of *Lumen Gentium*, see Richard Gaillardetz, *The Church in the Making: "Lumen Gentium," "Christus Dominus," "Orientalium Ecclesiarum"* (New York: Paulist, 2006).

metaphors as ways to appreciate the vast mystery of the church, the document then singles out one image, the "people of God," as central.[20] As the people of God, the church is more than a collection of persons: "God . . . does not make men holy and save them merely as individuals, without bond or link between one another. Rather has it pleased Him to bring men together as one people, a people which acknowledges Him in truth and serves Him in holiness."[21] The church is a community, a communion, more than the sum of its parts. Even so, the church is also situated in history and remains eschatologically incomplete. Rooted in the Old Testament covenant with ancient Israel and renewed in the new covenant sealed with Christ's blood, the church on earth remains a pilgrim people that "strains toward the completed Kingdom and, with all its strength, hopes and desires to be united in glory with its King."[22] The "not yet" character of the earthly church is held in tension with the as-yet-unrealized fullness of the church universal found in communion with Christ.

In a remarkable paragraph, *Lumen Gentium* connects the earthly variety of the "not yet" church to the riches of the church universal:

> Since the kingdom of Christ is not of this world, the Church or people of God in establishing that kingdom takes nothing away from the temporal welfare of any people. On the contrary it fosters and takes to itself, insofar as they are good, the ability, riches and customs in which the genius of each people expresses itself. Taking them to itself it purifies, strengthens, elevates and ennobles them. The Church in this is mindful that she must bring together the nations for that king to whom they were given as an inheritance, and to whose city they bring gifts and offerings. This characteristic of universality which adorns the people of God is a gift from the Lord Himself. By reason of it, the Catholic Church strives constantly and with due effect to bring all humanity and all its possessions back to its source in Christ, with Him as its head and united in His Spirit.[23]

The vision of the church that emerged from Vatican II goes hand in hand with the renewal of worship outlined in the *Constitution on the Sacred Liturgy*

20. *Lumen Gentium*, par. 2. This use of the phrase is more collective than Dulles's.
21. Ibid., par. 9.
22. Ibid., par. 5.
23. Ibid., par. 13.

and discussed in chapter 2. Worship, particularly the Eucharist, celebrated with "full, conscious, and active participation," knits worshipers into the body of Christ and constitutes them as the pilgrim people of God. The task of the council was to help congregations discover how to foster that full, conscious, active participation through renewed attention to corporate worship. Honoring the local conditions of the congregation was not only theologically correct, it was also a major way to foster participation in worship. Thus the several statements in the *Constitution* on making use of the "genius and talents of the various races and people" in the liturgy, including the acknowledgment that "[t]he art of our own days, coming from every race and region, shall also be given free scope in the Church, provided that it adorns the sacred buildings and holy rites with due reverence and honor; thereby it is enabled to contribute its own voice to that wonderful chorus of praise."[24]

In wrestling with this question, the Catholic Church has developed a helpful emphasis on the distinction between primary and secondary symbols. Primary symbols — water, bread, wine, fire or light, oil, the cross, the passing of Christ's peace, the gathered assembly of worshipers itself — are grounded in Scripture and belong to all Christians in every place and every time. Secondary symbols, like the use of incense, for example, or particular vestments for clergy, or historical symbols of the faith like the *ichthus* or *chi rho*, or visual motifs associated with a specific congregation, diocese, nationality, or geographic location, can enhance our worship and locate it in a particular time and place but should not have the same status or meaning as the primary symbols that embody the heart of our faith and witness.

Problems arise when secondary symbols are mistaken for primary, and primary symbols relegated to the status of secondary symbols. For the reformers of Vatican II, pre–Vatican II Catholic worship had relegated the gathered assembly to the status of a secondary symbol. Obscure liturgical rites performed by the clergy in Latin and lay devotional attention to a handful of saints who had gone before, vividly represented by the many statues and paintings in a typical sanctuary, seriously diminished worshipers' sense of the power and presence of God with them in the gathered assembly of living saints at worship. As the body of Christ, God's gathered

---

24. *Sacrosanctum Concilium (Constitution on the Sacred Liturgy)*, 37 and 123. See also 39, 119.

people at worship are themselves a primary symbol that manifests God's presence with us. When primary symbols are neglected, overlooked, or stingily used, no amount of compensation with secondary symbols can make up for their loss.[25] No amount of devotion to Mary or to one or two local saints can convey the majesty of the full communion of saints, the great cloud of witnesses, living and dead, we join in worship. When rightly used, however, secondary symbols can help us apprehend and express the depth and breadth of our faith. The Catholic ideal, then, is focused on worship that is ideally local in flavor but that expresses the oneness of the church universal through its liturgical integrity. Language can vary, colors can vary, music can vary, movements can vary, secondary symbols can vary, but the meaning of the liturgy cannot vary, because it is the liturgy itself that knits worshipers together into the church universal, the people of God. The arts are welcome — very welcome indeed — but *only* insofar as they support the liturgical integrity of the church's worship, and never when they distract from or compete with the liturgy. The words of Joyce Zimmerman again come to mind: "[t]he liturgical environment isn't the artistic playground for even the most gifted of artisans. It is the sacred space in which liturgy is celebrated so that the paschal mystery of Jesus Christ unfolds."[26] In the Catholic Church, the "operational ecclesiology" seeks to make manifest the universal character of the church through localized expressions of the liturgy.

Protestant

Though some have said the problem with Protestant ecclesiology is that there is no Protestant ecclesiology, that isn't really the case. The challenge of Protestant ecclesiology is that there are so many![27] Additionally, their typ-

---

25. Patrick Byrne, "Symbolic Actions in Christian Worship," in *Liturgy and Music: Lifetime Learning*, ed. Robin A. Leaver and Joyce Anne Zimmerman (Collegeville, MN: Liturgical Press, 1998), p. 87.

26. Joyce Ann Zimmerman, *The Ministry of Liturgical Environment* (Collegeville, MN: Liturgical Press, 2004), p. ix.

27. For Protestant ecclesiologies, see Veli-Matti Kärkkäinen's *An Introduction to Ecclesiology: Ecumenical, Historical, and Global Perspectives* (Downers Grove: InterVarsity, 2002). Miroslav Volf's *After Our Likeness: The Church as Image of the Trinity* (Grand Rapids: Eerd-

ical emphases render ecclesiology as such implicit rather than explicit, especially in comparison to Orthodox and Catholic ecclesiologies, with their clear emphases on the church universal, which draws attention to itself *as* ecclesiology. That there is no mention of "church" in the National Association of Evangelicals' Statement of Faith attests to the elusive character of ecclesiology in some Protestant traditions.[28]

Some Protestant ecclesiologies — Lutheran, Calvinist, and Anglican, in particular — resonate with the "people of God" imagery promulgated by the Second Vatican Council that, as Avery Dulles points out, "picks up many favorite themes of Protestant theology."[29] But in Dulles's analysis, two other images of "church" also find favor in Protestant circles: "church as herald" and "church as servant." In the herald model, the church is "gathered and formed by the word of God. The mission of the Church is to proclaim that which it has heard, believed, and been commissioned to proclaim. This type of ecclesiology . . . emphasizes faith and proclamation over interpersonal relations and mystical communion."[30] A congregation's identity as "church" is understood to be represented primarily in its proclamation and witness, and secondarily in its relationship to the body of believers stretching across time and space. In terms of governance, churches that emphasize word, faith, and proclamation are typically organized congregationally with most, if not all, authority granted to the local fellowship. This, in turn, creates room for "wide variations in the ways in which local communities of faith structure their creeds, their offices, and their worship."[31]

The servant model of church is even more radically oriented toward the temporal and local. Whereas the images of body of Christ, people of God, and herald assume God's initiative in determining the identity and character of the church in the world, the servant model gives as high a priority to the characteristics of the world around the church. As Dulles describes it, "[t]his model may be called 'secular-dialogic': secular, because the Church takes the world as a properly theological locus and seeks to discern the signs of the times; dialogic,

---

mans, 1997) and Harper and Metzger's *Exploring Ecclesiology* offer strong arguments for particular ecclesiologies.

28. http://www.nae.net/about-us/statement-of-faith, accessed July 30, 2013.
29. Dulles, *Models of the Church*, p. 46.
30. Ibid., p. 68.
31. Ibid., p. 75.

because it seeks to operate on the frontier between the contemporary world and the Christian tradition."[32] A servant ecclesiology "seeks to give the Church a new relevance, a new vitality, a new modernity, and a new sense of mission . . . [which] promises to bring about a great spiritual renewal within the Church itself. Not only individual persons in the Church, but the Church itself, can be transformed."[33] Paraphrasing one proponent of this view, Dulles writes, "the apostolate of the servant Church should not be primarily one of confessional proclamation or of cultic celebration, but rather discerning reflection on God's promise and presence in the midst of our own history."[34]

As a consequence of their muted emphasis on the church universal and their strong concern for effective proclamation and witness in their local context, both herald- and servant-oriented churches may not feel as strong a need to align either their organizational structures or their worship practices to the traditional structures and practices that many other Christian churches have used throughout the centuries.[35] There is instead a clear motivation for innovative experiments that look to the organizational structures and practices of the world in which the church finds itself to discover how to be "church" in a specific place and time. That innovative sensibility extends to the visual arts as well. Whatever the dominant understanding of the visual arts, however we organize and support artistic activity in our North American art system, according to these models, all of that has an absolutely legitimate place in the church if the church is to remain relevant, witness bearing, and effective in a modern context. It's no wonder, then, that we encounter such variety — everything from ArtPrize participation and cultural plunges to summer art camps, church-based galleries, and ambitious interpretive sanctuary installations — among Protestant churches in Grand Rapids.

Acknowledging the distinction between primary and secondary symbols

---

32. Ibid., p. 84.
33. Ibid., p. 91.
34. Ibid., p. 88.
35. A caveat is in order here. To make my basic point — that the universal/local orientation of a given congregation plays a large role in shaping what will or will not happen with the visual arts — I've been much more schematic than Dulles is in his discussion. Dulles makes very clear that confessional bodies and even individual congregations are rarely monolithic in their operative ecclesiologies. Most of the time, they combine two or more of these models in envisioning their mission and identity. Within his own Roman Catholic context, in fact, he can point to Catholic theologians who speak for each view.

might offer a salutary challenge for Protestant artists. Artists are particularly apt to lose sight of the primary symbol in search of the striking, novel, inventive secondary symbol. Innovation, originality, and creativity are, after all, at the heart of our art system's very definition of art. If, in the search for novelty, we lose sight of the core elements of our faith shared across time and space, we are in danger of actually trivializing the scope of our visual witness. What does it mean, for example, that in some parts of the Protestant world, the arts are used to brand a congregation? Is it a problem when a congregation's visual diet is meant to set it apart from every other Christian church in town, much less in the world? Working with familiar, shared symbols might seem like the antithesis of creativity. Doing it well, however, actually demands a tremendous amount of creativity. Furthermore, if all visual art is inherently local, if there is no universal Christian style, no single Christian kind of art, then looking to this inherently local art to underscore the universal elements of our Christian identity becomes even more of a creative challenge. Clearly, there is ample room for artistic innovation in our congregations. But that innovation is not the freewheeling experimentation generally lauded in our art system. It's more like the discipline of writing a sonnet. The parameters of the form itself become the source of the creativity.

Reflections for Congregations

Which primary symbols and secondary symbols are at work in your congregation's worship? Where do your worship patterns underscore the universal character of God's church, and where do they emphasize its local face? How do the arts play into these questions? These questions are complex, and ask us to engage the deep challenge that the universal/local dialectic raises, the twofold challenge of appropriately distinguishing, as best we can, in all humility, the local from the universal, as well as developing the ability to discern the universal in the local. Sometimes we mistake what is local for what is universal. I wonder, for example, if the particular late Roman/ early Christian stylistic vocabulary of Orthodox icons might not be an example of this challenge. Because that vocabulary, with a small number of regional variants, has been in place for so long, what was originally very local to a specific place and time is now taken as a universal norm. I offer this suggestion quite hesitantly, as an outsider to the Orthodox churches. I feel more confident in suggesting that too much Protestant writing on the visual arts and the church (as well as a lot of pre–Vatican II Catholic writing)[36] often takes as a universal norm our current North American understanding of "Art" with a capital *A*, when in fact this Art, with its supposed autonomy, its expressive freedom, and its apparently inherent spirituality and transcendence, is quite specific to post-Enlightenment Western culture. That position results in statements like this: "Art unearths, shakes up, keeps alive. . . . Art asks a question. . . . It is the intention of every artist to enlarge the parameters of our consciousness through an encounter with a work of art."[37] Or, art explores the "most primal and transcendental tasks" that link the human and the divine. Or, "[w]hen art is not understood as a significant component of a church's expression of itself, the vitality of the church is weakened."[38] Or this: "[t]he church doesn't have the courage of imagination that the artists have. . . . [Religion] has locked the door against imagination and the artists are sitting outside saying, I love this tradition, and I like the past, but the present really stinks. The life of the imagination is choked to death in modern religion, including Islam and Protestantism and the Roman Catholic Church."[39] Lauren Winner accurately diagnoses this problem, pointing out that such Christian apologias for art, grounded in claims for art's autonomous witness, its inherent transcendence, or its useless, "senseless beauty," in the end "obscure as much as they illuminate."[40]

---

36. See, for example, Susan White's masterful history of the Liturgical Arts Society (LAS), which was organized in 1928 and dissolved in 1972, in *Art, Architecture, and Liturgical Reform: The Liturgical Arts Society, 1928–1972* (New York: Pueblo Publishing Co., 1990). Frank Burch Brown summarizes part of White's point succinctly: LAS "fostered naive hopes for finding universally 'correct' standards of taste, it reflected class biases, and it sometimes indulged in vapid musings over the relationship between art, beauty, and divinity" (review of *Art, Architecture, and Liturgical Reform: The Liturgical Arts Society, 1928–1972*, by Susan White, *Encounter* 52 [Winter 1991]: 90–91).

37. Janet Walton, *Art and Worship: A Vital Connection* (Wilmington, DE: Michael Glazier, 1988), pp. 80–81.

38. Ibid., p. 69.

39. A prominent scholar of art and religion quoted in Amei Wallach, "Art, Religion and Spirituality: A Conversation with Artists," in *Crossroads: Art and Religion in American Life*, ed. Alberta Arthurs and Glenn Wallach (New York: Center for Arts and Culture, Henry Luce Foundation, 2001), pp. 253–54.

40. Lauren F. Winner, "Someone Who Can't Draw a Straight Line Tries to Defend Her Art-Buying Habit," in *For the Beauty of the Church: Casting a Vision for the Arts*, ed. W. David O. Taylor (Grand Rapids: Baker, 2010), pp. 80–81.

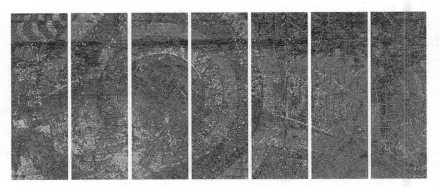

Fig. 19. John Nava, *New Jerusalem,* apse tapestry for Cathedral of Our Lady of the Angels, Los Angeles.

Nonetheless, local imagery can most certainly bear witness to the universal. Insofar as Orthodox icons attest to the reality of "the holy catholic church, the communion of saints," to quote the Apostles' Creed, their local visual vocabulary points to a universal, pan-Christian truth. Insofar as any church's local, in-house productions can orient a congregation to the story of the universal church grounded in the cosmic narrative of creation, fall, redemption, and consummation; insofar as any church's local, in-house productions point us toward the events of Christ's birth, death, and resurrection and the coming of the Spirit, that art can convey universal truths through specifically local imagery.

At this point, I can't help but think of an example from my Southern California context: the tapestries in the apse of the Cathedral of Our Lady of the Angels, in Los Angeles (fig. 19). Aligned behind the altar and the crucifix are seven woven panels called *New Jerusalem.* They superimpose the circular pattern associated with the mystical vision of the new Jerusalem onto a map of Los Angeles. Woven into the image is the text from Revelation 21:3: "See, God's dwelling is among mortals. God will dwell with them. They will be God's people and God will be with them." It's an image that captures the incarnational presence that sustains us in our local, everyday, "not yet" lives, even as we experience in worship the mystical, eschatological presence of God's holy reign, present in the worshiping church through the risen and ascended Christ.

CHAPTER 5

Story & Presence

*So that all people may know of your mighty acts
and the glorious splendor of your kingdom.*

— PSALM 145:12

A second dynamic that emerges in a side-by-side comparison of Orthodox, Roman Catholic, and Protestant ways of engaging the visual arts concerns the way in which the arts help mediate both the *story* of the faith, that is, the narrative of God's historically specific "mighty acts," and the *presence* of God in "the glorious splendor of the kingdom." As was the case with the universal and local character of the church, both story and presence are intimately connected with the fullness of our faith. Any congregation that celebrates only "God with us" and neglects to "tell the old, old story" risks sliding into presentist heresy. Any church that tells only the old, old story and fails to acknowledge the reality of God with us would eventually cease to be a church and devolve into some sort of historical society. All true churches worship diachronically, telling the story of the mighty saving acts of God throughout history; all true churches also worship synchronically, proclaiming the presence "now and forever" of Immanuel, God with us, in and through the power of the Holy Spirit.

In our limited human fashion, usually only one of these elements — story *or* presence, the timely *or* the timeless — provides the overarching framework for how worship is understood and experienced. Again, both are necessary; typically, however, one provides the lens through which the other is apprehended, and that lens focuses our expectations of what happens in worship. To use a description first offered by James White, story-oriented congregations approach worship "with hopes that it will be edifying," that "worship will provide new insights or emotions that will build one up in living a Christ-like life." Presence-oriented congregations "desire that [worship] will be sanctifying," that it will entail "being infused with Christ-likeness."[1]

Understanding the dynamics of story and presence in the worshiping life of a church often illuminates a congregation's use of the visual arts. Sometimes the arts mediate presence, sometimes they mediate story. And sometimes the visual arts are excluded from corporate worship altogether — particularly in strongly story-oriented congregations — because art is seen to invite a sense of presence that competes with or distracts from the story. In these cases, the visual arts might be very welcome in the life of the congregation, as long as they stay in the gallery or in the classroom, and out of the sanctuary on Sunday morning.

Orthodox

Orthodox worship is oriented strongly toward presence, in part, as a consequence of its ecclesiological emphasis on the eschatologically realized church universal. In Orthodox worship, one enters into the presence of God, joining in the eternal heavenly worship around the throne of God. The eternal heavenly character of the liturgy is reinforced by the myriad icons surrounding the gathered worshipers. Icons are primarily about presence. Paul Evdokimov explains that icons are "a structure through which the Other shines forth. . . . The icon expresses an energetic presence which is not localized nor enclosed but which shines out from a point of condensation." He contrasts that with the attitude of non-Orthodox churches, where, concerning images, "the accent [is] on *anamnesis,* memory, but not

---

1. James F. White, "Roman Catholic and Protestant Worship in Relationship," in *Christian Worship in North America: A Retrospective, 1955–1995* (Collegeville, MN: Liturgical Press, 1997), pp. 3–4.

on the epiphanic presence."[2] Leonid Ouspensky, according to his biographer Father Patrick Doolan, "showed in his painting and in his writing, that the essential meaning of the icon is not an intellectual construct, but rather, an encounter."[3] For Gennadios Limouris, "The icon, like the Liturgy, transcends time and is located at a perpetual 'today' — today, the first of the days remaining to us to live for eternity."[4]

Story is also present, but in Orthodox worship, even narrative can be transmuted to presence. Usually we associate narrative with words and look to Scripture to tell us our story. Bishop Ware writes, "It is sometimes thought that Orthodox attach less importance than western Christians to the Bible. Yet in fact Holy Scripture is read constantly at Orthodox services."[5] Indeed, the Orthodox lectionary, a one-year lectionary, emphasizes the four Gospels and the New Testament epistles in its schedule of readings. While the Gospel texts are very narrative in character, the epistles are often more didactic. Readings from the Old Testament do occur, but not very regularly, and even then, at services other than the regular Sunday liturgy.[6] Bishop Ware emphasizes that the liturgy itself is bathed in scriptural language; he cites 98 quotations from the Old Testament and 114 from the New.[7] Yet, those phrases, employed in the prayers, songs, and litanies of the liturgy, are excerpted from their narrative context to provide scriptural language for the worship of the eternal God. The Divine Liturgy itself, though less explicitly narrative in form than the Roman Catholic liturgy, has narrative elements. The Little Entrance and the Great Entrance, for example, are based on events in Christ's life. The Little Entrance is the movement of the Gospel books from the altar area to the sanctuary where the faithful are gathered,

---

2. Paul Evdokimov, *The Art of the Icon: A Theology of Beauty*, trans. Steven Bigham (Redondo Beach, CA: Oakwood Publications, 1990), pp. 179, 180.

3. Patrick Doolan, *Recovering the Icon: The Life and Work of Leonid Ouspensky* (Crestwood, NY: St. Vladimir's Seminary Press, 2008), p. 99.

4. Gennadios Limouris, "The Apocalyptic Character and Dimension of the Icon in the Life of the Orthodox Church," *Greek Orthodox Theological Review* 33, no. 3 (1988): 258.

5. Kallistos Ware, *The Orthodox Church,* new ed. (New York: Penguin Books, 1993), p. 201.

6. A few psalms are part of Sunday liturgy. But the Psalter as a whole is read during the Vespers and Matins liturgies, services that few Orthodox Christians who are not clergy attend.

7. Ware, *The Orthodox Church,* p. 201.

an action that represents Christ's incarnation. The Great Entrance is the action by which the eucharistic bread and wine are brought to the altar; it is understood as the triumphal entry of Christ into Jerusalem on Palm Sunday. Characteristically, though, these actions are engaged performatively, not as commemoration or memorialization.

Most tellingly, even festival icons — icons that represent moments in the Christian story (the annunciation, the nativity, and the crucifixion, for example) — like the actions of the Divine Liturgy, are understood not as illustrations, as mere remembrances of a past event, but rather as bringing the viewer into the very presence of the event. The saving deeds of God are enacted and experienced in worship, not merely remembered. As one worshiper explained, "We don't just retell the story. We relive it." Liturgical action *re*-presents events in our presence. The temporal laws of worship are not those of ordinary time. Past and future collapse into the now, into the perpetual "today" of Orthodox worship.

Roman Catholic

Presence has always been at the heart of Catholic worship, both before and after Vatican II, though with slightly different emphases. The *Constitution on the Sacred Liturgy* states clearly that God's presence is manifest in multiple ways — through the sacraments, through Scripture, and through the gathered assembly itself. Christ "is present in the sacraments, so that when a man baptizes it is really Christ Himself who baptizes. He is present in His word, since it is He Himself who speaks when the holy scriptures are read in the Church. He is present, lastly, when the Church prays and sings, for He promised: 'Where two or three are gathered together in my name, there am I in the midst of them' (Matthew 18:20)."[8] Like the Orthodox, Catholics also understand the worshiping church to be "celebrants of the heavenly liturgy."[9]

8. [Vatican Council II], *Sacrosanctum Concilium (Constitution on the Sacred Liturgy)* (Collegeville, MN: St. John's Abbey, 1963), par. 7; hereafter *Constitution*.

9. United States Catholic Conference, *Catechism of the Catholic Church*, 2nd ed. (Vatican City: Libreria Editrice Vaticana; Washington, DC: United States Catholic Conference, 2000), par. 1137.

This aspect of the liturgy — its mysterious, heavenly character — was particularly emphasized by the form of the pre–Vatican II Mass, which was not only ritually complex but also conducted largely in another language, Latin. This Tridentine Mass, as it is called, foregrounded the clergy's role and relegated the laity to contemplative, almost silent participation in worship. This gave rise to the circumstances discussed in chapter 2, where worshipers engaged in a number of private devotional practices parallel to the recital of the Mass by the clergy. Ordinary worshipers "saw the Mass as a quiet time to be alone with God while the priest did his stuff at the altar."[10]

Vatican II's concerted emphasis on "full, conscious, and active participation" was a direct attempt to remedy this situation, bringing the laity into the actions of worship and thereby lending the church's worship "new vigor to meet the circumstances and needs of modern times."[11] To that end, the council advised that its liturgical rites be revised to be "distinguished by a noble simplicity"; that the rites become "short, clear, and unencumbered by useless repetitions"; and that they meet "the people's powers of comprehension, and normally should not require much explanation."[12] This was achieved by giving churches permission to celebrate the liturgy in the local language, by simplifying the form of the liturgy, and, most importantly, by restoring to it a prominent role for Scripture and proclamation.

In simplifying the form of the liturgy, the Catholic Church exposed the underlying narrative structure of worship itself: God initiates, and we respond in confession, praise, and grateful service. The pre–Vatican II Mass was an elaborate, two-part structure (similar to that of the Orthodox Church), performed almost entirely by the clergy and their assistants around the altar. In revising the liturgy, the church transformed worship into a four-part service. New introductory rites included the entire worshiping community and created a clear, dramatic beginning to the worship event: the clergy enter in procession, carrying the Gospels. This is followed by a penitential rite performed by all present (not just the clergy) and a song of praise. After the introductory rite, the former Mass of the Catechumens became the "liturgy of the Word." The new liturgy of the Word

---

10. White, "Roman Catholic and Protestant Worship," p. 12.
11. *Constitution*, par. 4.
12. Ibid., par. 34.

increased the amount of Scripture read and mandated a sermon for all but the most exceptional circumstances. The liturgy of the Word also reintroduced congregational prayer, which had long since fallen out of use in the Tridentine Mass. The former Mass of the Faithful became the liturgy of the Eucharist, a simpler, more streamlined ceremony that augmented the actions of the clergy by requiring congregational participation. Inaudible prayers at the altar were changed to audible prayers with responses from the congregation, and the passing of the peace — which had formerly been done only by the clergy and servers at the altar — was now extended to the entire assembly. Finally, a new concluding rite provided a coherent and clear conclusion to worship, with the priest blessing the congregants and sending them out into the world. With this four-part arrangement — gathering, Word, table, sending — bookended by God's invitation at the beginning and God's blessing at the end, the Catholic Church recapitulates each Sunday the creation, fall, redemption, and consummation narrative of Scripture in the form of the liturgy.

Beyond the revision of the liturgy's form, however, the most remarkable achievement of Vatican II was its renewed attention to the centrality of Scripture for the worshiping church. In the language of the *Constitution on the Sacred Liturgy*, "The treasures of the bible are to be opened up more lavishly, so that richer fare may be provided for the faithful at the table of God's word. In this way a more representative portion of the holy scriptures will be read to the people in the course of a prescribed number of years."[13] Prior to Vatican II, the Catholic Church (like the Orthodox Church) used a one-year cycle of readings from the Gospels and Epistles; readings from the Old Testament were occasional and specified for services other than Sunday worship. After Vatican II, the Catholic Church developed a three-year lectionary that specified a psalm and a passage from the Old Testament as well as Epistle and Gospel readings for each Sunday. The Old Testament in particular needed restoration to the church's worship because, in the words of the *Catechism*: "Since Christ's Church was 'prepared in marvelous fashion in the history of the people of Israel and in the Old Covenant,' the Church's liturgy has retained certain elements of the worship of the Old Covenant as integral and irreplaceable, adopting them as her own: notably, reading the

13. Ibid., par. 51.

Old Testament; praying the Psalms; above all, recalling the saving events and significant realities which have found their fulfillment in the mystery of Christ (promise and covenant, Exodus and Passover, kingdom and temple, exile and return)."[14] The church finds its story not in the New Testament alone, but in the fulfillment of the Old Testament in the New.

And not only is Scripture to be read, it is to be proclaimed. Prior to Vatican II, a sermon was optional. After Vatican II, a sermon, rendered "with exactitude and fidelity," was required for all but a few extraordinary occasions, and "its character should be that of a proclamation of God's wonderful works in the history of salvation, the mystery of Christ, ever made present and active within us, especially in the celebration of the liturgy."[15]

The shape and clarity of the revised liturgy, together with a renewed emphasis on Scripture and proclamation, amplified the narrative character of Catholic worship. While worship still makes present the mystery of Christ and makes out of the liturgical assembly a "communion of faith," worship is also an act of *anamnesis* — of remembering God's saving events in history.[16] In comparison to the pre–Vatican II liturgy, in post–Vatican II worship the tension between the "already" and the "not yet" tilts a bit more clearly toward the "not yet." Note the language used to describe the liturgy in the *Constitution on the Sacred Liturgy*: "In the earthly liturgy we take part in a *foretaste* of that heavenly liturgy which is celebrated in the holy city of Jerusalem *toward which we journey* as pilgrims, where Christ is sitting at the right hand of God, a minister of the holies and of the true tabernacle; we sing a hymn to the Lord's glory with all the warriors of the heavenly army; venerating the *memory* of the saints, we *hope* for some part and fellowship with them; we eagerly *await* the Saviour, Our Lord Jesus Christ, until He, our life, shall appear and we too will appear with Him in glory."[17] Though we taste the fullness of God's kingdom in worship, we remain in a position of anticipation, of longing, and of hope for its consummation. We are not yet entirely there.

Simplifying the liturgy, accenting the Word, and underscoring the story of God's pilgrim people led to a reconceptualization of the role of the vi-

14. *Catechism*, par. 1093.
15. *Constitution*, par. 35.
16. *Catechism*, pars. 1100–1103.
17. *Constitution*, par. 8 (emphasis mine).

sual arts in worship. As recounted in chapter 2, Catholic sanctuaries before Vatican II had often communicated the mystery of holy presence through multiple statues or paintings of Jesus, Mary, and the saints with their side altars and banks of votive candles. After Vatican II, many of these elements were seen instead as distractions to the worshiping faithful, interfering with "full, conscious, and active participation" in the liturgy. Congregations were encouraged to move devotional imagery to the back of the sanctuary. Churches that before Vatican II had a tabernacle for the consecrated host on the main altar, after Vatican II often created a separate space for the tabernacle in some other prominent place in the sanctuary. This was meant to help emphasize the presence of Christ in the Word and in the gathered assembly, not only in the consecrated host. In place of devotional paintings, statues, and the eucharistic tabernacle, the visual qualities of the worship space itself were to help communicate "God with us": the spatial arrangement of the sanctuary, the placement of the altar and pulpit, the baptistery, the processional cross, and the Gospel books were to help represent the reality of God with us.

In addition to careful attention to architecture and to liturgical furniture, and the existence of a small number of liturgical objects, the art deemed most appropriate for the sanctuary became seasonal rather than devotional — keyed to the changing seasons of the church year. The church year is, of course, a narrative framework. Perhaps part of the "piety void" experienced by many Catholics was not so much a void as an unfamiliar shift in emphasis. The arts did not disappear altogether. They were, however, radically redirected. Whereas the pre–Vatican II liturgy and typical church sanctuary used the lens of presence to make sense of story, the postconciliar church redirected the use of the arts to emphasize story as much as presence, recognizing each as necessary for a robust expression of faith and worship.

Protestant

At this point, you may be wondering why I've been using "story" and "presence" rather than the more conventional dyad of "word" and "image" in my analysis. To some extent, story and presence align themselves to words and images, but that's really too neat. Even in the short discussions above, we've seen that images and visual environments can tell stories and that, for Christians, *Word* properly understood is most certainly a manifestation of holy presence. The word/image formulation has its roots in the Protestant Reformation. As such, it has buried within it a specious opposition, a suspicion of images as inherently ambiguous (as if words are always entirely straightforward), an assumption that words and images compete for our attention, that they operate in some sort of zero-sum theological field, that you either value the one *or* the other — to your peril.

It's a distinctly Protestant starting point for understanding the place of images in the church, and sometimes it obscures more than it reveals. Confident of their firm orientation to word, for example, Protestants have been blind to the myriad ways in which images circulate in their churches, ministries, and homes.[18] More importantly, the "word and image" formula tends to point us in essentialist directions — focusing our attention on words and images per se, on how they differ from one another (or less commonly, on how they are similar). Story and presence point us in a different direction. Story and presence help us notice the specific *expectations* within which words and images are received, used, and understood. Rather than trying to define the word relative to the image, we can look instead to *what words and images are doing* in our congregations. This allows us not only to see more clearly that some churches welcome images more than others, but to understand what those images are doing in and for that church.

Story and presence go together. As I stated above, the one without the other is at best an incomplete expression of the depth and richness of the Christian faith. At worst, it is outright heresy. Even though at the time of the Reformation, Martin Luther, John Calvin, John Knox, and, later, John Wesley paid close attention to the dynamics of story and presence, their heirs have not always been so careful. Today, Protestants — and here I'm speaking as a Protestant — with our Reformation heritage and our confi-

18. See, for example, the earlier work of David Morgan on the ways in which Protestants have consistently used — and overlooked their use of — the visual arts: *Visual Piety: A History and Theory of Popular Religious Images* (Berkeley: University of California Press, 1998); *Protestants and Pictures: Religion, Visual Culture, and the Age of American Mass Production* (Oxford: Oxford University Press, 1999); the volume edited with Sally M. Promey, *The Visual Culture of American Religions* (Berkeley: University of California Press, 2001); and the edited volume *Icons of American Protestantism: The Art of Warner Sallman* (New Haven: Yale University Press, 1996).

dence in our dedication to God's Word, have not always been attentive to the play of story and presence in our churches. The result? Story sometimes receives less attention than we would guess, and presence has shown up in some unexpected ways. Thoughtful attention to the potential of story and presence could, in fact, help us sort through some of our challenges in engaging the visual arts.

Whereas Orthodox and Catholic worship offer the experience of God's presence most clearly in the sacraments — especially the sacrament of the Eucharist — Protestant churches generally understand themselves to be oriented primarily toward Scripture as the mediator of God's living presence with us. In summarizing the views of a number of theologians, in his explication of the herald model for the church, Avery Dulles explains how, in this view, "Christian proclamation is therefore to be understood as a linguistic event in which the body of Christ is constituted and assembled."[19] He continues, "The word is [an] eschatological occurrence — that is to say, it makes God present here and now, giving life to those who accept it and death to those who refuse."[20] The encounter with God that Orthodox and Catholics experience most often through the Eucharist, Protestants expect to experience through proclamation. Though Luther, Calvin, and Wesley had a very high regard for the sacraments as means of God's gracious presence in our lives, the Word nonetheless stood central. "Thus," as church historian James White writes, "Sunday worship without the sacrament could be tolerated but Sunday worship without a sermon could not."[21]

But sermon is not necessarily story. In our discussion of the Catholic recovery of the Word after Vatican II, we noted several practices that reinforced the experience of story in worship in addition to the renewed emphasis on preaching: the four-part structure for worship that provides a clear narrative arc for the service as a whole; a lectionary that makes use of vast swaths of Scripture over the course of three years, including the Psalms and the other books of the Old Testament; renewed attention to the seasons of the liturgical year, which in themselves situate each worship service in a larger narrative arc. Lutheran and Anglican churches never rejected the

19. Avery Dulles, *Models of the Church* (Garden City, NY: Image Books, 1987), p. 72.
20. Dulles, *Models of the Church*, pp. 73–74.
21. James F. White, "Liturgical Reformation: Sixteenth Century and Twentieth," in *Christian Worship in North America: A Retrospective, 1955–1995*, p. 37.

lectionary or the church year, but most other ecclesial heirs of the Reformation did, substituting in its place the practice of *lectio continua* ("continuous reading"). With *lectio continua*, the sermon text becomes the primary locus for the reading of Scripture in worship, and the selection of texts is left to the pastor's discretion, thereby eliminating the need for a lectionary and any subsequent attention to the church year.[22] In many Protestant churches today, the only Scripture read in worship is the sermon text, which might amount to only a handful of verses. Without careful attention, it is easy for pastors to gravitate toward a particular biblical genre, a few favorite books (often from the New Testament), or a range of particular themes, neglecting the full scope of the Christian story. In churches with a heavy diet of topical preaching, story can easily be lost within a welter of "issues" if it is not reinforced by a lavish use of Scripture elsewhere in the service or supported by narrative liturgical structures — the shape of the service or the church year — that help tell our Christian story.

If the sermon, on its own, is not necessarily a robust encounter with story, neither is it always a medium of presence. Though committed in theory to the presence of God mediated by his Word, many Protestant churches diminish their sense of God's presence in the Word by conceptualizing the sermon as teaching. Teaching, rather than proclamation, is an activity that certainly *informs* us but does not necessarily *form* and *reform* us.[23] Explanation of historical context, attention to ancient language, exposition of doctrinal import — all these are laudable and worthy. But if they are not ultimately "good news," then the gospel has not been proclaimed. The proclamation of God's Word is not just teaching (though it certainly contains teaching). It is an encounter with the transformative presence of God in Christ through the power of the Holy Spirit.[24] It is the means through which

22. White, "Liturgical Reformation," p. 37. Some churches in the Reformed tradition, however, maintained the practice of psalm singing, which added considerably to the amount of Scripture encountered in worship. They also encouraged pastors to preach through a catechism at one of their Sunday services, which created a kind of alternate, doctrinally themed lectionary.

23. James K. A. Smith's exploration of culture, liturgy, and narrative in *Desiring the Kingdom: Worship, Worldview, and Cultural Formation* (Grand Rapids: Baker Academic, 2009), and *Imagining the Kingdom: How Worship Works* (Grand Rapids: Baker Academic, 2013), provides an extensive philosophical and sociological argument to support exactly this point.

24. Paul Scott Wilson, "Preaching as God's Event," *Vision* 10, no. 1 (Spring 2009): 12–19.

"[h]uman propositions can become the word of God."[25] Paul Scott Wilson writes of proclamation:

> The words of the gospel need to be inspired by the Holy Spirit, shaped for the individual time and place, prepared for by solid teaching in the sermon as one might prepare caringly for dinner guests, such that these precious words are heard to be spoken by God: "I love you. I died for you. I will not let you go. I forgive you. Come to me, all of you that are weary and heavy-laden, and I will give you rest. Take heart! Do not be afraid! Your faith has made you well. I am your Shepherd. Let not your hearts be troubled; neither let them be afraid. Well done, my good and faithful servant. I am with you to the end of the age. This is my body, broken for you. This is my blood, poured out for you." . . . The gospel is thus performed, and it transforms communities in the cruciform image of Christ.[26]

An index of a church's understanding of the sermon as proclamation and presence, and not just teaching, might be the use (or not) of a prayer for illumination before reading the text and preaching the sermon. The prayer for illumination is an act of worship that performs our relationship to Scripture, demonstrating our trust that "[t]he power of God's Word comes not from the ink and paper of our printed Bibles or from the creative rhetoric of a preacher, but from the work of the Holy Spirit."[27] In addition, "The prayer for illumination explicitly acknowledges the Spirit's work in this part of worship by requesting God's Spirit to act through the reading and preaching of Scripture."[28] Offered before the proclamation of the word, this prayer parallels the *epiclesis*, the prayer for the work of the Holy Spirit offered before communion. Together, the prayer for illumination before proclamation and the prayer for the work of the Holy Spirit before communion demonstrate the reciprocity between Word and table and acknowledge

---

25. Dulles, *Models of the Church*, p. 72.

26. Paul Scott Wilson, *Setting Words on Fire: Putting God at the Center of the Sermon* (Nashville: Abingdon, 2008), p. 81.

27. *The Worship Sourcebook* (Grand Rapids: Calvin Institute of Christian Worship, Faith Alive Christian Resources, and Baker Books, 2004), p. 139.

28. *The Worship Sourcebook*, p. 139.

the gracious action of the Holy Spirit, who brings us into union with God and one another.[29]

Protestants place an extraordinarily heavy burden on the Protestant sermon (and therefore on the pastor) when they tacitly expect it, single-handedly, to act as the only medium for both story and presence in worship. When the pastor is not a gifted preacher, worship as a whole is experienced as lacking. When the pastor is a gifted preacher, the congregation can some-times mistake the messenger for the message itself. The personality-driven church is, after all, almost an entirely Protestant phenomenon. The chal-lenge is even greater in Protestant churches with a two-part pattern for Sunday worship. A two-part structure generally consists of worship (that is to say, singing) followed by teaching. Two-part services may have few or no introductory or concluding elements, which obscures the narrative structure of worship, and they often practice infrequent or idiosyncratic celebration of the sacraments. It's no surprise, then, that the longing for presence finds an outlet elsewhere — most often in our experience of song. I would not be the first to observe that for many Protestant Christians, the closest thing to weekly communion might be singing. Music can help us experience God's presence. And songs can help tell us our story. But as pow-erful and true and moving and encouraging as music in worship can be, unless a church restricts itself entirely to biblical song (however that may be defined) and receives that song as proclamation, singing does not substitute for the specially privileged role of Word and sacrament.

But this is not a study of music in the church. This is an attempt to better understand the role that the visual arts play, and might play, in our churches. For Protestants, the visual arts in worship will probably never convey presence as icons do for the Orthodox without a radical and unlikely shift in liturgical theology. With the typical Protestant emphasis on the local congregation rather than the universal church, and the commitment to "presence" mediated through the proclamation of the Word, the forms and practices of much Protestant worship do not provide the theological or liturgical armature that allows icons to function as they do in Orthodoxy — as nonidolatrous mediators of holy presence. Even if we filled our Protestant

29. Alvin Hoksbergen, "Shedding Light on the Prayer of Illumination," *Reformed Worship* 52 (July 1999): 20–21.

sanctuaries with icons, we would not encounter them *as* icons, as dynamic partners in worship. We'd be more likely to see them as illustrations or, even worse, as decoration.[30]

All six art-committed Protestant congregations briefly described in chapter 3 understood the visual arts to be an important part of their identity, mission, and witness. But only two had regular practices that integrated the visual arts into Sunday worship. Both of those congregations tied the arts to story. At Church of the Servant, the visuals interpret the liturgical year, a framework for, in the words of their pastor, "remembering the mighty acts of God in Christ, and how we are the benefactors of these acts — remembering our place in the great story." In explaining the role of the arts in worship, he continued, "Art expresses what happens in worship. All week we live with ideas and understandings from the world around us, but in worship we are reconstituted as God's people. Art helps us visualize that difference."[31] Similarly, at Covenant Life, the visual arts serve to help interpret either a season of the church year or a specific sermon series. Insofar as the visual arts in these churches must engage more than a single sermon, must help interpret a larger theme in the life of the church, and must remain present for several weeks or several months, they have space and time to transcend simple decoration, illustration, and didacticism. They become embedded in the formative and reformative dynamics of corporate worship.

For the four other churches in our sample, engagement with the visual arts is less about story or presence than it is an expression of mission. Though Mars Hill recently introduced a large ArtPrize painting into its worship space, that painting is not a focal point for worship. In fact, it is at the back of "the Shed," out of the sight lines of almost all worshipers. The painting does not express story, and it certainly is not meant to mediate presence. It is a sign of mission, a reminder and a stimulus to engage with

30. For more on the problem of trivial uses of the arts, see Robin M. Jensen, "Beyond the Decorative and Didactic: The Uses of Art in the Church," which is chapter 4 in *The Substance of Things Seen: Art, Faith, and the Christian Community* (Grand Rapids: Eerdmans, 2004), pp. 75–100. For an explication of the resilience of the "imaginative traditions" that frame our encounters with the arts in worship, see William Dyrness's *Senses of the Soul: Art and the Visual in Christian Worship* (Eugene, OR: Cascade Books, 2008), especially pp. 161–70.

31. Interview with Rev. Jack Roeda, June 30, 2004. Interestingly, at the time of this interview, one of the most beloved seasonal paraments at Church of the Servant was an enormous, horizontal Pentecost banner featuring just the eyes of a Byzantine, mosaic Christ.

the visual arts *outside* the church, to look for the activity of God in the world around us.[32] Likewise, Mars Hill's elegant website and "cultural plunges," Orchard Hill's Arts Camp on the Hill, and the collections and exhibition programs at Fountain Street and First United Methodist are expressions of — and extensions of — each church's sense of its place and mission in the world. Few members of those congregations would look to the arts first and foremost as key mediators of the Christian story or as reliable mediators of God's presence with us. Rather, they would understand the visual arts as important vehicles for God-given creativity — and as such, a worthy arena for congregational witness and service.

Engaging with the visual arts in these ways becomes a way of enacting the servant model of the church that, reminding ourselves of Dulles's definition, "takes the world as a properly theological locus and seeks to discern the signs of the times" and "seeks to operate on the frontier between the contemporary world and the Christian tradition."[33] Taking the world as a properly theological locus, we also take it on its own terms, looking for God's leading and God's actions in the world as we find it. For the visual arts, that means taking the assumptions, the practices, and the commitments of our larger art system on their own terms. Primary among those commitments is our art system's commitment to "Art" with a capital *A*, to Art as an autonomous cultural realm with its own logic, its own authority, and its own integrity, which should not be subordinated to any aims other than its own. Collecting art, exhibiting art, teaching art — these are the core practices of our art system. When churches engage in these practices, they meet Art on its native ground. Congregations may tweak the practices a bit — collect and exhibit art made by church members, or collect and exhibit art exploring certain themes near and dear to the mission of the congregation, or teach art such that we link creative self-expression to the *imago Dei* — but none of these inflections challenge the norms of the system. When we collect and exhibit and teach, we affirm the goodness and the truth to be found in our art system. We build bridges that connect congregations to community in vital ways. We invigorate our

---

32. As one Mars Hill staff person stated, their approach to worship is "'less is more' and 'not in here, but out there'" (personal communication, July 23, 2013).

33. Dulles, *Models of the Church*, p. 84.

congregations with new perspectives and refreshing, sometimes challenging experiences.

But in collecting and exhibiting and teaching along these lines, we may also subtly reinforce the norms of our art system, norms that erect potential barriers between Art and church. Insofar as we imagine Art as a medium of individual self-expression, Art will sit awkwardly in the midst of our communal worship or reinforce whatever privatized, individualistic practices we already take to worship. Insofar as we imagine Art as autonomous, subordinating it to story makes us uncomfortable — as if we are asking Art to be merely illustrative or didactic, something less than it truly is. Insofar as we imagine Art as inherently spiritual and transcendent, we might accept it as a parallel mode of holy presence, turning the twinned pair of Word and sacrament into a triplet — Word, sacrament, and Art. Or, conversely, we might reject Art as a rival to Word and sacrament. Integrating Art into the worshiping church turns out to be a complex negotiation.

The felt need to accommodate Art on its own terms within the church is a uniquely Protestant challenge. It's not a challenge Orthodox churches face because icons are not Art and allow no Art. It's a challenge the Catholic Church faced at midcentury and legislated with church teachings that clearly subordinated Art to the purposes of worship, chastening it and channeling it toward specific roles that underscore story and presence in the liturgy. Catholic and Orthodox congregations remain entirely free to host exhibitions, to collect Art, or to offer instruction should they choose to. The Cathedral of Saint Andrew in downtown Grand Rapids, for example, also serves as an ArtPrize venue. Engagement with Art is entirely licit. But for both Catholic and Orthodox, it's clear that there is no direct, assumed connection between Art and the actions of corporate worship.

Protestant churches, on the other hand, with all their latitude and freedom to engage Art, have few internal resources to bring to the task and find themselves in a paradoxical position. An ecclesial orientation to the local congregation in its local context at once frees many Protestants from tight adherence to confessional identity or denomination or tradition while opening congregations up to the dynamics of the surrounding world. Convinced of Art's power and value, yet unconstrained by any ecclesial covenants with Art, we Protestants are left to negotiate with Art on its own terms. Thus, we look around for patterns and practices; we discover, mostly, the art museum, the gallery, the classroom, and the marketplace. And we welcome Art into our galleries and collections and classrooms and onto our websites where we know what we are dealing with. It's clear why it is there. We know how to receive it in these contexts and are able to embrace it as mission and witness. But sensing, perhaps, the potential disconnect between how we engage with Art in the gallery and what we do in worship, many of us find it more challenging to welcome Art, unbaptized, so to speak, into the sanctuary. We may, in fact, feel confused by our hesitation. As art lovers, we may not even be able to fully articulate the roots of our reluctance. But this is not philistinism. It is not hostility. It is not iconoclasm. It is an act of Christian discernment. It is, in truth, a hesitant gesture of wisdom.

"Worship painting," for example, is one method some Protestant congregations have tried in their desire to connect the visual arts to congregational worship. Worship painting typically occurs during the sermon, which aligns it with the presence-orientation of the proclaimed Word. The assumption that connects painting to preaching is the powerful idea of inspiration. It's not always clear, however, how artistic inspiration and spiritual inspiration relate to one another in the process of worship painting. Who is doing the inspiring? Is the Holy Spirit inspiring everyone — the preacher and the painter and the gathered faithful in their reception? Do the painter and the preacher each provide inspired responses to God's Word? Do the sermon and the painting have equal status as proclamation? Or — more likely — is the preacher inspiring the painter? If the preacher is inspiring the painter, is the painter's visual response meant to represent a collective or an individual response? If the painter's response is meant to encompass the entire congregation, how is that happening? If the painter's response is simply the painter's personal response, how does that facilitate corporate worship? How, exactly, does worship painting work? Without careful planning, execution, and follow-up, worship painting is prone to unwittingly collapse the Western, historically specific idea of artistic inspiration into the Christian idea of divine inspiration. In so doing, worship painting reaches toward the kind of authority and presence that Orthodox icons enjoy but without any of the ecclesial practices or theological frameworks that situate icons very precisely in relation to Scripture and liturgy. This is not to argue that worship painting can't be done, only that it needs to be done carefully, with a clear sense of why, how, and for whom it is being done.

Reflections for Congregations

How do story and presence play out in your congregational worship? Is one more easily discerned than the other? How? Where? Is one the lens through which the other is experienced? Perhaps both are woven into the structure of your worship but show up in unusual, idiosyncratic ways. How do the visual arts contribute to the ways in which you and your congregation encounter God's presence and God's story in worship?

Orthodoxy has the most stable, enduring liturgical framework for enacting both story and presence. In Orthodox worship, story becomes a manifestation of presence. Icons play a pivotal role, enacting these dynamics within the Orthodox liturgy. Lacking the Orthodox covenant with icons, however, it is impossible for non-Orthodox congregations to simply appropriate the use of icons to create a sense of God's presence and God's story in worship. Non-Orthodox Christians may admire icons, may even find them inspiring foci for their own personal devotions, but short of conversion, icons will always be some species of art rather than a species of holy revelation. Non-Orthodox congregations will have to look elsewhere, should they want to enhance story or presence in their worship through the visual arts.

Some Protestant churches have looked to the Catholics for guidance. The use of the visual arts in worship at Church of the Servant and at Covenant Life Church, for example, takes its cue from Vatican II. The four-part structure for worship that the Catholic Church adopted after Vatican II and that, through the liturgical movement, became the pattern for many Protestant congregations as well is basically a dramatic, story-shaped framework for worship. The opening act emphasizes God's gracious invitation to know and love him and our response to that invitation in praise and confession. These liturgical movements evoke creation, fall, and covenant. The next movement of the service emphasizes God's gracious self-revelation in the Word. The third act involves the lifting of our hearts in thanksgiving as we receive God's gracious gift of bread and wine at the table. These elements of the service evoke the journey of God's people through the promises of the Old Testament into the life, death, and resurrection of Christ in the New. The final act of the service returns us, fed and blessed, into the world, equipped to do God's work, evoking the coming consummation of Christ's kingdom. Every week, the back-and-forth movement of such a service —

God acts and we respond — reenacts the pattern of God's activity in human history, enfolding our small stories within God's larger story, from creation to consummation. How distinct is each of these acts in your congregation's worship? Would more careful attention to your congregation's patterns of worship deepen its ability to inhabit God's story? Are there ways in which artists could help mark and interpret this narrative arc?

Perhaps your congregation is heir to what church historian James White calls the frontier tradition of free-church worship and therefore uses a two- or three-part structure for worship.[34] Two-part structures typically involve a time identified as worship, usually enacted through singing, followed by a substantial sermon, often identified as teaching. Three part-services conclude with an altar call. In two- and three-part liturgies, the overall emphasis is often less oriented toward story than toward presence. The overall structure of the service is meant to create a space for worshipers to experience a life-changing encounter with God. In this respect, some free-church and charismatic congregations share the presence-oriented character of the Orthodox liturgy. Where, then, is there space for the narrative elements of Christian worship to come to the fore? If the basic liturgical pattern is not narrative, perhaps, as the Orthodox Church ably demonstrates, congregations with presence-oriented liturgical patterns can still bear witness to the great story of God's redeeming acts by making use of the church year.

Renewed appreciation for the church year, like renewed appreciation for the narrative shape of the four-part worship service, is also one of the gifts that flowed from the liturgical renewal movement. The seasons of Advent, Christmastide, and Epiphany, followed by Lent, Eastertide, Pentecost, and the long stretch of so-called ordinary time, provide yet another story-oriented structure through which churches can see their work and worship as part of God's story. The seasons of the church year also provide an ideal focus for the visual arts. Whether a congregation uses traditional vestments and paraments, banners and bulletins, or projected imagery, there is ample room here for the visual arts to signal our movement through the stories of Christ's birth, ministry, and death, and onward into the Spirit's continuing work in the church. Additionally, the church year connects congregations to the fellowship of churches around the world who are observing the same

---

34. White, *Christian Worship in North America*, pp. 105–14.

seasons. This also works toward helping a congregation appreciate the universality of the church.

Visualizing the seasons of the church year is a natural link to the visual arts. As a result, it is all too easy to purchase mass-manufactured sets of paraments or banners or find stock digital images to fulfill this task. But hopefully, given the opportunity and offered proper support, the artists in your congregation would be honored to lend their skills to the task. Beyond the sanctuary, however, many art-committed Protestant churches, like Fountain Street Church and First United Methodist, like Orchard Hill and Mars Hill, will continue to find it entirely natural and purposeful to engage Art as an extension of mission, accepting Art on its own terms, and encountering it via exhibitions and galleries and classrooms.

CHAPTER 6

Public Worship & Private Devotion

Personal prayer is possible only in the context of the community. Nobody is a Christian by himself, but only as a member of the body.

— GEORGES FLOROVSKY[1]

Indeed, many [Protestant] respondents did not in fact think first about the Sunday service at all when asked about their sense of worship.

— WILLIAM DYRNESS[2]

I did not expect to end up thinking about public and private in pursuing the question of how Christians have encountered the visual arts in the life of the church. That's probably because as a modern, Western, American, and, especially, Protestant Christian, I've been strongly and effectively socialized to imagine and experience both religion and art as largely private.

My sense of what is public and what is private forms the background context of my living and thinking. I'm rarely made aware of their operations. The fact that we have to call public art "public art," for example, exposes

1. Georges Florovsky, *Prayer: Private and Corporate* (Saint Louis: Ologos Publications, 1960), p. 3.
2. William Dyrness, *Senses of the Soul: Art and the Visual in Christian Worship* (Eugene, OR: Cascade Books, 2008), p. 24.

our normative assumption that our engagement with "Art" with a capital *A* is essentially individual, personal, and private. It's no surprise, then, that our most spectacular cultural arguments about Art have to do with what is permitted in venues understood to be "public." Likewise, arguments about the role of religion in American society turn on contested notions of what is properly private or properly public in American life. In both cases, the terms of the debate assume and perform the distinction, even as the results of such discussions often expose the frustrating limits of public and private as definitive categories for the analysis of religion or art in contemporary society.

If Art is a modern Western idea, with roots in the eighteenth-century Enlightenment, so too are current understandings of "public" and "private."[3] Historians have explored the emergence of public and private with respect to any number of social developments: the evolution of domestic architecture and city planning; the practices of letter writing and journalism; the development of specific notions of femininity and masculinity; and in the shift from the idea of people as subjects to the idea of people as citizens.[4] Entire worlds of association cluster around, underneath, and within our ideas of public and private. For "public," the public sphere, public service, the public square, civility, politics, the realm of facts, the market, and the world of work all come to mind. "Private" gives rise to notions of privacy, private property, private space, personal space, personal experience, interiority, domesticity, subjectivity, opinion, and individuality.

Public and private structure one another. One can't be private if there is no public, and vice versa. The reciprocity of private and public is built into

3. Two key texts for this discussion are the five volumes of *History of Private Life*, edited by Phillippe Ariés and Georges Duby et al. (Cambridge, MA: Harvard University Press, 1987–1991), and Jürgen Habermas's *The Structural Transformation of the Public Sphere: An Enquiry into a Category of Bourgeois Society*, trans. Thomas Burger with the assistance of Frederick Lawrence (Cambridge, MA: MIT Press, 1989). Harold Mah offers a summary and critique of historians' use of Habermas's theory in "Phantasies of the Public Sphere: Rethinking the Habermas of Historians," *Journal of Modern History* 72, no. 1 (March 2000): 153–82.

4. For examples of work in each of these areas, see Diana Webb, *Privacy and Solitude: The Medieval Discovery of Personal Space* (London: Continuum, 2007); Angela VanHaelen and Joseph P. Ward, eds., *Making Space Public in Early Modern Europe: Performance, Geography, Privacy* (New York and London: Routledge, 2013); Hannah Barker and Simon Burrows, eds., *Press, Politics, and the Public Sphere in Europe and North America, 1760–1820* (Cambridge: Cambridge University Press, 2002); James H. Kettner, *Development of American Citizenship, 1608–1870* (Chapel Hill: University of North Carolina Press, 1978).

Jürgen Habermas's famous definition of "public sphere": "The bourgeois public sphere may be conceived above all as the sphere of private people coming together as a public."[5]

Insisting on the historicity of Art is not to believe that no one made paintings or sculptures — not to mention stained-glass windows or illuminated manuscripts — before the eighteenth century. Similarly, insisting on the historicity of our contemporary experience of public and private is not to believe that prior to the eighteenth century, people never spent time alone or gathered together in shared spaces around shared activities. Far from it. It is to insist, however, that the *meaning* of being alone and being together, like the meaning of making a painting or sculpture, has not always been the same. Acknowledging the historicity of elements of my experience means that what I take for granted as perfectly obvious would not have seemed perfectly obvious to people who lived long before me, nor will it necessarily be taken for granted by people living elsewhere in the world today. "Art," "public," and "private" are historically and culturally relative terms.

Roman Catholic

The need to consider the meaning of public and private emerged in my attempt to understand the Catholic, post–Vatican II discussion about the relationship between public liturgy and private devotion with respect to the role of the visual arts in Catholic contexts. Hence, this chapter is ordered a bit differently, beginning with a discussion of the Catholic situation rather than the Orthodox context. The Second Vatican Council's strong emphasis on the "full, conscious, and active participation" of the gathered worshipers underscores the aim of corporate worship as an experience of *incorporation*, of being united in Christ as the "people of God." This emphasis was crucial, because the pre–Vatican II liturgy, it was thought, had come to be experienced as an affair of the clergy, leaving parishioners to sit in the pews engaging in personal, private devotion — a gathering of people, sitting side by side, each absorbed in individual religious experience, often facilitated by images found in the sanctuary.

5. Habermas, *Structural Transformation*, p. 27.

The concern articulated by the council, however, necessarily assumes particular meanings for public and private. And these assumed meanings, it turns out, have been a sticking point in the post–Vatican II debates about the role of devotion relative to the liturgy. In the years following the *Constitution on the Sacred Liturgy* and then *Environment and Art in Catholic Worship*, and especially after the publication in 2002 of the Vatican's *Directory on Popular Piety and the Liturgy: Principles and Guidelines*, Catholic scholars began to see the "problem with devotion" less as a problem with devotion per se and more as a manifestation of the challenge of inculturation. On the question of devotion, the Vatican documents, even while striving to speak to the worldwide Catholic communion, filtered their analysis of devotional practices through a Western, post-Enlightenment interpretive framework of what is public and what is private.

The term used most frequently in Vatican documents to discuss devotion is not "private devotion" but "popular devotion." As a term, "popular devotion" clearly points to the origin of these practices in the common life of local Christian communities. So far, so good. But popular devotion is most often contrasted in the documents to public worship and public prayer, by which is meant the Divine Liturgy. Contrasting popular devotion to public worship implies at once that popular devotion is not public, and that the liturgy is not popular (in its basic sense of being "of the people"). The language uncovers a tangle of fascinating questions.

This section from the *Directory on Popular Piety and the Liturgy* exposes some of the challenges:

> Indeed, "every liturgical celebration, because it is an action of Christ the Priest and of his Body, which is the Church, . . . is a sacred action surpassing all others. No other action of the Church can equal its efficacy by the same title or to the same degree" (SC 16). Hence, the ambivalence that the Liturgy is not "popular" must be overcome. The liturgical renewal of the council set out to promote the participation of the people in the celebration of the Liturgy, at certain times and places (through hymns, active participation, and lay ministries), which had previously given rise to forms of prayer alternative to, or substitutive of, the liturgical action itself. The faithful should be made conscious of the preeminence of the Liturgy over any other possible form of legitimate Christian prayer. While sacramental

actions are *necessary* to life in Christ, the various forms of popular piety are properly *optional.*[6]

This passage begins with a quote from the *Constitution* describing the liturgy as an action of Christ and the church universal: "every liturgical celebration, because it is an action of Christ the Priest and of his Body, which is the Church, . . . is a sacred action surpassing all others. No other action of the Church can equal its efficacy by the same title or to the same degree."[7] It then asserts that as such, the liturgy is inherently popular. Technically speaking, this is correct. The liturgy is "of the people." But this is not the sense in which "popular" is used throughout the documents. Most uses of the term "popular" in the *Constitution* and the *Directory* actually mean "local"; that is, "popular" is an expression of a regional or national culture within the Catholic Church. Popular practices in West Africa, we are to understand, will be different from popular practices in Maritime Canada. The insistence that the liturgy is popular because it is a manifestation of the church universal, but that local forms of popular devotion are always subordinate and secondary to the liturgy, obscures rather than illuminates the relationship between the universal and the local.

The *Directory* then continues with a one-sentence summary of the aims of liturgical reform — "to promote the participation of the people in the celebration of the Liturgy" — followed by a brief description of the conditions that necessitated reform — the rise of "forms of prayer alternative to, or substitutive of, the liturgical action itself." The description, though, is more apt for the European and North American church than for other parts of the Catholic communion. Mark Francis and John Empereur have pointed out that popular devotion as practiced in post-Enlightenment Europe and North America did indeed have many private aspects to it. Francis has suggested that this particular form of devotional practice, marked by individualism, subjectivity, and privacy, be called "European devotionalism."

---

6. *Directory on Popular Piety and the Liturgy: Principles and Guidelines* (Strathfield, Australia: St. Pauls Publications, 2002), par. 11. The "SC" in the quotation refers to *Sacrosanctum Concilium,* or *Constitution on the Sacred Liturgy.*

7. *The Constitution on the Sacred Liturgy of the Second Vatican Council and The Motu Proprio of Pope Paul VI with a Commentary by Gerard S. Sloyan* (Glen Rock, NJ: Paulist, 1964), par. 16; hereafter *Constitution.*

Recognizing European devotionalism as a particular, local form of popular devotion would make it easier for the Catholic Church as a whole to see the popular devotional practices of Catholics in other parts of the world as distinct from the typical European manifestation and not necessarily characterized by Western individualism and privatization — and therefore not necessarily problematic in relation to the celebration of the liturgy.[8]

The implicit public worship/private devotion distinction in these post–Vatican II documents exposes a genuine concern — the concern at the heart of the liturgical reform — of bringing individual worshipers into communion with Christ via the liturgical actions of the gathered assembly. But the implicit public worship/private devotion distinction also gives rise to additional challenges embedded in the very terms in which the distinction is drawn. What is a "public," other than a gathering of essentially "private" individuals — as Habermas's definition clearly indicates? "Public" does not necessarily entail unity, or commonality, or shared identity. For Habermas, in fact, the "public sphere" was understood primarily as a political space for individual expression, debate, contention, and free thought.[9] If we imagine "public worship" along those lines, we recognize exactly the atomized liturgical situation the Vatican documents were trying to foreclose! Curiously, the terms "corporate worship" and "corporate prayer" are never used in the English translations of either the *Constitution* or the *Directory*. "Public" is not the same as "corporate."[10] A street is public. A parade is corporate. We can worship publicly, side by side, and still not be "a people," not become the body of Christ. The documents are trying, in limited language, to point us to this very important truth.

The problems arise precisely when we imagine the people that we are becoming. In failing to adequately account for the diverse cultural aspects of the corporate church, or, more accurately, in mistaking the situation of

---

8. Mark R. Francis, *Shape a Circle Ever Wider: Liturgical Inculturation in the United States* (Chicago: Liturgy Training Publications, 2000), pp. 107–8. See also James Empereur's introduction to Peter C. Phan, ed., *Directory on Popular Piety and the Liturgy: Principles and Guidelines — a Commentary* (Collegeville, MN: Liturgical Press, 2005), pp. 1–17.

9. Later historians and sociologists using the concept shifted the definition to assume a space where common identity was practiced and forged. See Mah, "Phantasies," pp. 153–82.

10. Of course, the term "corporate" has problems as well — not least of which is its association in English with business. A non-Christian friend of mine once stopped me midsentence to ask if "corporate worship" was what televangelists did!

the Western Church as universal, the *Constitution, Environment and Art*, and the *Directory* uncover the imaginative challenge of inculturation. As James Empereur, a prominent scholar of liturgical inculturation, points out:

> In popular piety we are dealing with inculturated prayer, ritual, and specific religious sensibilities. If one were to search for a model for the process of liturgical inculturation, one would do well to start with popular piety. Yet the *Directory* states that popular religious practices should not be integrated into the liturgy. . . . Would not the integration of such practices keep them centered on Christ and also be a way for the liturgy to be grounded in the local culture? If not, what is one to make of the statement in chapter one that "the Church has never hesitated in incorporating into the liturgical rites forms drawn from individual, domestic and community piety"? Much of what is official liturgy today was popular piety at one time. Apparently, inculturation was acceptable in the early church, but not today.[11]

Private and public are categories native to a specific segment of the Catholic Church, the post-Enlightenment, Western part of the church that happens to have inherited a great deal of centralized ecclesial authority. Well acculturated to its own milieu, private and public appear simply as universal categories, normatively descriptive for everyone, everywhere. The problem with popular devotion as practiced in the West, it was assumed, was the problem with popular devotion everywhere else as well. The solutions to those problems — removing the visual and physical foci of those devotional practices from the sanctuary, for example — were apparently equally as global. Yet many popular devotional practices are overwhelmingly corporate in character. Many popular devotions are truly popular, telling the Christian story as part of local history, constituent of local identity, and animated by a local imagination. But as long as "popular devotion" *tout court* is viewed as secondary (optional, even) with respect to public worship and public prayer, then the worshipers imagined along these lines might very well turn out to be a collection of post-Enlightenment, Western, private, individual "I's" worshiping and praying in public, side by side, but hardly a corporate body united in Christ.

11. Empereur, introduction to *Directory . . . a Commentary*, p. 16.

The relationship between the uppercase "We" of the body of Christ and the "I" of individual experience in the liturgy is clear. The "I" is to become part of the "We." Much less clear in the Catholic documents is the place of the lowercase "we," the "we" of local community and local identity, the "we" of the particular, popular peoples of God.

This section began with an attempt to understand what was at stake for the Catholic Church in its desire to redirect the power of the visual arts in worship toward the liturgy and away from devotional activities. Grasping what was at stake led to a central observation and a resulting set of questions. The observation: key documents in the Catholic reform of the liturgy, especially the *Constitution on the Sacred Liturgy* and the later *Directory of Popular Piety and the Liturgy*, cast the analysis of the relationship between popular devotion and the liturgy within a tacit, Western framework of private versus public. While fully appreciating that the goal of these documents was to foster "full, conscious, and active participation" in the liturgy by discouraging private devotion during the liturgy, this construction also leads to a number of fascinating questions: First, is public worship necessarily corporate worship, and isn't *corporate* worship — worship that forms us as the "body of Christ" and the "people of God" — truly the goal of the reforms envisioned by Vatican II? Second, is popular devotion, as practiced around the world, always privatized as it tends to be in the West (along the lines of "European devotionalism") and thus in competition with "full, conscious, and active participation" in the liturgy? Or might popular devotion actually be deeply corporate, but also an expression of local cultural identity? Finally, if this is the case, how is the "we" of local culture and popular devotion properly expressed within (or on occasion effaced, or mistaken for) the mystical "We" of the church universal realized through the liturgy?

Orthodox

Orthodox practice immediately exposes the limits of the public/private distinction. An Orthodox Christian praying at home prays with images and prayers that connect him or her to the church as a whole. What one sees at home, one sees at church; what one sees at church, one sees at home. The strong reciprocity between the visual and verbal language of Sunday worship and the visual and verbal language of prayer outside of Sunday worship clearly situates the personal "I" at all times within the worshiping "We" of the church universal. While non-Orthodox Christians might be tempted to think that Orthodox icons help tie an individual's private devotional life to the public worship of the church, that formulation would distort the fundamental dynamic at work here: "Personal prayer is possible only in the context of the community. Nobody is a Christian by himself, but only as a member of the body. Even in solitude, 'in the chamber,' a Christian prays as a member of the redeemed community, of the Church. And it is in the Church that he learns his devotional practice."[12] Theologically, this dynamic embodies the Orthodox understanding of *theosis*, of being redeemed, transformed, and brought into full personhood through participation in the Trinitarian life of God in the worshiping church. As one Orthodox priest writes, "Orthodox doctrine affirms personal but not individual salvation." He continues, "No individual person can be 'like God,' for God is a community of persons."[13] The "I" can only come to full personhood in the "We" of God's triune presence in the church.

In light of the continuity and reciprocity between personal and corporate prayer, it's instructive to consider the reception of *The Orthodox Study Bible* among Orthodox Christians. Study Bibles, as a way of engaging scriptural text, originated with Protestantism. The 1599 English Geneva Bible, which contained descriptive introductions for each book, commentaries, indexes, maps, and cross-references, is sometimes referred to as the first study Bible. Study Bibles are meant to facilitate the use of Scripture for personal study and personal devotion. It's not entirely surprising to discover that the movers and shakers behind *The Orthodox Study Bible* were leaders among the group of evangelicals who joined the Orthodox Church in 1987 — Christians for whom a study Bible is an important companion in the experience of a genuine personal faith. Given the centrality of devotional Bible reading and study for evangelical Protestants, it makes perfect sense

---

12. Florovsky, *Prayer*, p. 3.

13. Father Michael Oleksa, "Orthodox Missiological Education for the Twenty-First Century," in *Missiological Education for the Twenty-First Century: The Book, the Circle, and the Sandals*, ed. J. Dudley Woodberry, Charles Van Engen, and Edgar J. Elliston (Maryknoll, NY: Orbis, 1996), pp. 83–90. Consulted via Father Oleksa's website, http://www.fatheroleksa .org/2.html, accessed April 12, 2012.

that these newly Orthodox Christians would want to continue this practice but with Orthodox reference points.

When the first volume was released in 1993 (the New Testament and Psalms), reviews from the Orthodox community at large were mixed.[14] Some critics quibbled with the translation, others with the content of the notes. But beneath those details was the chief worry that such a book "obscures the central point that for the Orthodox the Bible comes from the Church, exists in the Church, lives in the Church."[15] With Scripture, as with icons, the liturgical life of the church as a whole is the guiding force: "Orthodox Christians experience the Scriptures not so much through private reading and study, but visually, through tactile sense, orally, and aurally through the ritual, Biblical readings and hymnody that compose Orthodox liturgical worship."[16] The launch of *The Orthodox Study Bible* was perceived by some Orthodox Christians as undermining the authority of the liturgy. For what is the purpose of a study Bible except to encourage private engagement with God's Word? In the words of one critic, the whole enterprise "feels far too much like a piece of evangelical propaganda decked out in the trappings of Orthodoxy, like an eighteenth century New England chapel or meeting house with a golden onion dome stuck over the pediment of the porch."[17]

In spite of these misgivings, in the years since its publication, *The Orthodox Study Bible* has received official approval from the Standing Conference of the Canonical Orthodox Bishops in the Americas, has been embraced by most Orthodox jurisdictions, and has sold very well.[18] Perhaps *The Orthodox Study Bible* is an example of Orthodox inculturation into its North American context, demonstrating, in Matthew Francis's words, "the capability of the faith to graft into its midst people and concepts from the Evangelical Protestant community."[19] Even so, personal prayer and devotion in the Orthodox Church will always be dependent on and derivative of the language and imagery of corporate worship.

14. Matthew Francis, "The Orthodox Study Bible and Orthodox Identity in North America," *Canadian Journal of Orthodox Christianity* 2, no. 2 (June 1, 2007): 37–55.

15. Archimandrite Ephrem, review of *The Orthodox Study Bible: New Testament and Psalms*, *Sourozh* 54 (November 1993): 43.

16. Francis, "The Orthodox Study Bible," p. 41.

17. Ephrem, review of *The Orthodox Study Bible*, p. 43.

18. Francis, "The Orthodox Study Bible," pp. 47–48.

19. Ibid., p. 55.

The "I"/"We" dynamics of Orthodox worship exposes the limits of private and public as analytical categories. But, as with the Catholic Church, it leaves the "we" of local community less than clearly defined. The "We" of Orthodox liturgy is the uppercase "We" of the eternal, universal church. The role of icons in Orthodox worship is to make present this universal "We" using the traditional, visual vocabulary of the church, derived from late Roman/early Christian sources, as discussed in chapter 1. This leaves the lowercase "we" of local community in a complex and ambiguous position. If one's local Orthodox congregation is ethnically rooted in the historic lands of the Orthodox Church — Greece or Russia, for example — with their historic iconographic traditions, then the otherworldly universal "We" envisioned through icons is also the familiar "we" of local, national, or ethnic identity. In these lands and in these immigrant congregations, the church's holy images represent the church universal, even as they are experienced as local, as "our" images. Hence the old arguments about which iconographic variants were more appropriate, more spiritual, more beautiful than all others. Partisans in these debates always argued for the superiority of their own local idiom, betraying the identification of the local with the universal. As was the case in Catholic discussions of devotion and worship, it is possible for specific practices and particular assumptions to be taken as universal when they are in fact local. That's not necessarily a bad thing — unless those practices and assumptions are exported out of that local community as norms that preclude other local peoples from contributing their own unique cultural gifts to the church.

Let's imagine, however, a local congregation not predominantly rooted in the historical lands of the Orthodox Church. Or imagine an Orthodox worshiper new to the tradition — a convert or a reaffiliate from Catholicism or Protestantism. In these cases, icons look very otherworldly indeed. They are not "Art." They do not appear rooted in the worshiper's own local culture. They appear to transcend local identity and culture entirely and point to a mystical realm beyond space and time. The church universal is made very present. But where, in this case, might we find the charisms of local culture that Orthodox Christians insist are welcome, and even necessary, in the church? Is local identity represented primarily through language, through the use of the vernacular? Perhaps local culture shows up in the settings of the songs and hymns of the liturgy. Or perhaps it is represented mainly in the dress, gestures, and postures of the worshiping congregation. But could local culture ever show up as an iconographic style other than that rooted in the late Roman/early Christian Eastern Church? What might that look like? Or would the use of a local visual idiom come at the expense of the universal — which is the explicit focus of Orthodox worship?

Orthodox practice renders private/public distinctions nonsensical. Individual devotion flows from, and back into, the church's corporate worship of the triune God, in whom Christians ultimately find their personhood. Though one may have a personal experience of faith, this is in no sense a private experience of faith. True worship of the triune God is irreducibly communal, fundamentally corporate. Yet, as was the case in Catholicism, affirming the corporate character of worship can create its own challenges if we are not attentive to the ways in which we can mistake the local for the universal. In corporate worship, how do we properly envision the place of our local communion in the church universal? Or do we neglect this question and inadvertently end up imagining a church universal that merely looks like the most dominant local culture?

Protestant

Protestantism emerged in Western history alongside the interdependent modern notions of "private" and "public." As new or revised practices of prayer and devotion took root, early modern Protestants gradually assumed a greater sense of personal responsibility for their spiritual welfare. In addition to attending worship, the individual efforts of self-examination and of daily prayer and Bible study were strongly encouraged. This could be done in the context of the family or individually, and, early on, such activities followed the seasonal patterns of the church's worship. But over time, these exercises became increasingly independent of congregational activity or oversight, and were more and more understood as the responsibility of the individual Christian.[20] For many Protestants today, individual, private devotion is at the

20. Mary Hampson Patterson, *Domesticating the Reformation: Protestant Best Sellers, Private Devotion, and the Revolution of English Piety* (Madison, NJ: Farleigh Dickinson University Presses, 2007); Jessica Martin and Alec Ryrie, eds., *Private and Domestic Devotion in Early Modern Britain* (Burlington, VT: Ashgate, 2012); Cecile M. Jagodzinski, *Privacy and*

heart of true Christian piety. Personal reading of Scripture, private prayer, quiet time with God, and a course of devotional reading are fundamental disciplines of Protestant Christian life. Moreover, these activities are rarely understood as dependent on or pointed toward corporate worship but are rather viewed as separate activities, as different genres of Christian practice. If anything, the dynamics of church worship at its best mirrors that of private devotion. In *Senses of the Soul*, William Dyrness's study of how images and visual elements are actually received by ordinary Christians, he notes:

> While adherents of other traditions we interviewed could express their sense of worship in similar personal and individual terms, none insisted so radically on the immediate and inward character of worship as the Protestant respondents. . . . When put in these general terms, it would seem that worship has no *intrinsic* connection either with the time set aside for corporate services or for the physical setting in which it takes place. Indeed many respondents did not in fact think first about the Sunday service at all when asked about their sense of worship.[21]

Individual experience precedes and supersedes corporate identity. The purpose of the church and the purpose of public worship, then, are to support the individual in his or her walk of faith. It follows, then, that the most beneficial forms of public worship for many Protestants are those that share the intense personal focus of private devotion.

Either/or distinctions are rarely useful. Sunday worship is not *either* public *or* private, *either* individual *or* corporate. Worship is always both/and. Nonetheless, it can be useful to notice the ways in which our habits and assumptions may privilege one set of emphases and inadvertently diminish the other. Tracking the debates about the character of Roman Catholic worship since Vatican II does, I believe, give Protestants some useful lenses through

---

Print: Reading and Writing in Seventeenth-Century England (Charlottesville: University Press of Virginia, 1999); Lena Cowen Orlin, *Locating Privacy in Tudor London* (Oxford: Oxford University Press, 2007). For a historiographic critique of the scholarship on public spheres and private lives, see Dena Goodman, "Public Sphere and Private Life: Toward a Synthesis of Current Historiographical Approaches to the Old Regime," *History and Theory* 31 (1992): 1–20.

21. Dyrness, *Senses of the Soul*, p. 24.

which to view their own worship practices. I was moved to consider my own experience in some Protestant settings. I may be singing alongside everyone else, but the volume of the music (which makes it impossible to hear those around me) and the dim lighting (which makes it difficult to see those around me), combined with the often highly personalized lyrics (which encourage me to think of my relationship to Jesus as entirely personal), all encourage a private devotional experience. I could just as well be at home or in my car, singing prayerfully along with a recording of the same songs. Following the singing, the sermon might be presented as teaching, providing me with lessons and applications meant to support and equip me in my walk as a Christian, rather than as proclamation, the corporate assent of God's people to the presence of God in the Word. Communion, celebrated infrequently, might even be "self-serve," where worshipers absorbed in silent prayer and contemplation approach the table individually and help themselves to the elements. Listening in on the Catholic conversation about private devotion and public worship made me begin to ask whether some of our Protestant worship patterns facilitate private devotion rather than corporate worship. Then I began to wonder, "Do we truly appreciate what's at stake in gathering for worship?" In what ways do the worship practices of my church (and of my college) take seriously (or not) scriptural imagery of the church as "body of Christ" and "people of God"? Do we really take worshiping *together* as seriously as we should? What would that look like? Or do we imagine union with Christ as an exclusively intimate, private, individual affair?

The visual arts are directly implicated in questions about the individual or corporate character of our worship. If, as discussed in chapter 3, art is typically imagined as a product of and invitation to individual inspiration, and if a congregation's tacit understanding of worship is that it should foster inspirational, devotional experience, it would seem obvious that art and worship belong together. This is the argument of scholars like Robert Wuthnow: because art and religion both elicit what he calls "devotional effort" and because the experience of art and the experience of religion are, in modern Western culture, imagined so similarly, art can act as a carrier for religion.[22] This is also a standard argument for many artists and art lovers who

---

22. Robert Wuthnow, *All in Sync: How Music and Art Are Revitalizing American Religion* (Berkeley: University of California Press, 2003), p. 70.

support the visual arts as a legitimate component in worship. The theory fails in practice, however, precisely because of its underlying individualistic assumptions. We have precious few examples of *shared* viewing, of *shared* receiving of art that are not confined to the commercial or patriotic realm. How often, then, will the individual artistic vision of one artist facilitate the simultaneous private devotion of an entire congregation, much less foster *shared* corporate worship? Rarely. And at this point, art ceases to act as a devotional aid and becomes, to use the classic Protestant term of dismissal, a distraction. Scholars who point to growing Protestant enthusiasm for the arts in general also note that Protestants' "comfort level in discussing art decreases in direct proportion to its connection to formal worship."[23] Paradoxically, the assumption that art and religion share so much simultaneously creates and frustrates opportunities for art in corporate worship.

Reflections for Congregations

Setting Orthodox, Catholic, and various Protestant uses of the arts side by side highlights the complexity of how our plural identities relate to our sense of personal, individual Christian identity. In worship, the "I" of individual experience is expressed in part through the assumed "we" of local culture while also being knit to the mysterious, vast, and varied "We" of the church universal. The visual arts, as we saw, can clarify these levels of Christian experience — or confuse them.

How often do we mistake simultaneous individual devotion for true, corporate worship? This was the core concern of Vatican II's liturgical reform, with its emphasis on "full, conscious, and active participation" in worship. Though we discussed the complicated impact of Vatican II on the visual arts — in particular, the imposition of the modern, Western categories of "private" and "public" onto devotional practices that in many other cultures defy the distinction — the underlying question remains valid, especially for modern, Western Christians. Are we truly *a people* at worship? Or are we merely a Christian public, a collection of individuals next to each other in the same place at the same time, engaged in parallel but individual devotional activity? How do the visual arts help or hinder us in becoming a

23. Dyrness, *Senses of the Soul*, p. 121.

people in worship? And how do the arts help us relate our personal identity in Christ to our communal identity in Christ's church?

The emphasis in Orthodox worship, as we saw in chapter 1, is clearly on the relational character of Christian identity. Individuals find their true personhood in relationship to the triune God encountered in the worshiping church. Apart from that church, no one can hope to become a fully realized human. Icons play a key role in helping Orthodox worshipers undergo this holy, humanizing process. In both their content (Jesus, Mary, the saints, and the stories of the church) and their use in worship and devotion, icons foster in Orthodox believers a constant sense of the nearness of God and God's kingdom, which draws believers into sacred and sanctifying communion. The reciprocity between the verbal and visual language of corporate worship and the verbal and visual language of personal devotion constantly underscores, in turn, the reciprocity of personal and communal identity in the church. Though our discussion above raised the possibility that the strong emphasis on the universality of *what* icons represent might possibly obscure the local character of *how* they represent it, that point of discussion should not diminish the very real, strong, and positive dynamic by which the Orthodox covenant with icons helps Orthodox Christians become more profoundly themselves as persons in and through their love of God and God's church.

The Catholic Church, too, enjoys a rich and lively visual culture that connects individual believers to a communal, ecclesial identity. The prayers said at home and in private are also increasingly the prayers of the church at large. The Catholic imagery of the home is for the most part the imagery of the church. Unlike in the Orthodox Church, however, that imagery is much more stylistically varied. Though some of those variations are seen as problematic (such as the sentimental "Saint-Sulpice" and "Barclay Street" productions discussed in chapter 2), the very fact of culturally based stylistic variation is theologically significant. Crucifixes, images of saints, vestments, and altarpieces are more or less expected to reflect the character of the local community. A Catholic church in rural New Mexico will generally not look like a Catholic church in upstate New York, even though both might include an image of the Virgin of Guadalupe, depending on the makeup of the parish.

Where the Catholic Church has struggled is in discerning how certain devotional activities — like those associated with the Virgin of Guadalupe — relate to corporate worship. Are devotional activities that originate outside the liturgy inherently individualistic and "private," and therefore in tension with corporate worship? Or are they sometimes deeply communal in character? If the latter, might they, with some care and thought, be integrated into corporate worship where they would help express worshipers' varied local identities within the larger universal identity of the church?

Whatever challenges Orthodox and Catholic congregations may face regarding the relationship between personal devotion and corporate worship, Protestant congregations probably have the most thinking to do on this question. With little experience in how to engage images for worship or devotion, Protestants generally fall back on habits of looking learned from museums and galleries and from consumer culture. In the museum and gallery or in the Christian bookstore, images are meant to provoke individual, subjective encounters driven by personal taste. Depending on the object in question, those encounters might be contemplative or comforting or confrontational, but they are always imagined as fundamentally individual rather than communal. The viewer can engage or not, as she sees fit. The viewer can approve or not, as he sees fit. What happens, then, when we introduce images into worship? Do the images we see in worship create the kind of shared viewing that fosters corporate worship? Or do they invite a type of viewing that elicits an individual, subjective response, possibly at odds with the communal character of corporate worship?

Images designed for communal use and reception *can* invite powerful personal responses. The corporate does not preclude the individual. But it is harder to move in the opposite direction. If, for example, we understand images to be first and foremost about individual encounter and subjective interpretation, it becomes very difficult to corral all those individual responses into anything resembling a shared, communal encounter. Artists and art lovers who understand subjectivity to be at the heart of the artistic enterprise will strenuously resist any attempt to put interpretive boundaries around their art. This works very well for the church art gallery or for an art education program. But when this assumption shows up on Sunday morning in worship, it introduces a tension between individual and communal identity formation that could, if left unchecked, undermine the deeply communal character of worship. On the other hand, gifted artists who are aware of these dynamics are perfectly capable of creating works that engage the shared commitments of the congregation even as they invite congregants to respond personally to those commitments.

CHAPTER 7

Institutionalization & Professionalization

> In grammar school, teachers teach art; in my un-
> dergraduate college, artists taught art. In graduate
> school . . . artists teach artists.
>
> — HOWARD SINGERMAN[1]

So far, this compare-and-contrast exercise has focused attention on the ways we use the visual arts to illuminate the nature of the church: its local and universal character; its role as mediator of the story of redemption and as mediator of God's presence with us; and its role in forming us, through worship and devotion, as a people and as individual persons. In all three cases, these are both/and, not either/or, propositions. Recognizing the interplay among them, however, can help us see our own congregations in a new light and perhaps ask some new questions, especially if those questions have to do with the role of the visual arts in worship.

Beyond these ecclesiologically oriented questions, however, setting Orthodox, Roman Catholic, and Protestant patterns of engaging the visual arts side by side illuminates further questions that are less ecclesial in origin, but no less worthy of attention. These questions originate in social patterns of our art system. What kinds of artists do we have in our con-

---

1. Howard Singerman, *Art Subjects: Making Artists in the American University* (Berkeley: University of California Press, 1999), p. 3.

gregations? How has their training shaped them for work in the church? How do our churches prepare them? What are the potentials and pitfalls of various kinds of training? What assumptions about style enter the church from our larger art system? How do styles take on meaning in particular communities? What can we learn from the tangled legacy of Western naturalism in art destined for the worshiping church? How can attention to the visual arts sharpen our appreciation of the challenges of inculturation? When are we speaking the gospel message in our own visual idiom, and when are we merely advancing our own culture in the guise of the gospel? The following three chapters explore what cross-confessional comparisons help us notice more clearly about how artistic formation occurs and about why that matters for the visual arts in our congregations.

At first glance, the dynamics of institutionalization and professionalization may seem remote from the actual work of artists in congregations. The *Oxford English Dictionary* defines the verb "institutionalize" as establishing "something, typically a practice or activity, as a convention or norm in an organization or culture." Institutionalization is a form of routinization. It is not the same as professionalization, however. Professionalization is a concept with a distinguished if somewhat contentious sociological pedigree, but key to all understandings of professionalization is the importance of self-definition.[2] When a practice has been professionalized, the practitioners themselves determine standards of competence and excellence. As members of a self-regulated practice, professionals establish organizations with criteria for membership, often academic degrees, which distinguish professionals from amateurs.

"Institutionalization" and "professionalization" generally bring to mind ideas like oversight, routine, predictability, even bureaucracy — the very antithesis of how we tend to imagine art and art viewing. We imagine artists as free agents, as individuals whose work originates primarily in

2. For a brief introduction to key texts and historiographic trends concerning professionalization, see Julia Evetts, "Trust and Professionalism: Challenges and Occupational Changes," *Current Sociology* 54 (July 2006): 515–31. For a study emphasizing the trust dimensions of professionalization, see Samuel Haber, *The Quest for Authority and Honor in the American Professions: 1750–1900* (Chicago: University of Chicago Press, 1991). For a study emphasizing the economic aspects of professionalization, see Magali Sarfatti Larson, *The Rise of Professionalism: A Sociological Analysis* (Berkeley: University of California Press, 1977).

their own imagination and is unconstrained by external expectations and norms. Likewise, our art system encourages us to imagine that as viewers, our most meaningful encounters with art are deeply personal, individual experiences, also unconstrained by communal expectations and norms. Ironically, if we pause to notice, we might readily appreciate the degree to which both of these convictions are sustained and maintained by particular communities. Institutionalization and professionalization help us appreciate from yet another angle the social character of how the arts work in congregational settings. Learning to be an artist is to learn certain norms and conventions. Norms and conventions always exist, even if we are not always fully cognizant of them. And norms and conventions, by definition, are not the exclusive property of any one individual. They belong to a group. But which group? That is the key question. Do the norms belong to a communion of churches? To a specific congregation? To a professional guild responsible to a communion of churches? Or to a professional guild responsible primarily to itself?

The chapters in part 1 outline three different approaches to training artists for work in the church. Orthodox iconographers are taught by other iconographers, while, to paraphrase Howard Singerman, Protestant artists are taught by artists — that is, by members of the various art worlds represented in our colleges and universities. Catholic artists who work for the church typically have a both/and formation. They go to art school and are taught by artists, but to work in and for the church, they also receive additional artistic and liturgical education. What do each of these instructional patterns have to teach us?

Orthodox

Orthodox students of iconography may have formal artistic training, a BA or an MFA in art. But, as one iconographer put it, that training serves primarily technical purposes, providing a foundational understanding of color, media, and techniques.[3] In addition to mastering a repertoire of basic skills, becoming an iconographer, as opposed to becoming an artist, requires

3. Matushka Darya Carney, personal conversation, June 6, 2008.

the tutelage of the church through close study of its iconographic tradition and, ideally, instruction by one or more contemporary masters. In the United States, at least at the moment, there are no certificate programs, no degree-granting programs in the practice of iconography. Though various Orthodox seminaries offer iconography workshops, these are short-term courses of study — one or two weeks — designed to offer iconographers intense contact with a master iconographer. The pattern is one of master and apprentice. One cannot become an iconographer by earning a degree. But artists can become iconographers by immersing themselves in the tradition and then receiving the church's affirmation of the presence of that tradition in their work.

Sociologists might say that the training of iconographers (in the United States at least) is institutionalized but not professionalized. It is institutionalized insofar as it is not a random, free-form, autodidactic process that individuals could make up on their own. There are well-defined norms, expectations, and conventions in iconography that have to be learned from the inside out. It would be nonsensical for painters, no matter how skilled their hand and ardent their faith, to forgo immersion in the practices of iconography and simply declare themselves to be iconographers, fit for work in the church.

Insofar as iconography as a practice is maintained by the Orthodox Church as a whole, affirmed by those who receive as well as those who paint icons in prayerful obedience to tradition, professionalizing the practice could potentially create dissonance. It's easy to imagine that over time, unchecked by the reception of the wider church, a professionalized guild of iconographers would come to value the more esoteric aspects of the iconographic tradition, eventually moving the practice further and further from the community it is meant to serve.

Protestant

In Protestant settings, by contrast, professionalized artists, designers, and art educators are the norm. The MFAs, art teachers, and graphic designers at work in Protestant congregations, even if not card-carrying members of a professional association like the CAA (College Art Association), NAEA

(National Art Education Association), or AIGA (American Institute of Graphic Arts), have surely been trained by members of those guilds and have been taught to value the internally defined standards of excellence upheld by those guilds. In ecclesial settings with few or no institutionalized practices concerning the visual arts, the resulting vacuum is quickly filled by the standards of competence and excellence upheld by the dominant professional community, whether or not those standards are fully compatible with the expectations or needs of the congregation.

Professionalized art worlds by their very nature do not brook outside interference. The whole point of professionalism is that the "professors" themselves define the practice. How are Protestant congregations to begin a conversation about the role of art in the church if it is assumed from the start that only the professional artist's convictions count? Conversely, how are congregants to enter into helpful dialogue if their own expectations for art are unexamined? Chapter 3 discussed the complexities that might result from this situation where, for example, an arts ministry team might be internally divided between those with professionalized MFA identities and those with professionalized art educator identities, or where a pastor expecting a communication-oriented, graphic-design mentality on the part of the arts team encounters the sensibilities of other professionalized identities.

Roman Catholic

The American Roman Catholic Church finds itself betwixt and between. Recognizing that the standards of excellence upheld by various sectors of our larger North American art system, though valuable, may not be best suited to the needs of the church, and responding to the urgent need to staff diocesan liturgical committees with people sensitive to the needs of the church as well as to the importance of the arts, Catholics are well on their way toward establishing a new profession — liturgical consulting. Liturgical consultants are equipped to guide a congregation through a discernment process that simultaneously deepens its sense of the liturgy and explores its sense of identity, bringing both together through the process of designing environments for worship. A number of Catholic seminaries offer degrees or certificates in liturgical studies, and a new professional association, the Association of Consultants for Liturgical Space (ACLS), acts as a clearinghouse for those with appropriate expertise. ACLS defines itself as a society comprised of "working professionals who provide a liturgical education process including education on the importance, role and value of worship, the impact of the church building on worship, and with multidisciplinary expertise in some or all of the following areas of service: planning and design for the liturgical environment; collaborative work with the architect and related professionals; coordination of planning, design and fabrication of appropriate liturgical art, furnishings, and appointments."[4] Not surprisingly, many liturgical design consultants are architects. In our discussion in chapter 2 of the emphasis on worship space and liturgical furnishings that emerged after Vatican II, it was architects, not artists, who were among the first to be called on to help the church deal with its new questions.

In his discussion of the professionalization of artists in American colleges and universities, Howard Singerman contrasts two ways in which professionalization ensures high standards. One model supports the relationship between the expert and the client and is designed to establish a firm basis for trust in the expert's knowledge and experience. Medicine and architecture are examples of this professional idiom. A second model of ensuring high standards protects the autonomy of professional practice from outside influence. Science and, for Singerman, fine art are examples of this professional idiom. He writes of the

> opposing versions of the professional artist from the discourse of the artist in the university. One, the slightly older version, emphasizes the relation between professional and client: the professional puts to use a deep knowledge and a specific set of skills to solve a client's problems, to produce a particular outcome. The model is medicine or, closer to the tradition of the visual arts, architecture. The other emphasizes, not the client relationship — and the client's judgment — but the ideal of independent research within the field defined by a formal, theoretical discourse. It is modeled after the laboratory scientist or university professor, who

4. www.liturgical-consultants.org/membership.php, accessed July 30, 2014.

formulates problems in relation to the discipline's present and whose performance is judged by colleagues. Values attach to these positions: skill,
service, and quality to the first, intellectual autonomy and disciplinary
progress to the second.[5]

A professional association like ACLS, peopled by a critical mass of architects, functions along the lines of the older model in Singerman's description. It exists to support the field by ensuring trustworthy relationships between experts and clients. The congregation's goals, desires, and judgments
are at the heart of the process, and are guided, but not determined, by the
experienced expert. Unlike the model of professionalization that privileges
the expert's autonomy and creative freedom above all else, this older model
privileges the necessity for trust between the expert and the community he
or she has pledged to serve.

There is a lot to be said for the Catholic both/and process for forming artists for work in the church. Artists interested in working for the
Catholic Church typically undertake both a solid professional education
in the academy *and* additional professional formation in worship and
liturgy. Ideally, this dual formation creates experts who understand how
art works and how worship works, and who know how to bring the two
together with liturgical and artistic integrity. As beneficial as such an
arrangement is, however, professionalization can still have its drawbacks.
The principal drawback for the Roman Catholic Church in the United
States is its principal advantage; easy recourse to a national network of
certified, professional architects, artists, artisans, and designers often
means that local architects, artists, artisans, and designers — those sitting
in the parish pews — can be overlooked. While the artist in the pew will
certainly be valued as part of congregational dialogue, it might not occur
to the congregation or to the hired consultant, or even to the artist, to
actually use the artist's talents directly. And of course, none of these beneficial interactions take place at all unless a congregation is undertaking
a building project big enough to mandate consultation with the diocesan
liturgical committee.

5. Singerman, *Art Subjects,* pp. 193–94.

Reflections for Congregations

Institutionalization sounds anything but glamorous to the modern North American ear. Professionalism sounds much more attractive. But according to this analysis, the less-glamorous term is crucial for success, while the more attractive term needs some careful unpacking to lead to success. As social processes by which norms and assumptions are sustained in community, both institutionalization and professionalization represent a promise and a challenge. The promise is a shared, communally embedded vision for making and receiving the visual arts in the context of the congregation. The challenge is identifying what that shared vision is, and then figuring out how to sustain it over the long term. Who are the artists in your congregation? How have they been professionalized? What norms and assumptions sustain their work as artists? How congruent is the congregation's vision for the visual arts with the artists' vision? And how is the role of the arts institutionalized in your congregation?

Each of the art-interested Protestant congregations I profiled in chapter 3 succeeded in institutionalizing the arts such that artists and congregants shared a vision for what the arts were doing in their midst. They then embedded that vision in the finances, personnel, organizational structure, and activities of the congregation. In some cases, the shared vision was derived from the ecumenical conversation happening in the liturgical renewal movement, which is heavily influenced by developments in the Catholic Church. In other cases, one or another professional artist (MFA, graphic designer, art educator) put the defining stamp on the character of the program. Unlike Orthodoxy and Catholicism, in the Protestant world, visions for the arts are negotiable. But like Orthodoxy and Catholicism, institutionalization is not. Without institutional savvy, no vision for the arts, no matter how professional in character, will thrive.

Finally, how artists are socialized (or not) for work in the church also sheds light on the dynamic illuminated in chapter 3 — the ways in which a commitment to "Art" with a capital *A* in our North American art system generates activism and advocacy. To be an artist in our society is, in a very real sense, to proselytize on Art's behalf. Activism on behalf of Art finds little scope in the Orthodox Church. The Orthodox covenant with icons is not only incompatible with the notion of Art assumed by our art system, it also simultaneously satisfies artists' and worshipers' desire for a rich visual encounter with faith. Icons do not require the services of either artists or advocates. Icons require only disciples.

Roman Catholic and Protestant congregations, on the other hand, do have challenges connected to activism and advocacy on behalf of Art. Curiously, the challenges are mirror images of one another. Catholic congregations may need to encourage the activism of the artist in the pew and to learn to make room for more local expression than the liturgical consulting process might, at first glance, encourage; Protestant congregations may need to be more willing to examine their fundamental assumptions about church and Art to guide the lively and vital artistic energies in their midst to more fruitful and sustainable channels.

CHAPTER 8

Naturalism & Abstraction

*Beyond doubt there is the basis for a theological
aesthetic of style here. But whose aesthetic is it? The
answer, almost certainly, is* ours.

— JAMES TRILLING[1]

In addition to helping us appreciate the importance of how artistic training is institutionalized or professionalized in various ecclesial or artistic
communities, setting Orthodox, Roman Catholic, and various Protestant
practices side by side also illuminates the fascinating question of how artistic
styles accrue meanings in those communities. Naturalism in particular has
had a vexed history in our survey, particularly in the Orthodox and Roman Catholic traditions. Conversely, varieties of abstraction have appeared
throughout the history of the visual arts in the church as the appropriate
antidote to the problems perceived as intrinsic to naturalism. But is that
dyad — naturalism versus abstraction — helpful, or even accurate?

As discussed in chapter 1, the Orthodox tradition by and large eschewed
Renaissance naturalism in its icons, though I also noted the great exception
to this rule — the tradition of naturalistic icons that took root in Russia in
the seventeenth century and persisted well into the twentieth century. For

---

1. James Trilling, "Medieval Art without Style? Plato's Loophole and a Modern Detour,"
Gesta 34, no. 1 (1995): 58.

most of its history, in fact, the particular style of Orthodox icons remained untheorized. Very early on, some Russian Orthodox Christians rejected naturalistic icons as too "imaginative," but it wasn't until the early twentieth century that Orthodox iconographers and theologians articulated a systematic theoretical and theological rationale for such rejection based on the formal properties of icons.

As discussed in chapter 2, the Catholic Church's relationship with naturalism was also untheorized until the mid-twentieth century when, in the name of liturgical reform, some highly naturalistic images began to appear problematic. Though the grounds for this judgment were ostensibly liturgical and aimed at fostering "public worship," underneath the liturgical rationale the objections were just as often — if not more often — stylistic in origin. Brightly colored, sweetly naturalistic paintings and statues that had been unremarkable in the nineteenth century began to look naïve, if not embarrassingly tasteless, in light of developments in modern art. Consequently, a host of Marys and Josephs and other saints was ushered unceremoniously to the back of the sanctuary or out the door altogether, to be replaced by less naturalistic, more modern, and purportedly more liturgically suitable art.

The line of thinking behind both the twentieth-century theorization of icons in the Orthodox Church and the twentieth-century demotion of naturalistic popular art in the Catholic Church rests on twin assumptions, both of which are modern, and neither of which is historically tenable. The first assumption is that naturalism is inherently mundane and that it is too specific, too particular, too tied to the details of this world to bear the weight of the transcendent. Naturalistic art is therefore (according to this logic) always a lesser kind of achievement. The second assumption, linked to the first, is that abstraction transcends naturalism's limits and reaches toward the essential and the universal and is therefore more able to bear the weight of the sacred than naturalism.

Defining "Naturalism" and "Abstraction"

Before continuing, it may be helpful to clarify terms for the purposes of this discussion. "Naturalism" and "abstraction" are both quite slippery. Generally speaking, art historians use the term "naturalism" to describe images designed to mimic our optical experience of everyday life. The main techniques used to imitate this ordinary optical experience successfully create illusions of dimensionality. "Modeling" is the technical term artists and art historians use to describe using highlight and shadow to create the illusion of mass and volume in space. The term "perspective" describes a variety of techniques that create the illusion of depth on a flat surface. Linear, or one-point, perspective is the most well-known of these techniques. For most of art history's existence as an academic discipline, it was assumed that art's history *was* the history of (Western) naturalism.[2] Ernst Gombrich's enormously popular book *The Story of Art* is the most vivid and possibly the most influential portrayal of art's history as the rise and fall of naturalism in Western art. Introduced by the Greeks, perfected by the Renaissance Italians, and then overturned by modernism, Western naturalism was the assumed norm against which all other developments (medieval, baroque, romantic, not to mention non-Western) were judged — and often found wanting.

"Abstraction" is harder to pin down because the meaning of the word for artists and art theorists has shifted over time. Today, we generally assume abstract art is non- or even antinaturalistic. In common parlance, the phrase "abstract art" can call to mind anything from a Matisse or a Picasso to a Mondrian or a Pollock. Technically, artists would say the first two of these are properly abstract and the last two are nonrepresentational or nonobjective. But our sloppy, casual use of the term hides a host of instructive nuances. In its earliest uses in eighteenth-century art theory, "abstraction" was a component of naturalism, the process by which an artist transcended nature to create an idealized version of the visible world.[3] By "abstracting"

2. In casual speech, we tend to use the word "realism" as a synonym for "naturalism," describing art that "looks realistic." Artists and art historians, however, tend to restrict "realism" to a range of nineteenth-century artists committed to inventing an art they thought appropriate for their time — an art that refused idealization, an art that insisted on the particular, the ordinary, and especially the uncomfortable realities of the modern world.

3. The following discussion of abstraction is indebted to three essays by David Morgan tracing the history of this term in French, German, and British eighteenth- and nineteenth-century art theory: "Concepts of Abstraction in French Art Theory from the Enlightenment to Modernism," *Journal of the History of Ideas* 53, no. 4 (1992): 669–85; "The Rise and Fall of Abstraction in Eighteenth-Century Art Theory," *Eighteenth-Century Studies* 27, no. 3 (Spring 1994): 449–78; and "The Enchantment of Art: Abstraction and Empathy from German Romanticism to Expressionism," *Journal of the History of Ideas* 57, no. 2 (April 1996): 317–41.

the best, most beautiful elements from a number of exemplars, the artist created something beautiful that transcended ordinary, everyday experience. Theorists argued amongst themselves about how much of this achievement was mental or manual and how much should be credited to the study of nature or to the study of the art of the ancient Greeks, but all agreed that the artist's task was to see through and beyond nature to compose a more perfect, more complete, more universally true image. According to this view, which persisted through the eighteenth century, the artist's job was not to forgo naturalism but to perfect it, via abstraction.

By the turn of the nineteenth century, however, attention had shifted from the pursuit of ideal universal forms to the nature of those forms themselves. In the mysterious cauldron of the artist's imagination, ideal forms became less the idealized imitations of the world around the artist than the expressive essence of the artist's encounter with the world. Form, once tied to the world outside the artist, now became a visible trace of the world inside the artist. In the words of the French theorist Victor Cousin, "All is symbolic in nature: form is not form only, it is the form of something, it unfolds something inward. Beauty, then, is expression: art is the seeking after expression."[4] From there, it is but two short steps to the abstract art of a Matisse or a Picasso, then to the early twentieth-century nonrepresentational work of Mondrian or Pollock. David Morgan gives a succinct summary of the history of abstraction as a concept: "abstraction went from refining imitation to undermining it to eclipsing it altogether."[5]

Both of these views of abstraction — as the operation by which the artist achieves a more perfect naturalism and as the expressive trace of the artist's encounter with nature — share the conviction that art's task is the communication of ideals, that abstraction, whether idealistic or expressive, penetrates the visible world to determine the essence of a thing. "The artist was thought to arrive at this essence by a process of generalization whereby particulars were eliminated until only a subject's generic, universal qualities — its essence — remained."[6] It is this history, a relatively modern history,

---

4. From Cousin's 1818 *The Philosophy of the Beautiful*, as quoted in Morgan, "Concepts of Abstraction," p. 681.

5. Ibid., p. 685.

6. Morgan, "The Enchantment of Art," p. 319.

projected back into the distant past that fostered the widespread assumption that abstraction is inherently more spiritual than naturalism.

James Trilling has traced the impact of imposing this modernist history of abstraction retrospectively onto late Roman/early Christian art.[7] For the earliest generations of art historians, from Giorgio Vasari through Johann Winckelmann and beyond, the most salient characteristic of late Roman/ early Christian art was what Bernard Berenson called "the decline of form."[8] Measured against the naturalistic achievements of the Greco-Roman tradition, the lack of anatomical detail, the lack of modeling, the lack of dimensional projected space in most late Roman/early Christian art was explained variously by deficit of skill, by distance from the imperial center, and, significantly, by the advent of Christianity as a public religion supposedly ambivalent about visual representation. The dominant art-historical narrative for this era was the eclipse of artistic sophistication with no hope in sight until the subsequent renaissances of the following centuries.

After the nineteenth-century, expressivist turn in the art-historical understanding of abstraction, however, these very same characteristics of late Roman/early Christian art became powerful tokens of stylistic sophistication. Representational practices that had been judged defective were now understood to be precociously advanced. The same theoretical turn that made abstract, modern art possible also made possible the recovery of the icon.[9] Each required the same new way of seeing. But whose way of seeing is it? James Trilling is quite certain he knows: "Beyond doubt there is the basis for a theological aesthetic of style here. But whose aesthetic is it? The answer, almost certainly, is *ours*."[10]

A more historically grounded interpretation of this shift would emphasize the ways in which the viewers of the day responded to these more abstract forms, which appeared in secular and religious images alike. Trilling finds little evidence that late Roman viewers responded to abstraction as more intrinsi-

7. James Trilling, "Late Antique and Sub-Antique, or the 'Decline of Form' Reconsidered," *Dumbarton Oaks Papers* 41 (1987): 469–76.

8. Bernard Berenson, *The Arch of Constantine; or, The Decline of Form* (London: Chapman and Hall, 1954).

9. See, for example, Andrew Spira's *The Avant-Garde Icon: Russian Avant-Garde Art and the Icon Painting Tradition* (Burlington, VT: Lund Humphries and the Ashgate Publishing Company, 2008).

10. Trilling, "Medieval Art without Style?" 58.

cally spiritual than Greco-Roman naturalism. Discussing, for example, the ninth-century Byzantine patriarch Photios's description of the mosaic of the Virgin Mary in Hagia Sophia, Trilling points to the specificity of Photios's description and the way in which Photios reads expressive detail into the image: "His evocation of its human warmth does not bypass the stylistic features that we would consider non-naturalistic, e.g., the Virgin's 'detached and imperturbable mood.' Rather, it explicitly acknowledges and incorporates them, to the greater emotional and theological complexity of the image. The detached or passionless qualities of the mosaic contribute to its spiritual efficacy, but only because they are interpreted as *human* qualities. What we might see as transcendence, Photios treats as character exposition."[11] Abstraction represents a transfer of responsibility from artist to viewer, requiring more imaginative engagement from the viewer and less detail from the artist.[12] Trilling's conclusion? Our modern eagerness to rescue late Roman/early Christian art from the specter of decline by imagining its more abstract style as universal and transcendent, and therefore more advanced than Greco-Roman naturalism, is a projection of modern assumptions back onto a historical era that can't sustain them: "Abstraction as a universal language makes no allowance for cultures with different ideas of reality and different conventions for depicting it."[13]

Definitions and Their Effects

But what does all of this have to do with our discussion of icons? It returns us to questions of the universal and local character of the church raised in previous chapters. Twentieth-century theoretical and theological rationales for rejecting Western naturalism in icons rest on fundamentally modern assumptions about the meaning of abstraction that can't actually explain the persistence of the style in appropriately historical terms. Pre-

11. Ibid., p. 59.
12. Ibid., p. 60. Jas Elsner argues the same point in *Art and the Roman Viewer: The Transformation of Art from the Pagan World to Christianity* (Cambridge: Cambridge University Press, 1995). Trilling points out that John Onians reached much the same conclusion with respect to Roman literary forms already in 1980. For Onians's analysis, see "Abstraction and Imagination in Late Antiquity," *Art History* 3 (1980): 1–23.
13. Trilling, "Medieval Art without Style?" p. 60.

twentieth-century rejections of naturalism were not based on its supposedly this-worldly character or even on its lack of spirituality. Rather, naturalism was criticized because it was new, because it was perceived as "imaginative," and because it differed from tradition. Novelty, understood as imaginative invention, and foreignness were the problem, not any worldliness inherent in naturalism.[14] For its premodern proponents, iconic abstraction, it turns out, is just as particular, local, and culturally specific as naturalism, especially when the abstraction is "ours" and the naturalism "theirs."

The modern belief that abstract art is more universal and more spiritual than naturalistic art was also an important factor in the rejection of devotional art in the Roman Catholic Church after Vatican II. But the confrontation between nonnaturalistic, modern art and naturalistic traditional art in the Catholic Church began well before Vatican II. A handful of small churches in France dating from the 1940s and 1950s showcased the convictions of art-minded clergy and religiously sensitive critics, who argued for the compatibility of modern, abstract art in Christian churches, if not its superiority over naturalism. The church of Notre-Dame-de-Toute-Grâce in Assy is the most famous of these test cases, but Henri Matisse's little Chapel of the Rosary at Vence and Le Corbusier's grand Notre Dame du Haut are good pre–Vatican II examples as well. The reform-minded Dominican father Marie-Alain Couturier had a hand in all three. Assy, however, was the earliest and the most ambitious. As a new parish serving visitors to a local tuberculosis sanatorium, Assy was unencumbered by any deep tradition, existing structures, or long-standing parish community. With the encouragement of Father Couturier, the local chaplain managed to enlist the aid of an impressive roster of modern artists: Pierre Bonnard, Henri Matisse, Jean Lurçat, Fernand Léger, Jacques Lipchitz, Marc Chagall, Germaine Richter, and Georges Rouault — Rouault being the only Catholic among the notables. The dedication of the church in 1950 inaugurated several years of heated debate in the Catholic Church regarding the appropriateness of stylistically modern art in the church, a debate that ended with fairly drastic interventions from Rome that severely curtailed any further experiments with modern art until after the reforms of Vatican II.

14. See the section "Authorizing the Icon" in chapter 1 for a discussion of pre-twentieth-century objections to naturalism.

Though cast in stylistic terms, the main challenge presented by the art at Assy was not essentially stylistic. It was social. Father Couturier himself recognized that the issue was not so much the art itself as the society that produced it:

> To expect a truly sacred art of a society of our materialist type, and espe-
> cially a Christian art of nations once again become practically pagan, seems
> to me a chimera. . . . All sacred art implies certain essential elements of a
> collective and communicative order: rigorously *communal forms of sensibility
> and imagination*. And these forms are not produced except in societies of
> a type radically different from our own, societies in which religion forms
> a single body with the totality of the life of the group. . . . In the absence
> of a renaissance of art really sacred, I believe in the appearance among us,
> particularly in France, of works of a "religious" inspiration, very pure, but
> *rigorously individualistic and generally accidental*, works born spontaneously
> and by chance, here and there . . . that is to say, I believe in miracles.[15]

In the case of Assy, the miracles that materialized for Notre-Dame-de-Toute-Grâce were indeed "rigorously individualistic" and "generally acci-dental." In his study of the church, the art historian William Rubin con-cluded that good quality was the main criterion for the works commissioned for Assy.[16] There was no overarching program. There was little attention to the relationship between the theme of a piece and its physical location in the church. Nor, of course, was there any attempt to enforce stylistic continuity, a constraint that would have undermined the modernist autonomy of these modern artists. "At Assy," Rubin wrote, "though each choice has an appro-priate rationale, the decoration as a whole does not constitute a sequence, much less an inclusive affirmation of the essentials of the religion. . . . Sur-

15. Marie-Alain Couturier, "L'Art réligieux modern," *Le Figaro*, October 24, 1951, p. 3, as quoted in William Rubin, *Modern Sacred Art and the Church of Assy* (New York: Columbia University Press, 1961), p. 54 (emphasis mine).

16. Rubin, *Modern Sacred Art*, p. 33. That a young, ambitious, and well-connected scholar like Rubin chose this topic for his dissertation is also of interest. As a high school student, Ru-bin (1927–2006) was connected with Victor D'Amico, the director of education at MOMA. At Columbia, he studied under Mayer Schapiro. Today, most art historians know Rubin as the powerful director of MOMA's department of painting and sculpture (1967–1988) and a staunch defender of modernism.

veying the decoration from within the church, one is struck by a feeling of isolation of parts."[17] The haphazard development of the program at Assy mirrored in modern style the hodgepodge of disparate statues and paintings often found in more traditional parishes. Both traditional and modern practices lacked unity and subordination to the liturgy. Only the style differed.

Rubin published his study of Assy in 1961, a year before Vatican II was formally convened. His critique foreshadowed the direction the council would take with the arts — that arts brought into the church must be subordinated to the character of the space and the integrity of the liturgical rite. As discussed in chapter 2, however, that same emphasis on space and rite, on the "full, conscious, and active participation" of the gathered assembly in corporate worship, demoted any art that could be construed as devotional, which was imagined as private, and therefore in competition with the liturgy. Since most devotional art was rendered in a conventional nineteenth-century naturalistic style, relegating that art to the margins acted as a tacit endorsement of work that was more modern, more abstract — and purportedly more universal, more transcendent — in its place. The photographic appendix to *Environment and Art in Catholic Worship*, a frequent target of conservative critics of Vatican II, is a clear example of modernist bias. While the text endorsed no style in particular, the photographs, offered as examples of good liturgical design, clearly endorsed modernist styles.

In chapter 2, we saw this dynamic play itself out in two midcentury churches in western Michigan. Both Saint Frances de Sales in Muskegon (dedicated in 1967) and Saint Mary's in Spring Lake (dedicated in 1966) feature modernist visuals at the front of the sanctuary as a focal point for common worship (figs. 12 and 20). Both congregations moved naturalistic imagery to the back of the sanctuary, where its devotional function would not interfere with public worship (figs. 21 and 22). Four decades of controversy later, the pendulum has swung in the other direction, leading the congregation of Saint Sebastian in Byron Center to make a different choice. The visual focal point in the front of their sanctuary is a two-dimensional painted crucifix suspended over the apse (fig. 23). The placement and format of this crucifix mimic twelfth- and thirteenth-century hanging crosses from central Italy, painted by artists imitating the iconic style of the Eastern

17. Ibid., p. 39.

Fig. 20. Apse Mosaic at Saint Mary's Catholic Church, Spring Lake, Michigan. PHOTO-
GRAPH BY AUTHOR

Fig. 21. Devotional image at the rear of the sanctuary, Saint Mary's Catholic Church,
Spring Lake, Michigan. PHOTOGRAPH BY AUTHOR

Fig. 22. Devotional image at the back of the sanctuary, Saint Frances de Sales Catholic Church, Muskegon, Michigan. PHOTOGRAPH BY AUTHOR

Church. But rather than the flat, abstracted, iconic style of those ancient crosses, the crucifix at Saint Sebastian is naturalistic, complete with illusionistic, cast shadows and a portrait-like depiction of Christ.

The twentieth-century battle lines between abstract art and naturalistic art were more varied and less theologically tangled in the Protestant world. Fountain Street Church, for example, avidly supported the most contemporary, often highly abstract art. Yet the annual Celebration of the Arts exhibition at First United Methodist has always included naturalistic as well as abstract styles. While many artists and art lovers undoubtedly were personally convinced that abstraction was inherently more suited for truly religious work, the extent to which those convictions shaped the vision of an entire congregation would depend, as we discussed in chapter 3, on whether those individuals were in charge of arts programing at their church and what form the programming took.

It's clear, then, that styles have meanings. But as with our assumptions about art itself, our assumptions about the meaning of style are produced and maintained in community. Sometimes these communities are ecclesial. Orthodoxy, for example, assigns a universalized meaning to the basic, ab-

Fig. 23. Michael Northrop, crucifix, Saint Sebastian Catholic Church, Byron Center, Michigan. PHOTOGRAPH BY ARTIST

stracted style used for icons. But Orthodoxy is the exception rather than the rule. Most ecclesial communities profess an official agnosticism about style. They would agree with the Catholic pronouncement: "The Church has not adopted any particular style of art as her very own; it has admitted styles from every period according to the natural talents and circumstances of peoples."[18] Individual Christians, however, will have quite distinct opinions about style, and these are generally drawn from cultural communities outside our congregations. Nonartists might look to popular culture as a reference point for the meaning of style, or perhaps take cues from so-called high culture. Artists will look to the meanings ascribed to the styles that circulate in their particular art world — be that a craft community, the graphic design world, the educational community, or MFA-holding fine artists. Some artists and viewers will assume that naturalistic styles are best. They will assume that naturalism demonstrates artistic skill, or communicative clarity, or a kind of egalitarian, democratic appeal to the viewer. Abstract styles, for such viewers,

18. *Environment and Art in Catholic Worship* (Washington, DC: United States Catholic Conference, 1978), par. 8.

might signal an ersatz sophistication that is merely a cover for lack of skill or an alienating elitism inappropriate for a church context. Other viewers might look at those same naturalistically rendered images and see the visual vocabulary of popular, commercial art forms that compromise the potential of art to rise above mundane daily concerns. For them, abstraction is a way to disentangle art from the welter of commercial images that surround us every day and to raise it to a higher, independent plane of experience and inquiry. Given all the kinds of artists, viewers, and art worlds out there, it is no wonder, absent any clear ecclesial guidance, that we fight about style.

Reflections for Congregations

Is there a way out of our style wars? I believe so. But it's not easy. The first step is simply to acknowledge that the meanings we attribute to style are not absolute but are relative to the various communities that sustain them. If we've learned anything over the course of the last half-century, it is that all visual representation is local — whether abstract or naturalistic. There is no intrinsically universal artistic style. After accepting the fact that any style can be stunningly effective or wildly inappropriate, the next step is to acknowledge that members of one art world often oversimplify the views of those who belong to other art worlds. While it's true that abstraction *can* be ersatz sophistication masking lack of skill, it is also true that much abstract work comes out of long years of learning and experiment and manifests a range of skills less easily accessible to the eye but nonetheless meaningful and valid. While it is true that naturalism *can* uncritically perpetuate habits of viewing drawn from popular, commercial culture, it's also true that naturalistic art can powerfully redirect these habits of viewing, offering a revision or critique of popular culture and an expansion of ways of seeing. There's easy naturalism and sloppy abstraction. There's complex naturalism as well as accessible abstraction. No stylistic mode can be taken for granted. No style gets to claim universal authority or validity. All stylistic choices are intensely local and intensely communal. All are in need of careful, attentive engagement with respect to purpose.

But what does that careful and attentive engagement with respect to purpose look like? Orthodox and Catholic congregations have some support in negotiating this terrain within their own traditions. In Orthodoxy, the church simply maintains a commitment to one stylistic mode and, through its practices of making and receiving icons in faithful obedience to tradition, instructs both artists and congregants on what that stylistic mode means for the worshiper. Catholics embrace more stylistic diversity, but ideally, artists and congregants alike are equipped to engage that diversity through the liturgical education at the heart of the liturgical consulting process, anchoring discussions of style to a work's role in the liturgy. Protestants, on the other hand, have to hash through their stylistic commitments and differences with little guidance on the possible purposes for art. They need to begin by discerning the kinds of cultural convergence most likely to serve their congregation best. If the artistic commitments in the congregation lead to a bridging activity like an art gallery or art-education program, disputes over style are likely to be less destructive than if the artistic commitments point toward the use of visual arts for a bonding activity such as worship. If a congregation's artistic commitments point toward using the arts in worship, then it's imperative that the congregation engage in serious examination of its assumptions about worship and liturgy.[19] Productive conversations about stylistic possibilities can happen only *after* a congregation has determined the contours of its basic convictions about art and its basic convictions about worship.

After these foundational conversations have taken place, a congregation can move to discussions of purpose and style. At this point, two additional sets of tools might be useful. One set, drawn from Nicholas Wolterstorff's book *Art in Action: Toward a Christian Aesthetic*, can provide guidance in parsing what works of art *do*.[20] A second set of tools, drawn from the work of Frank Burch Brown, can clarify why we should care.[21]

Wolterstorff develops three terms — "artistic excellence," "aesthetic ex-

19. William Dyrness's *A Primer on Christian Worship: Where We've Been, Where We Are, Where We Can Go* (Grand Rapids: Eerdmans, 2009) is a great place to start. Leanne Van Dyk's edited volume, *A More Profound Alleluia: Theology and Worship in Harmony* (Grand Rapids: Eerdmans, 2004), offers an accessible but scholarly discussion of the ways in which worship enacts theology. Joyce Ann Zimmerman exemplifies the best of the Catholic Church's liturgical training, offered in an ecumenical voice in *Worship with Gladness: Understanding Worship from the Heart* (Grand Rapids: Eerdmans, 2014).

20. Nicholas Wolterstorff, *Art in Action: Toward a Christian Aesthetic* (Grand Rapids: Eerdmans, 1980). The following discussion draws from part 3, chapters 2 and 3. For excerpts from *Art in Action*, see appendix A.

21. Frank Burch Brown, *Good Taste, Bad Taste, and Christian Taste: Aesthetics in Religious Life* (Oxford: Oxford University Press, 2000); *Inclusive Yet Discerning: Navigating Worship Artfully* (Grand Rapids: Eerdmans, 2009). *Good Taste, Bad Taste, and Christian Taste* is aimed at an academic audience, while *Inclusive Yet Discerning* is aimed at a more general audience.

cellence," and "fittingness" — that make important distinctions for any discussion of art destined for use in worship. Briefly, "artistic excellence" has to do with how well an object serves the purpose for which it was initially made. Artistic excellence accommodates a wide range of purposes such as commemoration, documentation, ornamentation, and the like. "Aesthetic excellence," on the other hand, has to do with how well an object fulfills just one purpose — that of aesthetic contemplation. Wolterstorff defines aesthetic excellence in terms of a work's unity, internal richness, and fittingness intensity. "Fittingness" concerns the expressive potential of the elements of art. In the visual arts, this would include the expressive power of color, line, rhythm, texture, and the like, which inform a work's stylistic mode. As Wolterstorff defines them, artistic excellence and aesthetic excellence may overlap, but are not the same thing. Aesthetic excellence is a subspecies of artistic excellence insofar as a work intended for aesthetic contemplation fulfills that purpose well. Yet artistic excellence — the standard by which we should evaluate works of art intended for purposes beyond aesthetic contemplation — is always enhanced by aesthetic excellence. Unity, internal richness, and fittingness intensity, then, are relevant criteria for any work meant to serve the liturgy. But the larger question is how well they serve the liturgy, not how well they serve the aims of aesthetic contemplation.

Wolterstorff's analysis is helpful for clarifying *how* a work of art achieves its effects and to what end those effects are employed. His analysis will not, however, eliminate all dispute. People will still disagree about what counts as fitting with respect to art in the life of a congregation, even as they may understand more fully *why* someone else thinks differently.

At this point, Frank Burch Brown's books *Good Taste, Bad Taste, and Christian Taste* and *Inclusive Yet Discerning: Navigating Worship Artfully* offer additional tools. Burch Brown advocates the development of "ecumenical taste." Ecumenical taste does not reject standards, but rather understands that all standards are culturally embedded. Though Burch Brown is primarily interested in what's at stake in our arguments about music in worship, we can easily adapt his definition of ecumenical taste to the visual arts and "try to see in the art of others more of what they themselves are seeing."[22]

22. The exact quote is, "hear in the music of others more of what they themselves are hearing." Burch Brown, *Inclusive Yet Discerning*, p. 61.

His hope is that, chastened and disciplined, "our engagement with art participates in a spiritual conversion whereby aesthetic taste is transformed into something more: into faithful longing and joyful anticipation of a kind that Christians call 'eschatological' and perhaps 'apocalyptic.'"[23] To that end, he offers a list of twelve assumptions that provide ground rules for artistic discernment in congregational life. These assumptions include the following:

> There are many kinds of good taste, and many kinds of good religious art and music. In view of cultural diversity, it would be extremely odd if that were not true.[24]

> It is an act of Christian love to learn to appreciate or at least respect what others value in a particular style or work that they cherish in worship or in the rest of life. That is different, however, from personally liking every form of commendable art, which is impossible and unnecessary.[25]

> Aesthetic judgments begin with, and owe special consideration to, the community or tradition to which a given style or work is indigenous or most familiar. But they seldom end there; and they cannot if the style or work is to invite the attention of a wide range of people over a period of time.[26]

Neither Wolterstorff's analytical terms nor Burch Brown's ground rules for developing ecumenical taste will magically eliminate disagreements over artistic use and style, but they can prevent disagreements from turning toxic. At their best, these tools might even turn arguments about art into occasions for communal discernment and deepened discipleship.

Scholarship and experience have largely undermined the twentieth-century modernist assumption that abstraction entails spirituality and that naturalism is too mundane to bear the weight of the sacred. A savvy congregation can make "inclusive yet discerning" use of any variety of stylistic modes.[27] Once again, the Cathedral of Los Angeles, Our Lady of the Angels,

---

23. Burch Brown, *Good Taste, Bad Taste*, p. 96.
24. Ibid., p. 250.
25. Ibid., p. 251.
26. Ibid., pp. 250–51. For the full list of grounding assumptions, see appendix B.
27. The phrase mirrors the title of Frank Burch Brown's work, *Inclusive Yet Discerning*.

Bonaventure Peter
Claver Andrew
Felicitas Perpetua

Fig. 24. John Nava, panel from the *Communion of the Saints* tapestries on the north side of the nave, Cathedral of Our Lady of the Angels, Los Angeles.

provides a terrific example of what such discernment might look like in practice. Flanking the side aisles of the nave, long, large tapestries show naturalistically represented saints facing the altar (fig. 24). The tapestries surround worshipers with a great cloud of witnesses, a motif that dates back to the earliest Christian churches in Rome. Alongside those naturalistically represented saints, worshipers face an altar and a crucifix more abstract in character (fig. 25). And at the rear of the apse, behind the altar and the crucifix, the *New Jerusalem* tapestry (fig. 19) uses two kinds of abstraction, a symbol and a map, to represent God's eternal, incarnate presence in a very particular, earthly place — the city of Los Angeles. Naturalistic and abstract works all point toward the same profound mystery, the mystery of the worshiping church, which is already manifest in this local congregation while not yet fully realized in the new Jerusalem.

Fig. 25. Altar and crucifix, Cathedral of Our Lady of the Angels, Los Angeles.

CHAPTER 9

Inculturation & Enculturation

The reality that Christian worship is always cel-
ebrated in a given local cultural setting draws our
attention to the dynamics between worship and the
world's many local cultures.

— *NAIROBI STATEMENT ON WORSHIP AND CULTURE*[1]

If, as I've claimed in a previous chapter, all visual representation is local, what are the implications of this claim for the worshiping church? At the very least, it means that the visual arts are a prime site for *in*culturation, the "process of reciprocal assimilation between Christianity and culture and the resulting interior transformation of culture on the one hand, and the rooting of Christianity in culture on the other."[2] The visual arts, along with music and language, space and symbol, dress and gesture, are a means by which the specificity of local, human embeddedness in space and time is taken up into the universal, everlasting reign of God. When the arts are vehicles of *in*culturation, they speak the truth and force of the gospel in a local idiom. Equally true, however,

---

1. Department of Theology and Studies of the Lutheran World Federation, *Nairobi Statement on Worship and Culture: Contemporary Challenges and Opportunities* (Geneva: Lutheran World Federation, 1996), par. 1.2.

2. This is Anscar Chupungco's definition, taken from his *Liturgical Inculturation: Sacramentals, Religiosity, and Catechesis* (Collegeville, MN: Liturgical Press, 1992), p. 29, and first introduced in chapter 1.

the visual arts are a prime site for *en*culturation, "very largely an informal, even unconscious, experience . . . the rules of which are given by society."[3] When the arts are vehicles of *en*culturation, they run the risk of reenvisioning the gospel as entirely culturally compatible, forcing the Word into the normative, uncritically accepted forms of local culture. In this case, the gospel does not transform culture; rather, culture transforms the gospel. And perhaps, on occasion, the visual arts are also sites for what missiologist Aylward Shorter calls "cultural domination," which is "characterized by an ethnocentric posture on the part of the dominating culture that is so strong as to amount to the claim to be a 'world culture.'"[4]

Much of our human particularity is precious to God, an outgrowth of creation's intent. But some of our particularity, or, perhaps more precisely, *our interpretation of our particularity*, is sinful, requiring the Spirit's correction and chastening. It's especially problematic when we confuse what's local with what's universal. When we compare Orthodox, Catholic, and varied Protestant interactions with the visual arts to one another, what emerges quite clearly is the way in which the arts express ecclesial identities that are often unconsciously assumed to be universal but are in fact deeply particular to a specific culture. The particularity itself is not the problem. It's what we do with that particularity, what we make of it, that might require a bit more attention.

A word on terminology is in order here. There is little agreement on the best terms to describe the interaction of Christian faith and culture. Preferred terms have varied over time and continue to vary from discipline to discipline, from region to region, and from confessional community to confessional community.[5] For my purposes, I've chosen to adopt the widely used definitions provided by Aylward Shorter in his 1988 *Toward a Theology of Inculturation*. Shorter begins by defining "culture" as irreducibly human: "a transmitted pattern of meanings embodied in symbols, a pattern capable of development and change, and it belongs to the concept of humanness itself."[6] If culture belongs to the concept of humanness itself, then "Chris-

---

3. Aylward Shorter, *Toward a Theology of Inculturation* (Maryknoll, NY: Orbis, 1988), p. 5.

4. Ibid., p. 9.

5. I'm grateful for the insights of my Westmont colleague Reuben "Tito" Paredes-Alfaro, an anthropologist, on the difficult question of appropriate terminology.

6. Shorter, *Inculturation*, p. 5.

tian faith cannot exist except in a cultural form."[7] There is no "pure" gospel that is comprehensible to human beings that can be grasped outside of a cultural context. Inculturation, then, is unavoidable and is "the creative and dynamic relationship between the Christian message and a culture or cultures."[8] This dynamic relationship is "as relevant to the countries of Europe and North America, for example, which have been Christianized and now de-Christianized, as it is to the cultures of the Third World."[9]

Shorter himself would prefer the term "interculturation," which avoids the possibility of imagining that there is a pure, uninculturated gospel that is then inserted into varied cultural contexts. He writes, "'inculturation' by itself suggests merely the transfer of faith from one culture to another, the insertion of the Christian message into a given culture. In short, it seems to suggest that the process of mission or evangelization is a one-way process. To create such an impression is unfortunate, and it is the reason why some missiologists are dissatisfied with the term."[10] He continues, "'[I]nterculturation' correctly expresses the sociological and the theological reality, both at the individual and collective, cultural levels."[11] In spite of these drawbacks, Shorter concludes that "inculturation" is still the most useful term; it expresses the sense "that the Christian message transforms a culture. It is also the case that Christianity is transformed by culture, not in a way that falsifies the message, but in the way in which the message is formulated and interpreted anew."[12] While some scholars prefer other terms, "inculturation" remains the dominant term in the literature.

Orthodox

Chapter 1 recounted the Orthodox covenant with icons. We all have much to learn from the profoundly formative, ecclesial obedience reflected in the Orthodox understanding of icons. Orthodox Christians understand icons, both in their content and in their style, to be universal. Icons are seen as ve-

---

7. Ibid., p. 12.
8. Ibid., p. 11.
9. Ibid., p. 12.
10. Ibid., p. 13.
11. Ibid., p. 14.
12. Ibid., p. 14.

hicles of inculturation only insofar as they — through wood, pigment, color, and form — concretize the reality of the kingdom of God and "bring heaven down to earth," as Orthodox Christians are fond of saying. Icons are not understood as having inculturated the gospel into a particular late Roman/ early Christian strand of human culture. For Orthodox Christians, icons inculturate the gospel to human culture *tout court*. The Orthodox position has the virtue of clarity, consistency, and a certain elegant practicality.

There are few serious arguments about icons in Orthodox congregations. Near the end of my discussion in chapter 4, however, I hesitantly suggested that the formal constraints that govern Orthodox iconography might in fact represent a historically local style that, in ensuing centuries, acquired universalized status. Universalizing the basic traits of late Roman/ early Christian style forecloses the possibility that any other approach, that any other "native iconography," could ever be valid. Without diminishing the lively inculturation that icons do represent in their cultures of origin, might it also be the case that other cultures' indigenous styles could bear the weight of glory required for proper iconicity? That they, too, could be created and received in faithful obedience to Holy Tradition? If the naturalistic printed icons at Saint John Chrysostom can still function as icons, sanctified by generations of prayer, is it not possible that other cultures' visual vocabularies could as well? And without being labeled degenerate or deficient? What we would lose in such an expansion is a particular perception of universality, a stable, consistent way of imagining the church universal. But what we might gain is an expanded imagination for the breadth and reach of God's church throughout time and space.

Roman Catholic

Catholics have done more careful thinking about the entwinement of art and culture than any other confessional community, and chapter 2 recounted the important lessons the Roman Catholic Church learned in enacting the reforms of the Second Vatican Council. The Catholic Church's official stance toward cultural diversity in worship is heartening. But the Catholic discussion, turning on the relationship between devotional activity and corporate worship, has tended to assume that Western notions of "private" and "public" are stable, universal properties of human society and experience. This has created confusion both about artistic style and about the nature of devotional activity. Chapter 2 highlighted in particular the tension between the church's official openness to every culture's visual forms and practices and the assumption of local, post-Enlightenment, northern European norms that served at once to disenfranchise a range of visual practices (both Western and non-Western) and to privilege a more austere, modernist stylistic turn. The highly naturalistic styles associated with European devotionalism became, by extension, problematic as styles, and were rejected in favor of a supposedly more universal, more transcendent modernist style (which is, in fact, merely another kind of local style). Furthermore, the very real liturgical problems with European devotionalism were projected onto devotional practices around the globe, whether or not those practices were in fact marked by the same individualism and subjectivity as European devotionalism. That assumption has made it difficult to imagine how any communal devotional practice rooted in a non-Western culture can be appropriately integrated into corporate worship. In theory, the Catholic Church has clearly acknowledged the power of the visual arts to inculturate the gospel. In practice, its challenge has been to see past the local character of its own analytical categories. It is a testament to the depth of Roman Catholic commitment to these questions that some of the best literature on inculturation comes from Catholic theologians and missiologists, carefully working through these questions on the ground, in churches both in North America and around the world.

Protestant

Chapter 3 focused the discussion less on the internal practices and structures of Protestant churches concerning the visual arts than on the ways in which artists and art lovers are socialized by our North American art system. The assumptions nourished in our art system, I argued, shape what happens in Protestant congregations far more than any biblical or theological rationales we may provide to justify artistic engagement. The consequences of this situation generate, on the one hand, tremendous freedom for activist artists to experiment creatively in their congregations and, on the other, tremendous vulnerability. Even in confessional traditions that are theologically and historically more practiced with visual representation — Lutheranism and Anglicanism, for example — an art-interested congregation will not find much consistent institutional support or many officially endorsed resources. Art-interested Protestant congregations are generally on their own. But, forced to rely on their own initiative and resources, they are also free to experiment and discover cultural convergences that can make the visual arts part and parcel of their mission. There is often little reflection, however, on the nature of the cultural exchange that might be taking place and the extent to which the energy and direction of that exchange might be coming principally from outside the congregation. Art programs in Protestant settings, then, are vulnerable to uncritical adoption of art-system assumptions that may not be entirely compatible with art destined for congregational use. To what extent is a congregation's engagement with the visual arts a genuine inculturation of the gospel that transforms the art as well as the church? Or possibly, to what extent is it further enculturating Christians into local artistic norms that might in fact need to be challenged to be more fully and more richly transformed by the gospel?

Reflections for Congregations

There are no easy answers for any Orthodox, Catholic, or Protestant congregation to the questions raised by its confessional community. In all three cases, what passes for *in*culturation (the constant, Spirit-filled transformative dialogue between gospel and culture) may be, more often than not, *en*culturation (the unconscious reframing of the gospel to fit familiar cultural norms), or even, on occasion, cultural domination ("our" way is the only true, Christian way). Which term actually describes the engagement with the visual arts in any specific congregation depends entirely on how self-aware we are willing to be regarding the origins of our artistic practices, how attuned we are to the ecclesiologies our practices embody, and how thoughtful we are about the ways in which our visual representations foster our common worship, and shared mission.

One of the best tools currently available to help congregations sort through these questions is the *Nairobi Statement*, a document drafted in

1996 by the Lutheran World Federation's study team on worship and culture.[13] The statement begins with the conviction that "Worship is the heart and pulse of the Christian Church. In worship we celebrate together God's gracious gifts of creation and salvation, and are strengthened to live in response to God's grace. Worship always involves actions, not merely words. To consider worship is to consider music, art, and architecture, as well as liturgy and preaching" (par. 1.1). It then continues, "The reality that Christian worship is always celebrated in a given local cultural setting draws our attention to the dynamics between worship and the world's many local cultures" (par. 1.2). The final section of the introduction lays out four gospel/ culture relationships that churches should be aware of and be able to identify in their worship: "Christian worship relates dynamically to culture in at least four ways. First, it is *transcultural*, the same substance for everyone everywhere, beyond culture. Second, it is *contextual*, varying according to the local situation (both nature and culture). Third, it is *counter-cultural*, challenging what is contrary to the Gospel in a given culture. Fourth, it is *cross-cultural*, making possible sharing between different local cultures. In all four dynamics, there are helpful principles which can be identified" (par. 1.3). The ordering of these relationships is important. Beginning with the fundamentals of our shared faith (transcultural), the statement then acknowledges that our shared faith takes root in varied local cultures (contextual). Those cultures, in turn, need the purification of the gospel (countercultural), so that finally we can rejoice together, in the rich diversity of God's kingdom (cross-cultural).

What might you notice when you examine your congregation's use of the visual arts using these four cultural lenses? Perhaps some images, activities, or practices that you assumed to be transcultural are in fact contextual. Perhaps some of what you imagined as cross-cultural is actually transcultural. And perhaps you might see afresh ways in which the arts can engage in countercultural formation, fostering a deeper reciprocity between gospel and culture through which both are deepened, enriched, and enlivened with the quickening, life-breathing power of God's Holy Spirit.

---

13. Lutheran World Federation, *Nairobi Statement.* For the full text of the *Nairobi Statement*, see appendix C.

Faithful, Fruitful, and Sustainable

Let the favor of the Lord our God be upon us,
and prosper for us the work of our hands —
O prosper the work of our hands!

— PSALM 90:17

Prepare for the Journey

A core contention at the heart of this study is that having a biblical and theological rationale for being an artist or for introducing the visual arts into the worshiping church is not sufficient grounds for launching a meaningful arts program. I do not want to imply, however, that a biblical or theological rationale is not necessary. Far from it! We cannot neglect this task. All Christian artists, especially those of us working in and for the church, need to understand our work in light of our fundamental commitment to our triune God and to God's church.

Returning to our geographic metaphors from the introduction, solid biblical and theological grounds for what we do are like the passports and visas that grant us permission to travel. If we can't articulate to ourselves or to others why, as Christians, the arts matter, we probably shouldn't head off in their direction in the first place. But just as real-life passports and visas look different depending on their country of origin, so biblical and theological rationales differ as well, depending on their community of origin. Creation, redemption, incarnation, sacrament, Trinity — all these have been powerful, legitimate starting points for building a biblical and theological case for the visual arts in the life of the church. Not all of them are in circulation in all Christian communities; however, it can be inspiring and instructive to look at the passports issued by other Christian confessional communities. The aim of this study has not been to issue passports or visas. That's been the task of many, many other books on Christianity and the arts.[1]

In addition to having passport and visa in hand, savvy travelers anticipate the challenges they are likely to encounter. Sometimes special equipment or even immunizations are in order. That is to say — be prepared for the standard objections you will meet along your way. Depending on your congregation and its confessional orientation, the standard objections will differ. Some of you — probably very few — will need to offer defenses against accusations of idolatry. Many more will need to explain why spending money on the arts is not wasting resources that should go to other ministries. Still others may need to respond to the charge that visuals in worship are a distraction from pure, spiritual worship. All of us should be able to give a positive account for the stylistic choices we make. But once again, the purpose of this study has not been in the equipment or immunization

---

1. The following texts represent just handful of the myriad books and articles that offer biblical and theological rationales for art from varied confessional perspectives, Orthodox to free-church Protestant. They vary in length and difficulty, but each is representative of a typical approach: Leonid Ouspensky, *Theology of the Icon*, translated by Anthony Gythiel with selections translated by Elizabeth Meyendorff, 2 vols. (Crestwood, NY: St. Vladimir's Seminary Press, 1992); Pope John Paul II, "Letter to Artists," Easter Sunday, April 4, 1999; Richard R. Caemmerer, *Visual Art in the Life of the Church: Encouraging Creative Worship and Witness in the Congregation* (Minneapolis: Augsburg, 1983); Dorothy L. Sayers, *The Mind of the Maker* (New York: Harcourt, Brace and Co., 1941); Janet Walton, *Art and Worship: A Vital Connection* (Wilmington, DE: Michael Glazier, 1988); Nicholas Wolterstorff, *Art in Action: Toward a Christian Aesthetic* (Grand Rapids: Eerdmans, 1980); Francis A. Schaeffer, *Art and the Bible: Two Essays* (Downers Grove: InterVarsity, 1973); Colin Harbinson et al., "Redeeming the Arts: The Restoration of the Arts to God's Creational Intention," Lausanne Occasional Paper #46, Lausanne Movement, 2005; Jeremy Begbie, *Voicing Creation's Praise: Towards a Theology of the Arts* (Edinburgh: T. & T. Clark, 1991); Steven R. Guthrie, *Creator Spirit: The Holy Spirit and the Art of Becoming Human* (Grand Rapids: Baker Academic, 2011); and Harold M. Best, *Unceasing Worship: Biblical Perspectives on Worship and the Arts* (Downers Grove: InterVarsity, 2003).

department. There are other books and articles that have provided apologias for the arts on these questions.[2]

The aim of this study has been cartographic, a survey of the varied topographies of the visual arts in the worshiping church, a map of the landmasses and water features that push and pull us into distinct paths through the landscape. It is my hope that, with map in hand, you will have a better understanding of why your journey runs as it does in your particular landscape. I also hope that, now having a better way to navigate, you might want to visit other distinct topographies. So, assuming passports, visas, equipment, and immunizations are taken care of, what's left is to set off, to see what we can see.

Identify Governing Assumptions

The fundamental argument at the heart of this study has been that the social dimensions of both art and the church matter — and matter hugely — for the visual arts in Christian congregations. Ecclesiology, a congregation's operational theology of itself as "church," is one social lens on the question. The second social lens is comprised of the various art worlds that make up our larger art system and that, in turn, form different kinds of artists. Understanding how the two intersect is key to understanding what can and can't happen, what will and won't work, what is possible and what might be impossible concerning the visual arts in any given congregation. Where ecclesiologies are highly universal, for example, the visual arts are typically steered in particular directions to represent and preserve that unified identity across time and space. Where ecclesiologies are highly local, the sensibilities of local art worlds will determine the direction the arts take.

Step one, then, is to consider the governing assumptions about "church" and about "art" circulating in your congregation. What is the operational

2. As of the publication of this book, the most recent book to tackle the standard objections is Michael Bauer's *Arts Ministry: Nurturing the Creative Life of God's People* (Grand Rapids: Eerdmans, 2013). For a succinct appreciation of the many and varied roles that imagery already plays in religious life, turn to the introduction to David Morgan and Sally M. Promey, eds., *The Visual Culture of American Religions* (Berkeley: University of California Press, 2001), pp. 1–24.

ecclesiology in your congregation? It might be useful to use Avery Dulles's ecclesiological types (institutional, mystical communion, sacrament, herald, servant, and community of disciples) from his book *Models of the Church* as a framework for conversation in your congregation.[3] Do any of these types resonate with your congregation's character and commitments? Is your congregation's operational ecclesiology in line with its official ecclesiology? If not, where do they depart? What do those departures mean? Are the departures helpful corrections or problematic diversions?

In addition to *church*, what ideas of *art* and *artist* are in play in your congregation? This question is equally important. Do the art leaders and art lovers in your church bring the sensibilities of the master of fine arts (MFA) or the graphic designer or the art educator, or perhaps the liturgical consultant or iconographer, to their work? How do those assumptions and commitments play out in their work as artists in the congregation? How do those assumptions direct the arts programming in the congregation?

Learn from Other Traditions

Assumptions, by their very nature, are hard to identify. Assumptions are what we take for granted, not what we self-consciously name. That's where comparison helps. Comparisons can bring to light elements that are otherwise taken entirely for granted. The juxtaposition of Orthodox, Catholic, and various Protestant practices concerning the visual arts brought to light six themes that appeared unremarkable within their own contexts, but quite remarkable when viewed against the foil of other confessional communities. Three of these themes are ecclesial: how worship enacts the universal and local identity of a given congregation, how a congregation enacts story and presence in worship, and how a congregation relates (private) individual devotion to (public) corporate worship. The other three themes involve the cultural exchange between our churches and our larger North American art system: how churches institutionalize or professionalize the artists in their midst to channel and direct artistic activism toward particular ends; the meanings ascribed to naturalism and abstraction in our art system, and

---

3. Avery Dulles, *Models of the Church* (Garden City, NY: Image Books, 1987).

how these meanings have functioned in ecclesial settings; and, finally, the ways in which the visual arts participate in the process of inculturating and enculturating the gospel.

What intrigued you most about the traditions that are not your own described in this study? Why did those elements capture your attention? While remaining faithful to your own confessional community, what might these other ecclesial traditions have to teach you or your congregation? Answers to these questions will be different for every reader and every congregation. For myself, I'm drawn to the strongly institutionalized, ecclesial training of artists in the Orthodox tradition. I'm also intrigued by the way in which icons help foster the deep reciprocity between worship and daily life that expresses the profoundly communal character of Orthodox identity. I'm also convicted by the Roman Catholic Church's post–Vatican II concern that Sunday worship be truly corporate and communal rather than an exercise of simultaneous individual devotion. I'm equally impressed by the range of resources and materials that the Catholic Church has developed to enable such worship. Finally, I'm encouraged by the space for creative cultural convergence found in many Protestant churches, and I am humbled by the passion and energy that so many artists and art lovers in these settings willingly lavish on their congregations, often with little support for or understanding of the hard work involved. While some of the approaches to the visual arts detailed in the three descriptive chapters of part 1 are mutually exclusive, others are not. You may find in those other traditions tools to increase the efficacy and depth of your work with the arts in your congregation.

Faithful, Fruitful, Sustainable

I've imagined throughout this study that most readers will be Protestant artists and art-loving Protestant pastors and laypeople — those of us who have labored long and hard, sometimes without much support, out of sheer love of art as a part of God's good creation and out of a strong conviction that the arts deepen and enrich our worship and our congregational life. In some respects, this study has probably raised more questions than it has answered. What is the operational ecclesiology of your congregation? How do the visual arts enter into story and presence in the life of your church?

Conclusion

How genuinely communal is your congregation's worship? Do the arts facilitate reciprocity between personal devotion and corporate worship, helping form congregants as unique, individual persons but also as a people? What assumptions about art are in circulation? What art worlds are present in your congregation? What assumptions about style dominate the discussion? What kinds of cultural engagement do the visual arts enact in your setting? Willingness to consider these questions is an act of Christian faithfulness — faithfulness to God, to our churches, to the artists and worshipers in our midst, and to our lovely but broken world that we are called to serve.

I also hope, however, that for all the questions this study has raised, that in equal measure it has clarified challenges and pointed toward new opportunities for faithful, fruitful, and sustainable work with the arts in our congregations. Particularly for Protestant congregations, dependent as they often are on the vision of one or two artists or art lovers, the challenge of sustainability is acute. A congregation may enjoy a fantastic arts program — as long as those one or two people continue to make it happen. Longevity, however, requires embedding both the vision and the logistics of an art program into the larger life of the congregation — into its identity, its committee structure, and its budget. Successful integration, in turn, depends on the extent to which a program is fruitful. In their different ways, the Orthodox and Catholic Churches provide models for sustainability and fruitfulness that might with adjustment inspire Protestant readers. When the visual arts deepen a congregation's worship and strengthen a congregation's ministry, they will become the responsibility of the church as a whole and not just the special project of one or two visionaries. In honor of all those visionaries, past and present, Orthodox, Catholic, and Protestant, who have worked toward that day, let us pray with the psalmist,

> Let the favor of the Lord our God be upon us,
> and prosper for us the work of our hands —
> O prosper the work of our hands!

EPILOGUE

Three years after the project I described in the introduction to this study, my students and I tried again. Our second project was a direct outgrowth of the learning that happened our first time around. We designed it to improve both our process and our product. Whereas our first project had used three groups of artists, each tasked with creating one work of art, the "Stations of Christ's Life" project featured fourteen groups, each composed of one student artist with three or four friends who were interested in art but not artists themselves.

Changing the composition of the working groups changed the character of the conversations that happened in those groups. The in-house, artist-to-artist arguments that hobbled our first project were transformed into more productive artist-audience dialogues. Whereas our first project gave each group of artists a blank slate, provided that in the end the group's piece was ultimately somehow about worship in a college context, our second project anchored each group in a biblical text and tied the design process to investigation of that text. Whereas our first project focused almost entirely on the process of making the work and was quite vague about how members of the college community were actually supposed to engage the finished works, our second project was devised from the outset to have a number of specific goals: connecting Christ's passion, death, and resurrection to the character of his entire ministry; connecting our personal Lenten devotions to our life together as a college community; and, finally, connecting our majority Protestant college to the local Catholic community by using the format of the Stations of the Cross and by pointing to various Catholic stations near campus for use during Holy Week.

It is tempting to say that our second project was much more successful than our first and leave it at that. It's undeniably true that by any number of measures, our second project was indeed more successful. It's equally true that our first project was supremely successful in exposing our assumptions and revealing where the real questions lurked. Intuitively, moving from our first experiment into our second, we were feeling our way toward the "now what?" questions that emerged in this study.

Our solutions were tentative, but being so, they were also characterized by more artistic humility, more sensitivity to our context, and greater accountability to our community than was the case for our first attempt. Such humility and tentativeness didn't always feel comfortable, but, in the end, they were deeply instructive. One student commented, "Dependence on an audience is something I have never been quite comfortable with, but this was a great learning experience. The more I love my neighbor, the more I will be willing to reach them." Another noted how freeing it was "to go to the community instead of convincing the community to come to me." A third named the difficulty of giving up his assumed artistic autonomy: "Flexibility is absolutely necessary when working with a group. This was truly a challenge to my self-centered tendencies." Finally, summing up her learning, one student artist discovered, to her delight, that art could "make a hospitable space for God to have a conversation with his people."

What might be next for your congregation?

Artistic Excellence, Aesthetic Excellence, and Fittingness

These quotes from *Art in Action: Toward a Christian Aesthetic* (Grand Rapids: Eerdmans, 1980) provide Nicholas Wolterstorff's definitions of the three terms ("artistic excellence," "aesthetic excellence," and "fittingness") I used in chapter 8, "Naturalism & Abstraction." They are taken from part 3: "Art in Christian Perspective." All italics in these excerpts are in the original text. I recommend this book to any artist or congregation looking for a broad explanation for why and how the arts function as they do in modern Western society.

On Artistic Excellence

[W]orks of art are human artifacts, produced and distributed for a purpose — objects and instruments of intentional action . . . proving generally good and satisfying to use for [their] purpose. (p. 156)

A good hymn is one that serves well the purpose of hymns. A good concerto is one that serves well the purpose of concertos. A good piece of background music is one that serves well the purpose of background music. A good drinking song is one that serves well the purpose of drinking songs. Let us say that a work of art has *artistic excellence* if it serves well the purpose for which it was made or distributed. (p. 157)

On Aesthetic Excellence

Concertos are produced, and presented or distributed to us, in order to provide satisfaction upon aesthetic contemplation. On the theory just offered, a good concerto is one that serves its purpose well. It is effective in yielding satisfaction when submitted to aesthetic contemplation and it proves generally good and satisfying to use in this way. (p. 158)

An *aesthetically excellent* object is one that effectively serves the purpose of contemplation for aesthetic delight. (p. 158)

On the Relationship between Artistic and Aesthetic Excellence

A hymn is a *good* hymn if it serves its purpose effectively and then in addition proves good and satisfying to use for this purpose, that purpose being to enable a congregation to offer praise to God — *not, be it noted, to give delight upon aesthetic contemplation.* Thus the quality of a hymn is to be judged first of all by its effectiveness in serving its purpose. Likewise the quality of a concerto is to be judged first of all by its effectiveness in serving its particular purpose, that of giving delight upon aesthetic contemplation. In general, hymns serve aesthetic contemplation less effectively than do concertos. But that no more decisively determines their quality as hymns than does the fact that a concerto serves poorly the purpose of enabling a congregation to praise God decisively determine its quality as a concerto.

I added, however, that if a hymn is to be good, it must, like any other artifact, not only serve its purpose effectively, but also prove *good and satisfying to use for this purpose.* Can we say, then, that if a hymn is to prove good and satisfying to use for praising God, it must in general be aesthetically good? To prove generally good and satisfying to use for its intended purpose, must it be such that if it were contemplated aesthetically it would give us satisfaction, perhaps not as much as works made deliberately for this purpose, yet some satisfaction nonetheless, not just boredom or disgust? In brief, must a good hymn be *aesthetically* good?

I think the answer is Yes . . . [as] it is for human artifacts in general. Relatively few have as their dominant purpose to give delight upon aesthetic contemplation. But the rest do not simply escape our attention. With infinite gradations of degree they lure our awareness, or force themselves upon it. And the aesthetic merits in them produce their effects on us whether or not we submit them to aesthetic contemplation. There is no such thing as a *good* artifact . . . which is aesthetically poor. Or to put it more cautiously, and more accurately: If an artifact occupies a significant place in our perceptual field, then, it is a better artifact if it is an *aesthetically* better artifact. (pp. 169–70)

On Fittingness

Artists are workers in *fittingness* — all artists, inescapably, not indeed in the sense that their work is *made out of* fittingness, but rather in the sense that fittingness is a feature of the reality within which we all exist. (p. 96)

Fittingness is similarity across modalities. *Fittingness is cross-modal similarity.* To say that *large* fits better with *loud* than with *soft* (in sound) is to say that the cross-modal similarity between *large* and *loud* is closer than that between *large* and *soft*. (p. 99)

[I]n what respect do qualities resemble each other across modalities? The answer is that they resemble each other with respect to preferability, . . . with respect to potency, and with respect to activity. Previously it was obscure in what respect *loud* resembles *large* more than *small*. Now there is clarity: with respect to potency. And now it is clear that it is with respect to *activity* that a jagged line resembles restlessness, and an undulating one, tranquility. (pp. 107–8)

[T]he expressiveness of objects inheres . . . in the *relations of fittingness* that the aesthetic characters of those objects bear to the qualities which those objects express. (p. 112)

Christian Taste

The excerpt below comes from Frank Burch Brown's *Good Taste, Bad Taste, and Christian Taste: Aesthetics in Religious Life* (Oxford: Oxford University Press, 2000), pp. 250–51. *Good Taste, Bad Taste, and Christian Taste* is an academic exposition of Burch Brown's idea of cultivating *ecumenical taste*, which he also develops for a more general audience in *Inclusive Yet Discerning: Navigating Worship Artfully* (Grand Rapids: Eerdmans, 2009).

[L]et me conclude this penultimate portion of our study by setting forth twelve assumptions that I hope could fruitfully guide discussions of aesthetic taste as they arise in the next stage of religious, and specifically Christian, development in relation to the arts. None of these should come as a surprise to readers who have come this far in the present book. I regard them as assumptions or premises rather than as goals; but one could also look on them as habits of mind useful for exercising Christian taste in healthy ways. By calling them assumptions I do not mean that they do not require support (which the rest of the book has been intended to provide), only that such points cannot immediately be argued from the ground up when matters of Christian taste are in dispute.

1.   There are many kinds of good taste, and many kinds of good religious art and music. In view of cultural diversity, it would be extremely odd if that were not true.

2.   Not all kinds of good art and music are equally good for worship, let alone for every tradition or faith community. In terms of worship,

therefore, it is not enough that a work or style of art be likeable; it must also be appropriate.

3. There are various appropriately Christian modes of mediating religious experience artistically — from radically transcendent to radically immanent in a sense of the sacred; from exuberantly abundant to starkly minimal in means; from prophetic to pastoral in tone; from instructive to meditative in aim.

4. Every era and cultural context tends to develop new forms of sacred music and art, which to begin with often seem secular to many people.

5. Because every musical/aesthetic style calls for a particular type of attunement, no one person can possibly be competent to make equally discerning judgments about every kind of music or art. Yet almost everyone is inclined to assume or act otherwise. That impulse is related to the sin of pride.

6. It is an act of Christian love to learn to appreciate or at least respect what others value in a particular style or work that they cherish in worship or in the rest of life. That is different, however, from personally liking every form of commendable art, which is impossible and unnecessary.

7. Disagreements over taste in religious music (or any other art) can be healthy and productive; but they touch on sensitive matters and often reflect or embody religious differences as well as aesthetic ones.

8. The reasons why an aesthetic work or style is good or bad, weak or strong (and in what circumstances), can never be expressed fully in words; yet they can often be pointed out through comparative — and repeated — looking and listening.

9. Aesthetic judgments begin with, and owe special consideration to, the community or tradition to which a given style or work is indigenous or most familiar. But they seldom end there; and they cannot if the style or work is to invite the attention of a wide range of people over a period of time.

10. The overall evaluation of any art used in worship needs to be a joint effort between clergy, congregation and trained artists and musicians, taking into account not only the aesthetic qualities of the art itself but also the larger requirements and contours of worship,

which should at once respond to and orient the particular work of art or music.

11. While relative accessibility is imperative for most church art, the church also needs art — including "classic" art of various kinds — that continually challenges and solicits spiritual and theological growth in the aesthetic dimension. This is art that the Christian can grow into but seldom out of.

12. Almost every artistic style that has been enjoyed and valued by a particular group over a long period of time and for a wide range of purposes has religious potential. That is because life typically finds various and surprising ways of turning religious. As Augustine said, our hearts are restless until they rest in God.

Nairobi Statement on Worship and Culture:
Contemporary Challenges and Opportunities

Below, I reproduce the *Nairobi Statement on Worship and Culture* in its entirety,[1] including the preamble that situates the statement with respect to the work of the Lutheran World Federation in the mid-1990s.

This statement is from the third international consultation of the Lutheran World Federation's Study Team on Worship and Culture, held in Nairobi, Kenya, in January 1996. The members of the Study Team represent five continents of the world. . . . The initial consultation, in October 1993 in Cartigny, Switzerland, focused on the biblical and historical foundations of the relationship between Christian worship and culture, and resulted in the "Cartigny Statement on Worship and Culture: Biblical and Historical Foundations." (This Nairobi Statement builds upon the Cartigny Statement; in no sense does it replace it.) The second consultation, in March 1994 in Hong Kong, explored contemporary issues and questions of the relationships between the world's cultures and Christian liturgy, church music, and church architecture and art. The papers of the first two consultations were published as "Worship and Culture in Dialogue."[2] The papers and statement from the Nairobi consultation were published as "Christian Worship: Unity in Cultural Diversity."[3] In 1994–95, the Study Team conducted regional research, and prepared reports on that research. Phase IV of

1. Reprinted with permission of the Lutheran World Federation.
2. Geneva: Lutheran World Federation, 1994. Also published in French, German, and Spanish.
3. Geneva: Lutheran World Federation, 1996. Also published in German.

the Study commenced in Nairobi and will continue with seminars and other means to implement the learnings of the study, as LWF member churches decide is helpful. The Study Team considers this project to be essential to the renewal and mission of the Church around the world.

1. Introduction

1.1. Worship is the heart and pulse of the Christian Church. In worship we celebrate together God's gracious gifts of creation and salvation, and are strengthened to live in response to God's grace. Worship always involves actions, not merely words. To consider worship is to consider music, art, and architecture, as well as liturgy and preaching.

1.2. The reality that Christian worship is always celebrated in a given local cultural setting draws our attention to the dynamics between worship and the world's many local cultures.

1.3. Christian worship relates dynamically to culture in at least four ways. First, it is transcultural, the same substance for everyone everywhere, beyond culture. Second, it is contextual, varying according to the local situation (both nature and culture). Third, it is counter-cultural, challenging what is contrary to the Gospel in a given culture. Fourth, it is cross-cultural, making possible sharing between different local cultures. In all four dynamics, there are helpful principles which can be identified.

2. Worship as Transcultural

2.1. The resurrected Christ whom we worship, and through whom by the power of the Holy Spirit we know the grace of the Triune God, transcends and indeed is beyond all cultures. In the mystery of his resurrection is the source of the transcultural nature of Christian worship. Baptism and Eucharist, the sacraments of Christ's death and resurrection, were given by God for all the world. There is one Bible, translated into many tongues, and biblical preaching of Christ's death and resurrection has been sent into all the world. The fundamental shape of the principal Sunday act of Christian worship, the Eucharist or Holy Communion, is shared across cultures: the people gather, the Word of God is proclaimed, the people intercede for the needs of the Church and the world, the eucharistic meal is shared, and the people are sent out into the world for mission. The great narratives of Christ's birth, death, resurrection, and sending of the Spirit, and our Baptism into him, provide the central meanings of the transcultural times of the church's year: especially Lent/Easter/Pentecost, and, to a lesser extent, Advent/Christmas/Epiphany. The ways in which the shapes of the Sunday Eucharist and the church year are expressed vary by culture, but their meanings and fundamental structure are shared around the globe. There is one Lord, one faith, one Baptism, one Eucharist.

2.2. Several specific elements of Christian liturgy are also transcultural, e.g., readings from the Bible (although of course the translations vary), the ecumenical creeds and the Our Father, and Baptism in water in the Triune Name.

2.3. The use of this shared core liturgical structure and these shared liturgical elements in local congregational worship — as well as the shared act of people assembling together, and the shared provision of diverse leadership in that assembly (although the space for the assembly and the manner of the leadership vary) — are expressions of Christian unity across time, space, culture, and confession. The recovery in each congregation of the clear centrality of these transcultural and ecumenical elements renews the sense of this Christian unity and gives all churches a solid basis for authentic contextualization.

3. Worship as Contextual

3.1. Jesus whom we worship was born into a specific culture of the world. In the mystery of his incarnation are the model and the mandate for the contextualization of Christian worship. God can be and is encountered in the local cultures of our world. A given culture's values and patterns, insofar as they are consonant with the values of the Gospel, can be used to express the meaning and purpose of Christian worship. Contextualization is a necessary task for the Church's mission in the world, so that the Gospel can be ever more deeply rooted in diverse local cultures.

3.2. Among the various methods of contextualization, that of dynamic equivalence is particularly useful. It involves re-expressing components of Christian worship with something from a local culture that has an equal meaning, value, and function. Dynamic equivalence goes far beyond mere translation; it involves understanding the fundamental meanings both of elements of worship and of the local culture, and enabling the meanings and actions of worship to be "encoded" and re-expressed in the language of local culture.

3.3. In applying the method of dynamic equivalence, the following procedure may be followed. First, the liturgical ordo (basic shape) should be examined with regard to its theology, history, basic elements, and cultural backgrounds. Second, those elements of the ordo that can be subjected to dynamic equivalence without prejudice to their meaning should be determined. Third, those components of culture that are able to re-express the Gospel and the liturgical ordo in an adequate manner should be studied. Fourth, the spiritual and pastoral benefits our people will derive from the changes should be considered.

3.4. Local churches might also consider the method of creative assimilation. This consists of adding pertinent components of local culture to the liturgical ordo in order to enrich its original core. The baptismal ordo of "washing with water and the Word," for example, was gradually elaborated by the assimilation of such cultural practices as the giving of white vestments and lighted candles to the neophytes of ancient mystery religions. Unlike dynamic equivalence, creative assimilation enriches the liturgical ordo — not by culturally re-expressing its elements, but by adding to it new elements from local culture.

3.5. In contextualization the fundamental values and meanings of both Christianity and of local cultures must be respected.

3.6. An important criterion for dynamic equivalence and creative assimilation is that sound or accepted liturgical traditions are preserved in order to keep unity with the universal Church's tradition of worship, while progress inspired by pastoral needs is encouraged. On the side of culture, it is understood that not everything can be integrated with Christian worship, but only those elements that are connatural to (that is, of the same nature as) the liturgical ordo. Elements borrowed from local culture should always undergo critique and purification, which can be achieved through the use of biblical typology.

4. Worship as Counter-cultural

4.1. Jesus Christ came to transform all people and all cultures, and calls us not to conform to the world, but to be transformed with it (Romans 12:2). In the mystery of his passage from death to eternal life is the model for transformation, and thus for the counter-cultural nature of Christian worship. Some components of every culture in the world are sinful, dehumanizing, and contradictory to the values of the Gospel. From the perspective of the Gospel, they need critique and transformation. Contextualization of Christian faith and worship necessarily involves challenging of all types of oppression and social injustice wherever they exist in earthly cultures.

4.2. It also involves the transformation of cultural patterns which idolize the self or the local group at the expense of a wider humanity, or which give central place to the acquisition of wealth at the expense of the care of the earth and its poor. The tools of the counter-cultural in Christian worship may also include the deliberate maintenance or recovery of patterns of action which differ intentionally from prevailing cultural models. These patterns may arise from a recovered sense of Christian history, or from the wisdom of other cultures.

5. Worship as Cross-cultural

5.1. Jesus came to be the Savior of all people. He welcomes the treasures of earthly cultures into the city of God. By virtue of Baptism, there is one Church; and one means of living in faithful response to Baptism is to manifest ever more deeply the unity of the Church. The sharing of hymns and art and other elements of worship across cultural barriers helps enrich the whole Church and strengthen the sense of the communion of the Church. This sharing can be ecumenical as well as cross-cultural, as a witness to the unity of the Church and the oneness of Baptism. Cross-cultural sharing is possible for every church, but is especially needed in multicultural congregations and member churches.

5.2. Care should be taken that the music, art, architecture, gestures and postures, and other elements of different cultures are understood and respected when they are used by churches elsewhere in the world. The criteria for contextualization (above, sections 3.5 and 3.6) should be observed.

6. Challenge to the Churches

6.1. We call on all member churches of the Lutheran World Federation to undertake more efforts related to the transcultural, contextual, counter-cultural, and cross-cultural nature of Christian worship. We call on all member churches to recover the centrality of Baptism, Scripture with preaching, and the every-Sunday celebration of the Lord's Supper — the principal transcultural elements of Christian worship and the signs of Christian unity — as the strong center of all congregational life and mission, and as the authentic basis for contextualization. We call on all churches to give serious attention to exploring the local or contextual elements of liturgy, language, posture and gesture, hymnody and other music and musical instruments, and art and architecture for Christian worship — so that their worship may be more truly rooted in the local culture. We call those churches now carrying out missionary efforts to encourage such contextual awareness among themselves and also among the partners and recipients of their ministries. We call on all member churches to give serious attention to the transcultural nature of worship and the possibilities for cross-cultural sharing. And we call on all churches to consider the training and ordination of ministers of Word and Sacrament, because each local community has the right to receive weekly the means of grace.

6.2. We call on the Lutheran World Federation to make an intentional and substantial effort to provide scholarships for persons from the developing world to study worship, church music, and church architecture, toward the eventual goal that enhanced theological training in their churches can be led by local teachers.

6.3. Further, we call on the Lutheran World Federation to continue its efforts related to worship and culture into the next millennium. The tasks are not quickly accomplished; the work calls for ongoing depth-level research and pastoral encouragement. The Worship and Culture Study, begun in 1992 and continuing in and past the 1997 LWF Assembly, is a significant and important beginning, but the task calls for unending efforts. Giving priority to this task is essential for evangelization of the world.

BIBLIOGRAPHY

Ackerman, James. "The Arts in Higher Education." In *Content and Context: Essays on College Education*, edited by Carl Kaysen, pp. 219–66. New York: McGraw-Hill, 1973.

Anderson, Fred. "Protestant Worship Today." *Theology Today* 43, no. 1 (April 1986).

Antonova, Clemena. *Space, Time, and Presence in the Icon: Seeing the World with the Eyes of God*. Farnham, UK: Ashgate, 2010.

Ariés, Phillippe, and Georges Duby, et al., eds. *History of Private Life*. 5 vols. Cambridge, MA: Harvard University Press, 1987–1991.

Baggly, John. *Doors of Perception: Icons and Their Spiritual Significance*. Crestwood, NY: St. Vladimir's Seminary Press, 1988.

Barker, Hannah, and Simon Burrows, eds. *Press, Politics, and the Public Sphere in Europe and North America, 1760–1820*. Cambridge: Cambridge University Press, 2002.

Barrett, David B., ed. *World Christian Encyclopedia*. 2nd ed. Oxford: Oxford University Press, 1999.

Basil the Great. *On the Holy Spirit*. Crestwood, NY: St. Vladimir's Seminary Press, 1980.

Bätschmann, Oscar. *The Artist in the Modern World: The Conflict between Market and Self-Expression*. New Haven: Yale University Press, 1997.

Bauer, Michael. *Arts Ministry: Nurturing the Creative Life of God's People*. Grand Rapids: Eerdmans, 2013.

Baxandall, Michael. *Giotto and the Orators: Humanist Observers of Painting in Italy and the Discovery of Pictorial Composition (1350–1450)*. Oxford: Oxford University Press, 1971.

Begbie, Jeremy. *Voicing Creation's Praise: Towards a Theology of the Arts*. London: T. & T. Clark, 1991.

Bell, Clive. *Art*. London: Chatto and Windus, 1914.

Beltings, Hans. *Likeness and Presence: A History of the Image before the Era of Art*. Chicago: University of Chicago Press, 1994.

Berenson, Bernard. *The Arch of Constantine; or, The Decline of Form*. London: Chapman and Hall, 1954.

Best, Harold M. *Unceasing Worship: Biblical Perspectives on Worship and the Arts*. Downers Grove: InterVarsity, 2003.

Bigham, Steven. *Heroes of the Icon*. Torrance, CA: Oakwood Publications, 1998.

———. "The Icon: Sign of Unity or Division?" *Ecumenism* 176 (Winter 2009–2010).

Black, Lydia. *Russians in Alaska*. Fairbanks: University of Alaska Press, 2004.

Bolshakov, S. T. *An Icon Painter's Notebook: The Bolshakov Edition (An Anthology of Source Materials)*. Translated and edited by Gregory Melnick. Torrance, CA: Oakwood Publications, 1995.

Boyer, Mark. *The Liturgical Environment: What the Documents Say*. 2nd ed. Collegeville, MN: Liturgical Press, 2004.

Brink, Emily, and John D. Witvliet. "Music in Reformed Churches Worldwide." In *Christian Worship in Reformed Churches Past and Present*, edited by Lukas Vischer, pp. 324–47. Grand Rapids: Eerdmans, 2003.

Burch Brown, Frank. Review of *Art, Architecture, and Liturgical Reform: The Liturgical Arts Society, 1928–1972*, by Susan White. *Encounter* 52 (Winter 1991): 90–91.

———. *Good Taste, Bad Taste, and Christian Taste: Aesthetics in Religious Life*. Oxford: Oxford University Press, 2000.

———. *Inclusive Yet Discerning: Navigating Worship Artfully*. Grand Rapids: Eerdmans, 2009.

Byrne, Patrick. "Symbolic Actions in Christian Worship." In *Liturgy and Music: Lifetime Learning*, edited by Robin A. Leaver and Joyce Anne Zimmerman, pp. 70–101. Collegeville, MN: Liturgical Press, 1998.

Caemmerer, Richard R. *Visual Art in the Life of the Church: Encouraging Creative Worship and Witness in the Congregation*. Minneapolis: Augsburg, 1983.

Canons and Decrees of the Council of Trent. Translated by H. J. Schroeder. Saint Louis and London: Herder, 1941.

Catholic Church. *Directory on Popular Piety and the Liturgy: Principles and Guidelines*. Strathfield, Australia: St. Pauls Publications, 2002.

Cavarnos, Constantine. Review of *The Meaning of Icons*, by Leonid Ouspensky and Vladimir Lossky. *Speculum* 32, no. 3 (July 1957).

Chatzidakis, Manolis, and Gerry Walters. "An Encaustic Icon of Christ at Sinai." *Art Bulletin* 19 (September 1967).

Chaves, Mark. *Congregations in America*. Cambridge, MA: Harvard University Press, 2004.

Chinnici, Joseph P. "The Catholic Community at Prayer, 1926–1976." In *Habits of Devotion: Catholic Religious Practice in Twentieth-Century America*, edited by James M. O'Toole, pp. 9–87. Ithaca, NY: Cornell University Press, 2004.

Chupungco, Anscar. *Liturgical Inculturation: Sacramentals, Religiosity, and Catechesis*. Collegeville, MN: Liturgical Press, 1992.

The Constitution on the Sacred Liturgy of the Second Vatican Council and The Motu Proprio of Pope Paul VI with a Commentary by Gerard S. Sloyan. Glen Rock, NJ: Paulist, 1964.

Coomler, David. *The Icon Handbook: A Guide to Understanding Icons and the Liturgy*. Springfield, IL: Templegate Publishers, 1995.

Couturier, Marie-Alain. "L'Art réligieux modern." *Le Figaro*, October 24, 1951.

Crichton, James. *Lights in the Darkness: Forerunners of the Liturgical Movement*. Collegeville, MN: Liturgical Press, 1996.

Davenport, Nancy. "The Revival of Fra Angelico and Matthias Grünewald in Nineteenth-Century French Religious Art." *Nineteenth-Century French Studies* 27, no. 1–2 (Fall 1998/Winter 1999).

DeHass, Medeia Csoba. "Daily Negotiation of Traditions in a Russian Orthodox Sugpaiq Village in Alaska." *Ethnology* 46 (Summer 2007).

Department of Theology and Studies of the Lutheran World Federation. *Nairobi Statement on Worship and Culture: Contemporary Challenges and Opportunities*. Geneva: Lutheran World Federation, 1996.

Devine, George. *American Catholicism: Where Do We Go from Here?* Englewood Cliffs, NJ: Prentice-Hall, 1974.

———. *Liturgical Renewal: An Agonizing Reappraisal*. New York: Alba House, 1973.

Didron, Adolphe-Napoléon. Original preface to the first edition of the *Manuel d'iconographie chrétienne, grecque et latine, traduit du manuscript byzantine, le guide de la peinture par P. Durand*. Paris: Imprimerie Royal, 1845.

Dillenberger, John. "Artists and Church Commissions: Rubin's *The Church at Assy* Revisited." In *Art, Creativity, and the Sacred*, edited by Diane Apostolos-Cappadona, pp. 193–204. London and New York: Bloomsbury Academic, 1995.

————. *A Theology of Artistic Sensibilities: The Visual Arts and the Church.* Norwich, UK: SCM, 1987.

————. *The Visual Arts and Christianity in America: From the Colonial Period to the Present.* Eugene, OR: Wipf and Stock, 2004.

DiMaggio, Paul, et al. "The Role of Religion in Public Conflicts over the Arts in the Philadelphia Area, 1965–1997." In *Crossroads: Art and Religion in American Life,* edited by Alberta Arthurs and Glenn Wallach, p. 130. New York: Center for Arts and Culture, Henry Luce Foundation, 2001.

DiMaggio, Paul, and Becky Pettit. "Public Opinion and Political Vulnerability: Why Has the National Endowment for the Arts Been Such an Attractive Target?" Working Paper #7. Princeton: Center for Arts and Cultural Policy Studies, Princeton University, 1999. www.princeton.edu/~artspol/workpap7.html.

Dionysius of Fourna. *The "Painter's Manual" of Dionysius of Fourna.* Translated and with commentary by Paul Hetherington. Codex gr. 708 in the Saltykov–Shchedrin State Public Library, Leningrad. Redondo Beach, CA: Oakwood Publications, 1989.

Directory on Popular Piety and the Liturgy: Principles and Guidelines. Strathfield, Australia: St. Pauls Publications, 2002.

"The Divine Liturgy of Saint John Chrysostom." Greek Orthodox Archdiocese of America. www.goarch.org/chapel/liturgical_texts/liturgy_hchc.

Doolan, Patrick. *Recovering the Icon: The Life and Work of Leonid Ouspensky.* Crestwood, NY: St. Vladimir's Seminary Press, 2008.

Dorn, Charles. *Art Education: The Development of Public Policy.* Miami: Barnhardt and Ashe, 2005.

Driskel, Michael. *Representing Belief: Religion, Art, and Society in Nineteenth-Century France.* University Park: Pennsylvania State University Press, 1992.

Drobot, Georges. "Icons: Lines, Language, Colours, and History." In *Icons: Windows on Eternity,* edited by Gennadios Limouris, pp. 160–69. Faith and Order Paper 147. Geneva: WCC Publications, 1990.

Dulles, Avery. *Models of the Church.* Garden City, NY: Image Books, 1987.

Dyrness, William. "Hope That Is Seen Is Not Hope: Visual Explorations of Advent." *Interpretation* 62, no. 4 (October 2008).

————. *A Primer on Christian Worship: Where We've Been, Where We Are, Where We Can Go.* Grand Rapids: Eerdmans, 2009.

————. *Reformed Theology and Visual Culture: The Protestant Imagination from*

Calvin to Edwards. Cambridge and New York: Cambridge University Press, 2004.

———. *Senses of the Soul: Art and the Visual in Christian Worship*. Eugene, OR: Cascade Books, 2008.

———. *Visual Faith: Art, Theology, and Worship in Dialogue*. Grand Rapids: Baker Academic, 2001.

Efland, Arthur D. *A History of Art Education: Intellectual and Social Currents in Teaching the Visual Arts*. New York: Teachers College Press, 1990.

Elkins, James. *On the Strange Place of Religion in Contemporary Art*. New York: Routledge, 2004.

Elsner, Jas. *Art and the Roman Viewer: The Transformation of Art from the Pagan World to Christianity*. Cambridge: Cambridge University Press, 1995.

Environment and Art in Catholic Worship. Washington, DC: United States Catholic Conference, 1978.

Ephrem, Archimandrite. Review of *The Orthodox Study Bible: New Testament and Psalms*. *Sourozh* 54 (November 1993).

Erickson, Craig Douglas. *Participating in Worship: History, Theory, and Practice*. Louisville: Westminster John Knox, 1989.

Evdokimov, Paul. *The Art of the Icon: A Theology of Beauty*. Translated by Steven Bigham. Redondo Beach, CA: Oakwood Publications, 1990.

———. *L'orthodoxie*. Paris: Desclée de Brower, 1979.

Evetts, Julia. "Trust and Professionalism: Challenges and Occupational Changes." *Current Sociology* 54 (July 2006).

Evseyeva, Lilia, et al. *A History of Icon Painting: Sources, Traditions, Present Day*. Translated by Kate Cook. Moscow: Grand-Holding Publishers, 2005.

Fagerberg, David. *Theologia Prima: What Is Liturgical Theology?* Mundelein, IL: Hillenbrand Books, 2004.

Falconer, Alan D. "Word, Sacrament, and Communion: New Emphases in Reformed Worship in the Twentieth Century." In *Christian Worship in Reformed Churches Past and Present*, edited by Lukas Vischer, pp. 142–58. Grand Rapids: Eerdmans, 2003.

Farbman, Michael S. *Masterpieces of Russian Painting: Twenty Colour Plates and Forty-Three Monochrome Reproductions of Russian Icons and Frescoes from the XI to the XVIII Centuries*. London: Zwemmer Publications, 1930.

Fenwick, John R. K., and Bryan D. Spinks. *Worship in Transition: The Liturgical Movement in the Twentieth Century*. New York: Continuum, 1995.

Finney, Paul Corby. *Seeing beyond the Word: Visual Arts and the Calvinist Tradition.* Grand Rapids: Eerdmans, 1999.

Fitzgerald, Michael. *Making Modernism: Picasso and the Creation of the Market for Twentieth-Century Art.* Berkeley: University of California Press, 1995.

Florensky, Pavel. *Iconostasis.* Translated by Donald Sheehan and Olga Andrejev. Crestwood, NY: St. Vladimir's Seminary Press, 1996.

Florovsky, Georges. *Prayer: Private and Corporate.* Saint Louis: Ologos Publications, 1960.

Foley, Edward. *From Age to Age: How Christians Celebrated the Eucharist.* Chicago: Liturgy Training Publications, 1991.

Foster, Ann T. "Louise Nevelson's Worship Environment for St. Peter's Church: A Transformative Space." *Arts* 11, no. 2 (January 1, 1999).

Foster, John J. M. "Diocesan Commissions for Liturgy, Music and Art: An Endangered Species?" *Worship* 71, no. 2 (March 1997).

Foucart, Bruno. *Le Renouveau de la peinture religieuse en France (1800–1860).* Paris: Arthéna, 1987.

Francis, Mark R. *Shape a Circle Ever Wider: Liturgical Inculturation in the United States.* Chicago: Liturgy Training Publications, 2000.

Francis, Matthew. "The Orthodox Study Bible and Orthodox Identity in North America." *Canadian Journal of Orthodox Christianity* 2, no. 2 (June 1, 2007).

Freedberg, David. *The Power of Images: Studies in the History and Theory of Response.* Chicago: University of Chicago Press, 1989.

Gaillardetz, Richard. *The Church in the Making: "Lumen Gentium," "Christus Dominus," "Orientalium Ecclesiarum."* New York: Paulist, 2006.

Galadza, Peter. "Restoring the Icon: Reflections on the Reform of Byzantine Worship." *Worship* 65 (1991).

Galavaris, George. *The Icon in the Life of the Church: Doctrine, Liturgy, Devotion.* Leiden: Brill, 1981.

Gardener, Johann. *Russian Church Singing.* Vol. 1 of *Orthodox Worship and Hymnography.* Translated by Vladimir Morosan. Crestwood, NY: St. Vladimir's Seminary Press, 1980.

Gillis, Chester. *Roman Catholicism in America.* New York: Columbia University Press, 1999.

Gillquist, Peter. *Becoming Orthodox: A Journey to the Ancient Christian Faith.* Ben Lomond, CA: Conciliar Press, 1992.

Gioia, Dana. "How the United States Funds the Arts." Washington, DC: National Endowment for the Arts, 2007.

———. Preface to *The Arts and Civic Engagement: Involved in Arts, Involved in Life*, by National Endowment for the Arts. Washington, DC: National Endowment for the Arts, 2006.

Gombrich, Ernst. *Norm and Form: Studies in the Art of the Renaissance*. London and New York: Phaidon, 1971.

Goodman, Dena. "Public Sphere and Private Life: Toward a Synthesis of Current Historiographical Approaches to the Old Regime." *History and Theory* 31 (1992).

Gorky, Maxim. *In the World*. Translated by G. Foakes. New York: Century Co., 1917.

Greeley, Andrew. *Catholic Imagination*. Berkeley: University of California Press, 2000.

———. *Come Blow Your Mind with Me*. Garden City, NY: Doubleday, 1970.

———. *Religion as Poetry*. New Brunswick, NJ, and London: Transaction Publishers, 1995.

Guthrie, Steven R. *Creator Spirit: The Holy Spirit and the Art of Becoming Human*. Grand Rapids: Baker Academic, 2011.

Haber, Samuel. *The Quest for Authority and Honor in the American Professions: 1750–1900*. Chicago: University of Chicago Press, 1991.

Habermas, Jürgen. *The Structural Transformation of the Public Sphere: An Enquiry into a Category of Bourgeois Society*. Translated by Thomas Burger with the assistance of Frederick Lawrence. Cambridge, MA: MIT Press, 1989.

Harakas, Stanley. *Living the Liturgy: A Practical Guide for Participating in the Divine Liturgy of the Eastern Orthodox Church*. Minneapolis: Light and Life Publishing, 1974.

Harbinson, Colin, John Franklin, James Tughan, and Phyllis Novac. "Redeeming the Arts: The Restoration of the Arts to God's Creational Intention." Lausanne Occasional Paper #46. Lausanne Movement, 2005. http://www.lausanne.org/wp-content/uploads/2007/06/LOP46_IG17.pdf.

Harper, Brad, and Paul Louis Metzger. *Exploring Ecclesiology: An Evangelical and Ecumenical Introduction*. Grand Rapids: Brazos, 2009.

Hart, Aidan. "Iconography for the Twenty-First Century." Talk delivered at Sidney Sussex College, Cambridge, UK, 2005. www.aidanharticons.com/articles/Iconography%20for%2021st%20century.pdf.

Heller, Steven, and Nathan Gluck. "Seventy-Five Years of AIGA." 1989. www.aiga
.org/content.cfm/about-history-75thanniversary.

Herr, Dan. "Stop Pushing." *Critic* 24 (October-November 1965).

Hitchcock, James. *The Recovery of the Sacred.* New York: Seabury, 1974.

Hoksbergen, Alvin. "Shedding Light on the Prayer of Illumination." *Reformed Worship* 52 (July 1999).

Holt, Elizabeth. *A Documentary History of Art.* Vol. 2, *Michelangelo and the Mannerists.* New York: Doubleday, 1958.

Jagodzinski, Cecile M. *Privacy and Print: Reading and Writing in Seventeenth-Century England.* Charlottesville: University Press of Virginia, 1999.

Janzen, John M. "Mennonite Icon – an Oxymoron." *Mennonite Life* 59 (March 2004). www.bethelks.edu/mennonitelife/2004Mar.

Jensen, Robin Margaret. *Face to Face: Portraits of the Divine in Early Christianity.* Minneapolis: Fortress, 2005.

―――. *The Substance of Things Seen: Art, Faith, and the Christian Community.* Grand Rapids: Eerdmans, 2004.

John Paul II. "Letter to Artists." Easter Sunday, April 4, 1999. Chicago: Liturgy Training Publications, 1999.

Johnston, Cheryl. "Digital Deception." *American Journalism Review* 25, no. 4 (May 2003).

Kalokyris, Constantine. *The Essence of Orthodox Iconography.* Brookline, MA: Holy Cross Orthodox Press, 1985.

Kan, Sergei. *Memory Eternal: Tlingit Culture and Russian Orthodox Christianity.* Seattle: University of Washington Press, 1999.

―――. "Russian Orthodox Brotherhoods among the Tlingit: Missionary Goals and Native Response." *Ethnohistory* 32 (Summer 1985).

Kärkkäinen, Veli-Matti. *An Introduction to Ecclesiology: Ecumenical, Historical, and Global Perspectives.* Downers Grove: InterVarsity, 2002.

Kauffman, Gordon. *Jesus and Creativity.* Minneapolis: Fortress, 2009.

Kettner, James H. *Development of American Citizenship, 1608–1870.* Chapel Hill: University of North Carolina Press, 1978.

Kitchel, Karen. "The M.F.A.: Academia's Pyramid Scheme." *New Art Examiner* 26 (Fall 1999).

Kitzinger, Ernst. "The Cult of Images before Iconoclasm." *Dumbarton Oaks Papers* 8 (1954).

Bibliography

Koerner, Joseph. *Caspar David Friedrich and the Subject of Landscape.* New Haven: Yale University Press, 1990.

Krindatch, Alexei. "'American Orthodoxy' or 'Orthodoxy in America'? Profiling the Next Generation of Eastern Clergy in the USA." 2004. www.hartford institute.org/research/orthodoxarticle2.html.

———. *Atlas of American Orthodox Christian Churches.* Brookline, MA: Holy Cross Orthodox Press, 2011.

———. *Evolving Visions of the Orthodox Priesthood in America.* Berkeley, CA: Patriarch Athenagoras Orthodox Institute, 2006.

———. *The Orthodox Church Today.* Berkeley, CA: Patriarch Athenagoras Orthodox Institute, 2008.

———. "The Orthodox (Eastern Christian) Churches in the USA at the Beginning of a New Millennium." (2002.) www.hartfordinstitute.org/research/orthodoxpaper.html.

Kristeller, Paul Oskar. "The Modern System of the Arts." *Journal of the History of Ideas* 12 (1951).

Küng, Hans, Yves Congar, and Daniel O'Hanlon, eds. *Council Speeches of Vatican II.* Glen Rock, NJ: Paulist, 1964.

Larson, Magali Sarfatti. *The Rise of Professionalism: A Sociological Analysis.* Berkeley: University of California Press, 1977.

Lathrop, Gordon. "Worship: Local Yet Universal." In *Christian Worship: Unity in Cultural Diversity,* edited by Anita Stauffer, pp. 47–66. Geneva: Lutheran World Federation, 1996.

Latour, Bruno, and Peter Weibel, eds. Catalogue for the *Iconoclash* exhibition. Cambridge, MA: MIT Press, 2002.

Ledogar, Robert. "The Question of Daily Mass." *Worship* 43, no. 5 (May 1969).

Lefchick, Basil. "The Resurgence of Icons: Why Now?" *Environment and Art Newsletter* 14 (September 2001).

Limouris, Gennadios. "The Apocalyptic Character and Dimension of the Icon in the Life of the Orthodox Church." *Greek Orthodox Theological Review* 33, no. 3 (1988).

Liturgical Art and Environment Commission, Diocese of Grand Rapids, Michigan. *A House of Prayer: Building and Renovation Guidelines.* 1998.

Lock, Charles. Review of *Theology of the Icon,* by Leonid Ouspensky. *Canadian Slavonic Papers/Revue Canadienne des Slavistes* 37, no. 1/2 (March-June 1995).

Logan, Frederick M. *Growth of Art in American Schools*. New York: Harper and Brothers, 1955.

Lossky, Vladimir. *In the Image and Likeness of God*. Crestwood, NY: St. Vladimir's Seminary Press, 1985.

Maguire, Henry. *The Icons of Their Bodies: Saints and Their Images in Byzantium*. Princeton: Princeton University Press, 1996.

Mah, Harold. "Phantasies of the Public Sphere: Rethinking the Habermas of Historians." *Journal of Modern History* 72, no. 1 (March 2000).

Martin, Jessica, and Alec Ryrie, eds. *Private and Domestic Devotion in Early Modern Britain*. Burlington, VT: Ashgate, 2012.

Mathews, Thomas. "Early Icons of the Holy Monastery of Saint Catherine at Sinai." In *Holy Image, Hallowed Ground*, edited by Robert Nelson. Los Angeles: J. Paul Getty Trust Publications, 2007.

———. "Psychological Dimensions in the Art of Eastern Christendom." In *Art and Religion: Faith, Form, and Reform*, edited by Osmund Overby, pp. 1–21. Columbia: Curators of the University of Missouri–Columbia, 1986.

McDannell, Colleen. *Material Christianity: Religion and Popular Culture in America*. New Haven: Yale University Press, 1995.

McGuckin, John Anthony. *The Orthodox Church: An Introduction to Its History, Doctrine, and Spiritual Culture*. Oxford: Blackwell, 2008.

Merton, Thomas. "Liturgy and Spiritual Personalism." *Worship* 34 (October 1960).

Metzger, Marcel. *History of the Liturgy: The Major Stages*. Collegeville, MN: Liturgical Press, 1997.

Meyendorff, John. *Living Tradition: Orthodox Witness in the Contemporary World*. Crestwood, NY: St. Vladimir's Seminary Press, 1978.

———. "The Orthodox Church and Mission: Past and Present Perspectives." *St. Vladimir's Theological Quarterly* 16, no. 2 (1972).

Mikulay, Jennifer Geigel. "Another Look at *La Grande Vitesse*." *Public Art Dialogue* 1, no. 1 (March 2011).

———. "Producing *La Grande Vitesse*: Civic Symbolism, Vernacular Archives and Public Sculpture in Grand Rapids, Michigan." In "Focus: Public Art," special issue, *Collections: A Journal for Museum and Archives Professionals* 4, no. 3 (Summer 2008).

Montefiore, Hugh. *The Gospel and Contemporary Culture*. London: Mowbray, 1992.

Morgan, David. "Concepts of Abstraction in French Art Theory from the Enlightenment to Modernism." *Journal of the History of Ideas* 53, no. 4 (1992).

————. "The Enchantment of Art: Abstraction and Empathy from German Romanticism to Expressionism." *Journal of the History of Ideas* 57, no. 2 (April 1996).

————, ed. *Icons of American Protestantism: The Art of Warner Sallman.* New Haven: Yale University Press, 1996.

————. *Protestants and Pictures: Religion, Visual Culture, and the Age of American Mass Production.* Oxford: Oxford University Press, 1999.

————. "The Rise and Fall of Abstraction in Eighteenth-Century Art Theory." *Eighteenth-Century Studies* 27, no. 3 (Spring 1994).

————. *The Sacred Gaze: Religious Visual Culture in Theory and Practice.* Berkeley: University of California Press, 2005.

————. *Visual Piety: A History and Theory of Popular Religious Images.* Berkeley: University of California Press, 1998.

Morgan, David, and Sally M. Promey, eds. *The Visual Culture of American Religions.* Berkeley: University of California Press, 2001.

Morosan, Vladimir. "Liturgical Singing or Sacred Music? Understanding the Aesthetic of the New Russian Choral School." In *Christianity and the Arts in Russia*, edited by William C. Brumfield and Milos M. Velimirovic, pp. 124–30. Cambridge: Cambridge University Press, 1991.

Morrison, Pat. "Trademarking Holiness." *National Catholic Reporter* 92, no. 1 (August 15, 2003).

National Association of Evangelicals. "Statement of Faith." http://www.nae.net/statement-of-faith/.

Neff, David. "The Fullness and the Center: Bishop Kallistos Ware on Evangelism, Evangelicals and the Orthodox Church." *Christianity Today* 55 (July 2011).

Nelson, Robert, and Kristen Collins, eds. *Holy Image, Hallowed Ground: Icons from Sinai.* Los Angeles: J. Paul Getty Museum, 2006.

Newbigin, Lesslie. *Foolishness to the Greeks: The Gospel and Western Culture.* Grand Rapids: Eerdmans, 1986.

Nichols, Robert L. "The Icon and the Machine in Russia's Religious Renaissance." In *Christianity and the Arts in Russia*, edited by William C. Brumfield and Milos M. Velimirovic, pp. 131–44. Cambridge: Cambridge University Press, 1991.

Nikolaou, Theodor. "The Place of the Icon in the Liturgical Life of the Orthodox Church." *Greek Orthodox Theological Review* 35, no. 4 (1990).

Noll, Mark A., and Carolyn Nystrom. *Is the Reformation Over? An Evangelical Assess-*

ment of Contemporary Roman Catholicism. Grand Rapids: Baker Academic; Bletchley, UK: Paternoster, 2005.

Oleksa, Michael. "Orthodox Missiological Education for the Twenty-First Century." In *Missiological Education for the Twenty-First Century: The Book, the Circle, and the Sandals,* edited by J. Dudley Woodberry, Charles Van Engen, and Edgar J. Elliston, pp. 83–90. Maryknoll, NY: Orbis, 1996.

Onians, John. "Abstraction and Imagination in Late Antiquity." *Art History* 3 (1980).

Orlin, Lena Cowen. *Locating Privacy in Tudor London.* Oxford: Oxford University Press, 2007.

Ouspensky, Leonid. *Theology of the Icon.* Translated by Anthony Gythiel with selections translated by Elizabeth Meyendorff. 2 vols. Crestwood, NY: St. Vladimir's Seminary Press, 1992.

Ouspensky, Leonid, and Vladimir Lossky. *The Meaning of Icons.* 2nd ed. Crestwood, NY: St. Vladimir's Seminary Press, 1999.

Patterson, Mary Hampson. *Domesticating the Reformation: Protestant Best Sellers, Private Devotion, and the Revolution of English Piety.* Madison, NJ: Farleigh Dickinson University Presses, 2007.

Petraru, Gheorghe. "Missionary Theology in the Theological University Education of the Romanian Orthodox Church." *International Review of Mission* 95 (July 2006).

Petras, David. "Eschatology and the Byzantine Liturgy." *Liturgical Ministry* 19 (Winter 2010).

Phan, Peter C., ed. *Directory on Popular Piety and the Liturgy: Principles and Guidelines – a Commentary.* Collegeville, MN: Liturgical Press, 2005.

Philippart, David. "Like Living Stones." Series of essays in *Environment and Art Letter* 15, no. 2–7 (2002).

Popova, Olga. "Byzantine Icons of the 6th to 15th Centuries." In *A History of Icon Painting: Sources, Traditions, Present Day*, edited by Lilia Evseyeva, pp. 41–94. Moscow: Grand Holding Publishers, 2005.

Promey, Sally M. "Pictorial Ambivalence and American Protestantism." In *Crossroads: Art and Religion in American Life*, edited by Alberta Arthurs and Glenn Wallach, pp. 189–230. New York: New Press, 2001.

Rathbun, Robert R. "The Russian Orthodox Church as a Native Institution among the Koniag Eskimo of Kodiak Island." *Arctic Anthropology* 18 (1981).

Rubin, William. *Modern Sacred Art and the Church of Assy.* New York: Columbia University Press, 1961.

Russian Icons. New York: American Russian Institute, 1931.

The Russian Primary Chronicle: Laurentian Text. Translated by Samuel Hazzard Cross and Olgerd P. Sherbowitz-Wetzor. Cambridge, MA: Mediaeval Academy of America, 1953.

Ruth, Lester. "A Rose by Any Other Name: Attempts at Classifying North American Protestant Worship." In *The Conviction of Things Not Seen: Worship and Ministry in the 21st Century*, edited by Todd E. Johnson, pp. 33–51. Grand Rapids: Brazos, 2002.

Sayers, Dorothy L. *The Mind of the Maker.* New York: Harcourt, Brace and Co., 1941.

Schaeffer, Francis A. *Art and the Bible: Two Essays.* Downers Grove: InterVarsity, 1973.

Schineller, Peter, SJ. *A Handbook on Inculturation.* Maryknoll, NY: Orbis, 1990.

Schloeder, Steven. *Architecture in Communion.* San Francisco: Ignatius, 1999.

Schmemann, Alexander. *The Journals of Father Alexander Schmemann.* Crestwood, NY: St. Vladimir's Seminary Press, 2000.

Schwind, Monica, OP. *In God's Own Time: St. Francis de Sales Parish, Muskegon, Michigan.* Muskegon, MI: Saint Francis de Sales Parish, 1997.

Seasoltz, R. Kevin, OSB. "From the Bauhaus to the House of God's People: Frank Kacmarcik's Contribution to Church Art and Architecture." *U.S. Catholic Historian* 15, no. 1 (Winter 1997).

Segal, Robert A. "In Defense of the Comparative Method." *Numen* 48 (2001).

Sendler, Egon. *The Icon, Image of the Invisible: Elements of Theology, Aesthetics, and Technique.* Translated by Fr. Steven Bigham. Redondo Beach CA: Oakwood Publications, 1988. First published as *L'icone: Image de l'invisible* (Paris: Editions Desclée De Brouwer, 1981).

Sevcenko, Nancy. "Icons in the Liturgy." *Dumbarton Oaks Papers* 45 (1991).

Shea, William. *The Lion and the Lamb: Evangelicals and Catholics in America.* Oxford: Oxford University Press, 2004.

Sherry, Patrick. *Spirit and Beauty: An Introduction to Theological Aesthetics.* Oxford: Clarendon, 1992.

Shiner, Larry. *The Invention of Art: A Cultural History.* Chicago: University of Chicago Press, 2001.

Shorter, Aylward. *Toward a Theology of Inculturation.* Maryknoll, NY: Orbis, 1988.

Singerman, Howard. *Art Subjects: Making Artists in the American University.* Berkeley: University of California Press, 1999.

Slagle, Amy. *The Eastern Church in the Spiritual Marketplace: American Conversions to Orthodox Christianity.* De Kalb: Northern Illinois University Press, 2011.

―――. "Imagined Aesthetics: Constructions of Aesthetic Experience in Orthodox Christian Conversion Narratives." In *Aesthetics as a Religious Factor in Eastern and Western Christianity*, edited by Wil van den Bercken and Jonathan Sutton, pp. 53–63. Leuven: Peeters, 2005.

Smith, Holmes. "Problems of the College Art Association." *Bulletin of the College Art Association* 1 (1913).

Smith, James K. A. *Desiring the Kingdom: Worship, Worldview, and Cultural Formation.* Grand Rapids: Baker Academic, 2009.

―――. *Imagining the Kingdom: How Worship Works.* Grand Rapids: Baker Academic, 2013.

Soteriou, George, and Maria Soteriou. *Icones du Mont Sinai.* Athens: Institut Français d'Athènes, 1956–1958.

Spackman, Betty. *A Profound Weakness: Christians and Kitsch.* Carlisle, UK: Piquant, 2005.

Spinks, Bryan D. "Liturgical Theology and Criticism – Things of Heaven and Things of Earth: Some Reflections on Worship, World Christianity and Culture." In *Christian Worship Worldwide: Expanding Horizons, Deepening Practices*, edited by Charles E. Farhadian, pp. 230–52. Grand Rapids: Eerdmans, 2007.

Spira, Andrew. *The Avant-Garde Icon: Russian Avant-Garde Art and the Icon Painting Tradition.* Burlington, VT: Lund Humphries and the Ashgate Publishing Company, 2008.

Staniszewski, Mary Anne. *Believing Is Seeing: Creating the Culture of Art.* New York: Penguin Books, 1994.

St. Athanasius Church, Santa Barbara, California. "Our History." http://www.stathanasius.org/about/our-history/.

Stoichita, Victor. *Visionary Experience in the Golden Age of Spanish Art.* London: Reaktion Books, 1995.

Stokoe, Mark, and Leonid Kishkousky. *Orthodox Christians in North America (1794–1994).* Syosset, NY: Orthodox Christian Publications, 1995.

Storr, Robert. "View from the Bridge." *Frieze* 92 (June-August 2005). www.frieze.com/issue/article/view_from_the_bridge4.

Summers, David. *Real Spaces: World Art History and the Rise of Western Modernism.* New York: Phaidon, 2003.

Taft, Robert. "The Liturgical Enterprise Twenty-Five Years after Alexander Schmemann (1921–1983): The Man and His Heritage." *St. Vladimir's Theological
Quarterly* 53, no. 2–3 (2009).

Tarasar, Constance, and John Erickson. *Orthodox America, 1794–1976: Development
of the Orthodox Church in America.* Syosset, NY: Orthodox Church in America Department of History and Archives, 1975.

Tarasov, Oleg. *Icon and Devotion: Sacred Spaces in Imperial Russia.* Translated and
edited by Robin Milner-Gulland. London: Reaktion Books, 2002.

Taylor, Michael J. *Liturgical Renewal in the Christian Churches.* Baltimore and Dublin: Helicon, 1967.

Taylor, W. David O., ed. *For the Beauty of the Church: Casting a Vision for the Arts.*
Grand Rapids: Baker, 2010.

Thiessen, Gesa Elsbeth. *Theological Aesthetics: A Reader.* Grand Rapids: Eerdmans,
2004.

"Thirty Years after *The Constitution on the Sacred Liturgy.*" *Worship* 68 (March 1994).

Tischler, Linda. "Target Practice." *fastcompany.com* 85 (August 2004). http://www
.fastcompany.com/magazine/85/graves_qa.html.

Torgerson, Mark A. *An Architecture of Immanence: Architecture for Worship and Ministry Today.* Grand Rapids: Eerdmans, 2007.

Tracy, David. *Analogical Imagination: Christian Theology and the Culture of Pluralism.*
New York: Crossroad, 1981.

Trilling, James. "Late Antique and Sub-Antique, or the 'Decline of Form' Reconsidered." *Dumbarton Oaks Papers* 41 (1987).

———. "Medieval Art without Style? Plato's Loophole and a Modern Detour."
Gesta 34, no. 1 (1995).

Tuzik, Robert L., ed. *How Firm a Foundation: Leaders of the Liturgical Movement.*
Chicago: Liturgy Training Publications, 1990.

Ugolnik, Anthony. *The Illuminating Icon.* Grand Rapids: Eerdmans, 1989.

United States Catholic Conference. *Built of Living Stones: Art, Architecture, and Worship.* Washington, DC: United States Catholic Conference, 2000.

———. *Catechism of the Catholic Church.* 2nd ed. Vatican City: Libreria Editrice
Vaticana; Washington, DC: United States Catholic Conference, 2000.

Uspensky, Boris. *The Semiotics of the Russion Icon.* Lisse: Peter de Ridder Press, 1976.

Van Dyk, Leanne, ed. *A More Profound Alleluia: Theology and Worship in Harmony.*
Grand Rapids: Eerdmans, 2004.

Van Gelder, Craig. *The Essence of the Church: A Community Created by the Spirit.* Grand Rapids: Baker, 2000.

VanHaelen, Angela, and Joseph P. Ward, eds. *Making Space Public in Early Modern Europe: Performance, Geography, Privacy.* New York and London: Routledge, 2013.

Van Proyen, Mark. "The Educators Educated." *New Art Examiner* 27 (Fall 2000).

Varacalli, Joseph, Salvatore Primeggia, Salvatore J. LaGumina, and Donald J. D'Elia, eds. *The Saints in the Lives of Italian-Americans: An Interdisciplinary Investigation.* Stony Brook, NY: Forum Italicum, 1999.

Vasileios of Stavronikita, Archimandrite. *Hymn of Entry: Liturgy and Life in the Orthodox Church.* Translated by Elizabeth Briere. Crestwood, NY: St. Vladimir's Seminary Press, 1984.

[Vatican Council II]. *Dogmatic Constitution on the Church: Lumen Gentium.* Boston: Pauline Books and Media, 1998.

————. *Sacrosanctum Concilium [Constitution on the Sacred Liturgy].* December 4, 1963. Collegeville, MN: St. John's Abbey, 1963.

Volf, Miroslav. *After Our Likeness: The Church as Image of the Trinity.* Grand Rapids: Eerdmans, 1997.

Vosko, Richard. "*Built of Living Stones*: Seven Years Later." *Liturgical Ministry* 17 (Spring 2008).

Wainwright, Geoffrey. *Is the Reformation Over? Catholics and Protestants at the Turn of the Millennium.* Milwaukee: Marquette University Press, 2000.

Wallace, Fern. *The Flame of the Candle: A Pictorial History of the Russian Orthodox Churches in Alaska.* Chilliwack, BC: Saints Kyril and Methody Society, 1974.

Wallach, Amei. "Art, Religion and Spirituality: A Conversation with Artists." In *Crossroads: Art and Religion in American Life,* edited by Alberta Arthurs and Glenn Wallach, pp. 233–62. New York: Center for Arts and Culture, Henry Luce Foundation, 2001.

Walton, Janet. *Art and Worship: A Vital Connection.* Wilmington, DE: Michael Glazier, 1988.

Ware, Kallistos. *The Orthodox Church.* New ed. New York: Penguin Books, 1993 (first published in 1963).

————. *The Orthodox Way.* Crestwood, NY: St. Vladimir's Seminary Press, 1990.

Webb, Diana. *Privacy and Solitude: The Medieval Discovery of Personal Space.* London: Continuum, 2007.

Webb-Mitchell, Brett. "True Kitsch Is Catholic Kitsch." *Regeneration Quarterly* 3, no. 3 (Summer 1997).

Weiss, Amy Levin. "Breaking Boundaries: Louise Nevelson and the Erol Beker Chapel of the Good Shepherd." *Arts* 23, no. 3 (January 1, 2012).

Weitzmann, Kurt. "Byzantine Scholarship and Art in America." *American Journal of Archaeology* 51 (Autumn 1947).

————. *The Monastery of Saint Catherine at Mount Sinai, the Icons.* Princeton: Princeton University Press, 1976.

Welten, Ruud. "Toward a Phenomenology of the Icon." In *Aesthetics as a Religious Factor in Eastern and Western Christianity*, edited by Wil van den Bercken and Jonathan Sutton, pp. 395–403. Leuven: Peeters, 2005.

White, James F. "Liturgical Reformation: Sixteenth Century and Twentieth." In *Christian Worship in North America: A Retrospective, 1955–1995*, pp. 34–43. Collegeville, MN: Liturgical Press, 1997.

————. "Roman Catholic and Protestant Worship in Relationship." In *Christian Worship in North America: A Retrospective, 1955–1995*, pp. 3–15. Collegeville, MN: Liturgical Press, 1997.

White, Susan J. *Art, Architecture, and Liturgical Reform: The Liturgical Arts Society, 1928–1972.* New York: Pueblo Publishing Co., 1990.

Williams, Rowan. *The Dwelling of the Light: Praying with Icons of Christ.* Grand Rapids: Eerdmans, 2004.

————. *Ponder These Things: Praying with Icons of the Virgin.* Brewster, MA: Paraclete Press, 2006.

————. "The Theology of Vladimir Nikolaievich Lossky: An Exposition and Critique." DPhil thesis, University of Oxford, 1975.

Wilson, Charles. "U.S. Bishops' New Art and Architecture Document." *AD2000* 13, no. 6 (July 2000).

Wilson, Paul Scott. "Preaching as God's Event." *Vision* 10, no. 1 (Spring 2009).

————. *Setting Words on Fire: Putting God at the Center of the Sermon.* Nashville: Abingdon, 2008.

Winner, Lauren. "Someone Who Can't Draw a Straight Line Tries to Defend Her Art-Buying Habit." In *For the Beauty of the Church: Casting a Vision for the Arts*, edited by W. David O. Taylor, pp. 69–82. Grand Rapids: Baker, 2010.

Witvliet, John D. *Worship Seeking Understanding: Windows into Christian Practice.* Grand Rapids: Baker Academic, 2003.

Wolterstorff, Nicholas. *Art in Action: Toward a Christian Aesthetic.* Grand Rapids: Eerdmans, 1980.

The Worship Sourcebook. Grand Rapids: Calvin Institute of Christian Worship, Faith Alive Christian Resources, and Baker Books, 2004.

Wuthnow, Robert. *All in Sync: How Music and Art Are Revitalizing American Religion.* Berkeley: University of California Press, 2003.

———. *Creative Spirituality: The Artist's Way.* Berkeley: University of California Press, 2001.

Wybrew, Hugh. "The Orthodox Liturgy: The Development of the Eucharistic Liturgy in the Byzantine Rite." Crestwood, NY: St. Vladimir's Seminary Press, 1990.

Yannoulatos, Anastasios. "Discovering the Orthodox Missionary Ethos." *St. Vladimir's Theological Quarterly* 8 (1964).

Yates, Wilson. *The Arts in Theological Education: New Possibilities for Integration.* Atlanta: Scholars Press, 1987.

Yiannias, John. "Icons Are Not 'Written.'" orthodoxhistory.org/2010/06/08/icons –are–not–written.

Zibawi, Mahmoud. *The Icon: Its Meaning and History.* Collegeville, MN: Liturgical Press, 1993.

Zimmerman, Joyce Ann. *The Ministry of Liturgical Environment.* Collegeville, MN: Liturgical Press, 2004.

———. *Worship with Gladness: Understanding Worship from the Heart.* Grand Rapids: Eerdmans, 2014.